The State in Ancient Egypt

DEBATES IN ARCHAEOLOGY
Series editor: Richard Hodges

Against Cultural Property, John Carman
The Anthropology of Hunter-Gatherers, Vicki Cummings
Archaeologies of Conflict, John Carman
Archaeology: The Conceptual Challenge, Timothy Insoll
Archaeology and International Development in Africa, Colin Breen and Daniel Rhodes
Archaeology and State Theory, Bruce Routledge
Archaeology and Text, John Moreland
Archaeology and the Pan-European Romanesque, Tadhg O'Keeffe
Beyond Celts, Germans and Scythians, Peter S. Wells
Bronze Age Textiles, Klavs Randsborg
Building Colonialism, Daniel T. Rhodes
The Byzantine Dark Ages, Michael J. Decker
Changing Natures, Bill Finlayson & Graeme M. Warren
Combat Archaeology, John Schofield
Debating the Archaeological Heritage, Robin Skeates
Early European Castles, Oliver H. Creighton
Early Islamic Syria, Alan Walmsley
Empowering Communities through Archaeology and Heritage, Peter G. Gould
Ethics and Burial Archaeology, Duncan Sayer
Evidential Reasoning in Archaeology, Robert Chapman and Alison Wylie
Fishing and Shipwreck Heritage, Sean A. Kingsley
Fluid Pasts, Matthew Edgeworth
Gerasa and the Decapolis, David Kennedy
Heritage, Communities and Archaeology, Laurajane Smith & Emma Waterton
Houses and Society in the Later Roman Empire, Kim Bowes
Image and Response in Early Europe, Peter S. Wells
Indo-Roman Trade, Roberta Tomber

Loot, Legitimacy and Ownership, Colin Renfrew
Lost Civilization, James L. Boone
Museums and the Construction of Disciplines, Christopher Whitehead
The Origins of the Civilization of Angkor, Charles F. W. Higham
The Origins of the English, Catherine Hills
Pagan and Christian, David Petts
The Remembered Land, Jim Leary
Rethinking Wetland Archaeology, Robert Van de Noort and Aidan O'Sullivan
The Roman Countryside, Stephen L. Dyson
Roman Reflections, Klavs Randsborg
Shaky Ground, Elizabeth Marlowe
Shipwreck Archaeology of the Holy Land, Sean A. Kingsley
Social Evolution, Mark Pluciennik
State Formation in Early China, Li Liu and Xingcan Chen
Towns and Trade in the Age of Charlemagne, Richard Hodges
Tradition and Transformation in Anglo-Saxon England, Susan Oosthuizen
Vessels of Influence, Nicole Coolidge Rousmaniere
Villa to Village, Riccardo Francovich and Richard Hodges

The State in Ancient Egypt

Power, Challenges and Dynamics

Juan Carlos Moreno García

BLOOMSBURY ACADEMIC
LONDON • NEW YORK • OXFORD • NEW DELHI • SYDNEY

BLOOMSBURY ACADEMIC
Bloomsbury Publishing Plc
50 Bedford Square, London, WC1B 3DP, UK
1385 Broadway, New York, NY 10018, USA

BLOOMSBURY, BLOOMSBURY ACADEMIC and the Diana logo are trademarks of Bloomsbury Publishing Plc

First published in Great Britain 2020

Copyright © Juan Carlos Moreno García, 2020

Juan Carlos Moreno García has asserted his right under the Copyright, Designs and Patents Act, 1988, to be identified as Author of this work.

Cover image © Menkaura Triad, Pharaoh Menkaure with Goddesses. Danita Delimont / Alamy Stock Photo

All rights reserved. No part of this publication may be reproduced or transmitted in any form or by any means, electronic or mechanical, including photocopying, recording, or any information storage or retrieval system, without prior permission in writing from the publishers.

Bloomsbury Publishing Plc does not have any control over, or responsibility for, any third-party websites referred to or in this book. All internet addresses given in this book were correct at the time of going to press. The author and publisher regret any inconvenience caused if addresses have changed or sites have ceased to exist, but can accept no responsibility for any such changes.

A catalogue record for this book is available from the British Library.

Library of Congress Cataloging-in-Publication Data

Names: Moreno Garcia, Juan Carlos, author.
Title: The state in ancient Egypt : power, challenges and dynamics / Juan Carlos Moreno Garcia.
Description: London : Bloomsbury Publishing Plc, 2019. | Series: Debates in archaeology | Includes bibliographical references and index.
Identifiers: LCCN 2019004465 (print) | LCCN 2019005590 (ebook) | ISBN 9781350075016 (epub) | ISBN 9781350075009 (epdf) | ISBN 9781350074989 (pbk.) | ISBN 9781350074996 (hardback)
Subjects: LCSH: Egypt—Politics and government—To 332 B.C. | Egypt—History—To 332 B.C.
Classification: LCC DT83 (ebook) | LCC DT83 .M56 2019 (print) | DDC 932/.01—dc23
LC record available at https://lccn.loc.gov/2019004465

ISBN: HB: 978-1-3500-7499-6
PB: 978-1-3500-7498-9
ePDF: 978-1-3500-7500-9
eBook: 978-1-3500-7501-6

Series: Debates in Archaeology

Typeset by RefineCatch Ltd, Bungay, NR35 1EF, UK

To find out more about our authors and books, visit www.bloomsbury.com and sign up for our newsletters.

To my niece Sandra and my nephew Javier, with love.

Contents

List of Figures x
Maps xi
Preface xiii

1 State Theory, Archaeology and the Pharaonic States   1
2 Integrating Spaces   15
3 Managing Resources   37
4 Co-opting Leaders   61
5 Hidden Forces? Invisible Actors and Their Impact on
   the State   87
6 Creating Authority   109
7 Building Statehood Through Culture   137
8 Sociopolitical Change and the State   163
9 The Pharaonic State(s) in Comparative Perspective   187

Bibliography   203
Index   213

Figures

0.1	Map of Egypt	xi
0.2	Map of the Near East	xii
2.1	Egyptian landscape showing the sharp contrast between the flood plain and the adjacent desert	17
3.1	Royal pyramid at Dahshur, built from poor-quality materials. A sign of a weakened tax-system in the early second millennium BC?	43
3.2	Djoser's step pyramid at Saqqara, a sign of the lavish investment of resources in royal monuments around 2650 BC	51
4.1	Scribes represented the ruling class at the service of kings	76
4.2	Officials depicted themselves on costly prestigious monuments. Here, we see one shown as a receiver of funerary offerings	78
6.1	Colossal royal statue at Memphis, symbol of the pharaohs' power	112
6.2	Akhenaten and his wife, Nefertiti, represented in a more informal, even intimate attitude	118
7.1	Nefertiti and her husband, Akhenaten, introduced considerable – but ultimately short-lived – religious innovations	142
7.2	Pyramid texts from the pyramid of King Pepi I at Saqqara	147
8.1	Lists of titles of rank and function expressed the social position of officials and their place in the hierarchical structure of the kingdom	166

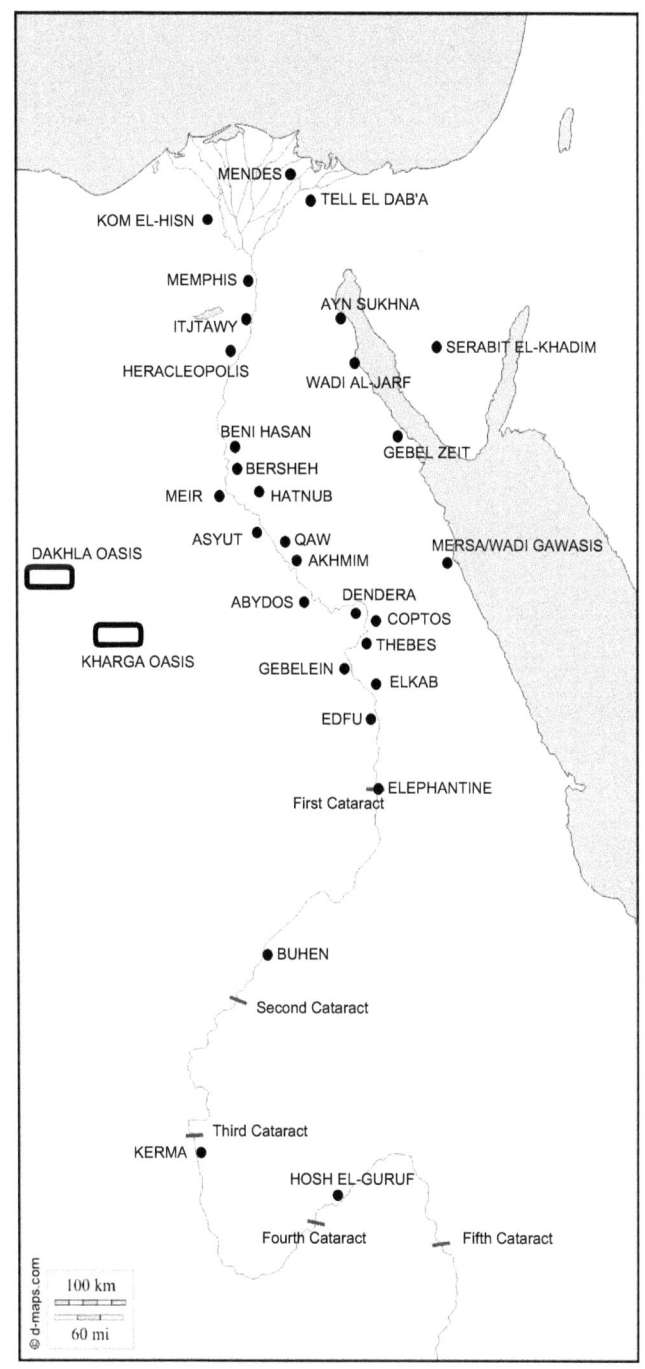

Figure 0.1 Map of Egypt.

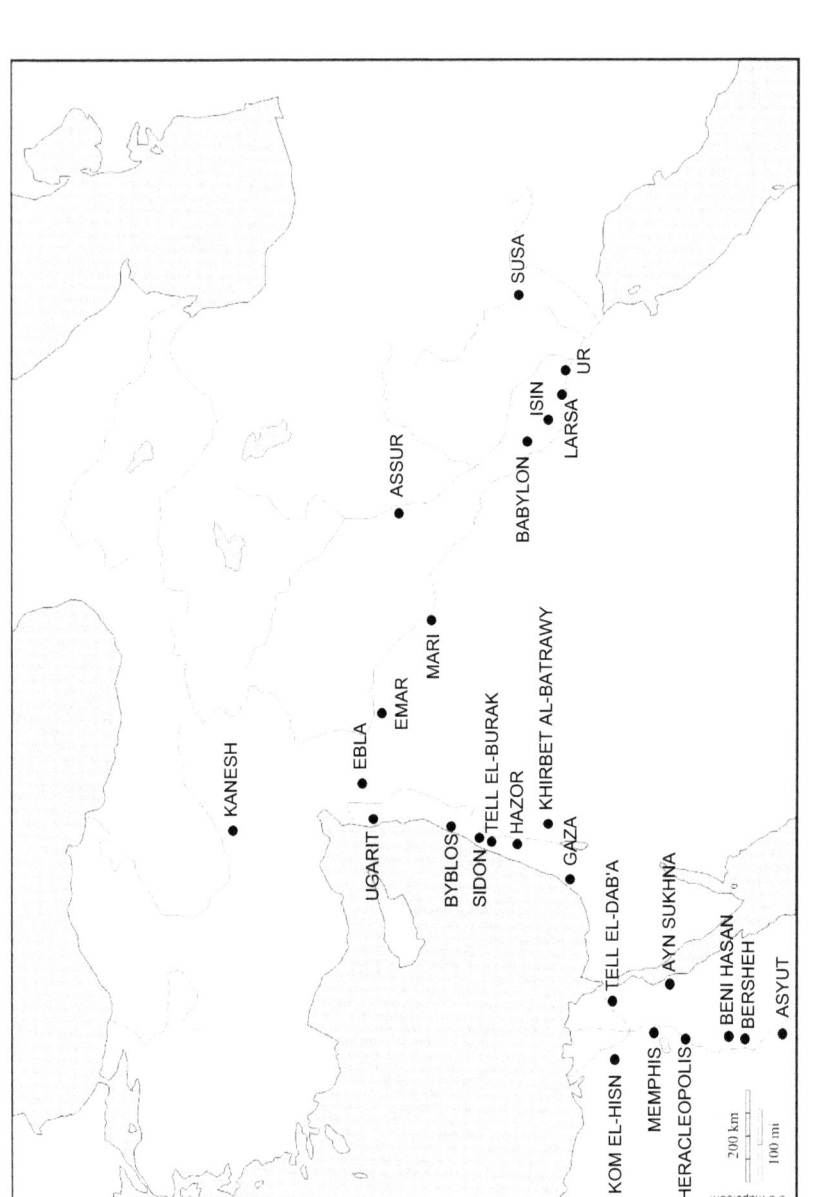

Figure 0.2 Map of the Near East.

Preface

In the primatologist Frans de Waal's book *Chimpanzee Politics* (1982), based on his own fieldwork, he summarized his observations in a single but disturbing statement: the roots of human's political behaviour went back to our closest kin – chimpanzees. Almost four decades later, Craig Stanford (Stanford 2018) confirmed this conclusion, in part inspired by the study of the largest community of chimpanzees known today, at Ngogo, in the Kibale National Park, Uganda. Here, some males develop individual strategies that aim to acquire and preserve power by a variety of means, such as forging hierarchies through the promotion of allies and exclusion of potential rivals, the selective distribution of meat to prospective allies in exchange for their 'political' support (for instance, to attack, overthrow and replace the dominant alpha male), and the organization of hunting expeditions to help build alliances and strengthen bonds between a close group of males. As for collective strategies, repeated 'war' expeditions pursue territorial expansion and capture of resources at the expense of neighbouring chimpanzee communities through a ruthless use of violence, including systematic killing. Recent field studies in West Africa have also revealed a formerly unknown cultural behavioural trait. Adult males throw, and then stack, stones inside hollow trees (referred to as 'shrine trees') in the context of ritualized displays that include particular gestures and vocalizations.

Over the course of thousands of years, a long evolutionary path led to the emergence of a very particular political entity, the state, which was also characterized by a marked social hierarchy, a selective use of violence, territorial control, expansion at the expense of other communities, capture of resources and ritual behaviour. Some authors believe that 'state' as a term should be reserved for a particular political entity created in Europe around the late fifteenth and early sixteenth centuries, consolidated at the Peace of Westphalia in 1648, and theorized by the pioneering work of Machiavelli and Hobbes. According to this view, political formations that do not fit this particular historical trajectory cannot be considered true states and as a result should be seen as belonging to other categories, such as 'monarchies'. However, other authors think that states first appeared in the ancient Near East sometime around 3000 BC, that they shared characteristics usually ascribed to 'tributary states', and that from roughly 500–600 AD onwards, Western Europe began to follow a distinctive political path that departed from this model and ultimately led to the modern state. Since the middle of the nineteenth century, passionate discussions have revolved around the definition and characterization of these and other forms of state according to the degree of political complexity they had achieved, but also around the 'transitions' between them (with the Western state considered the referential epitome of modernity), their divergences and, finally, around the distinctive forms that the exercise of power took in them, as exemplified in the work of authors such as Karl Marx and Max Weber. Anthropology and archaeology also made their own contributions to these discussions as they proposed a parallel line of reasoning, inspired by biology. Thought of as social organisms, political formations were ranged on an evolutionary scale leading from 'primitive' (tribe) to 'complex' (state) through intermediate steps, 'chiefdom' being the most popular (and problematic) of them. In reality, such taxonomies sought to draw a clear contrast between the 'uniqueness' of the West and its supposed economic, political and cultural supremacy, and a backward non-Western Other, located both in the past and in an 'underdeveloped' and/or 'traditional' present. The weight carried by these views is still considerable, because they obscure the role of alternative forms of social organization that do not fit the Western model and its classification criteria, from non-hierarchical and non-centralized agglomerations that were none the less 'cities' to regions and groups of people impervious to any firm control by a political power (Scott 2009; Rodríguez López 2018). Even worse, these views also tend to minimize the role of informal institutions and dense communal bonds that, in the absence of Western-like institutions (codified laws, contracts, division of powers, property, etc.), nonetheless guaranteed security and ensured the reproduction of society's structure and sources of power (among others), despite being dismissed as inefficient or primitive.

As one of the most long-lived political entities recorded in history, pharaonic Egypt (3100–343 BC) constitutes an ideal case study of a society that went through extraordinary changes in the *longue durée*. It was a society that experienced many different configurations of power (unified monarchy, regional kingdoms, empire, vassal of foreign powers, etc.) but which claimed regardless political and cultural continuity based on beliefs, foundational myths and values that forged its identity. It was a society that developed a complex set of institutions (including kingship) as well as governmental and administrative bodies that proved remarkably adaptable to changing political, economic and social conditions under the cover of conservatism and the formal respect of traditions. Ultimately, this society was a vigorous political actor in the international sphere, recognized as such by other polities and capable of developing strategies and deploying the tools necessary to achieve its goals – from war to trade and diplomacy – in the face of other powers. However, the contribution of pharaonic Egypt to the study of statehood and, in general, to comparative research in social sciences has been marginal despite its rich historical and archaeological record, probably because most of Egyptological research has focused traditionally on philology, religion, works of art and factual history.

That is why the aim of this book is threefold. First, it intends to show how ancient Egyptian data might be of use to social scientists and show its extraordinary potential for comparative research. Second, it addresses themes and concepts habitually discussed in social sciences so as to make this information more easily accessible for an audience of non-specialists in Egyptology. Third and finally, the book focuses on how state power was built and organized, how it reproduced itself, the limits and weaknesses it faced and the diverse political forms it took in the long term, depending on the balance of power prevailing at each time. The perspective adopted is thus a dynamic one, far from the still-popular image of an absolutist, rigid and highly centralized monarchy, an image derived mainly from monumental art and official sources. In consequence, this book focuses on the realities of power, its construction, negotiation and exercise, the challenges it encountered, the role played by formal and informal actors, and the elaboration of an official culture that aimed to draw together the ruling elite around the king and, to a lesser degree, to provide the indispensable 'ICT-pack' (Identity, Cohesion, Transcendence) essential for the reproduction and survival of any society. Other components also discussed – and which are present in almost all societies and that assumed specific contents, shapes and interdependencies in each historical context – are territory, authority and rights: the 'TAR-pack' analysed by Saskia Sassen (Sassen 2008). In this sense, the rich theoretical and conceptual framework provided by authors such as Bob Jessop, Michael Mann, Saskia Sassen and others has been a continuous source of inspiration. All in all, I hope that this introductory study to statehood in ancient Egypt will stimulate the interest of social scientists in the rich pharaonic past and help to integrate it more effectively in future comparative research.

1

State Theory, Archaeology and the Pharaonic States

Pharaonic Egypt (3100–343 BC) has traditionally played a marginal role in discussions about ancient states, about the distinctive nature of the state as a particular form of political organization or about the very pertinence of the term 'state' when referring to the political entities that flourished in the Near East during the Bronze and Iron Ages. From the very beginnings of Egyptology, ancient Egypt was considered unique, a society that stood apart from any other of the ancient world, a successful monarchy that lasted for more than three millennia and that represented, together with China, an exceptional case of political continuity in history. Its longevity, which stood in stark contrast to the succession of monarchies and empires prevalent in other parts of the ancient world, was equated with cultural endurance (based on solid moral values), immobility (pharaohs had found the perfect formula to build their power), abundance (Egypt was 'the gift of the Nile') and a model bureaucratic regime. Pharaohs had thus accomplished an extraordinary achievement, that of building, keeping and transferring, from one ruler to the next, the secret of perfect order, social stability, economic prosperity and a successful redistributive state.

For a Western world embarked on the transition from the discredited absolutist order to the new liberal regimes, from an agrarian to an industrial economy in a context of colonial expansion across most of the world, ancient Egypt was regarded in the nineteenth century as an astonishing paradox. In stark opposition to an ancient world characterized by shortage, violence and arbitrary absolutism, Egypt emerged as an outpost of modernity (centralization, efficient administration and resource management, power limited by an ideal of justice) in the most improbable of settings (Africa). At the same time, it also became a sort of refuge from this very modernity and its uncertainties, a repository of a conservative and hierarchical social order, of an elevated spiritual life (exquisite art, sophisticated beliefs in the afterworld) and of submission to an authoritarian but paternal king. It was a welcome contrast to the irruption of the masses in politics, to the crisis of the liberal order in the late 1800s and to the cultural anxieties of a *fin de siècle* sensibility that adumbrated the war and revolutions to come. In other words, pharaonic Egypt was regarded as a kind of venerable Other engaged in a continuous dialogue with the present. The myth of 'eternal Egypt', of its 'uniqueness', of its strange modernity *avant la lettre*, mean that the cultural construction of ancient Egypt was far from being the dispassionate fruit of scientific reflection. And the burden of such a perception is probably nowhere more evident than in the analysis of the organization of the state (Moreno García 2014a).

In fact, it has been taken for granted that ancient Egypt was a state, so much so that the very concept has been barely discussed seriously in Egyptology, for several reasons. As an outpost of modernity, as the very expression of political and cultural sophistication in an otherwise backward African setting, Egypt had all the ingredients needed to be regarded as a state: a centralized and bureaucratic order surrounded by tribal primitive peoples; an 'advanced' society in the evolutionist scale ranging from tribe to (modern) state; a well-defined territory over which pharaohs ruled uncontested; an efficient society replete with solid institutions, governmental offices, hierarchically organized duties and sophisticated administrative practices that had been developed by an impersonal bureaucracy, epitomized by the ubiquitous scribe. In short, it was a world in which kings collected taxes, administered justice and enacted laws. The contrast was apparent with Mesopotamia and its world of rival city-states, ruthless absolutist rulers (Naram-Sin, Shamshi-Adad, Hammurabi, Sennacherib, Nebuchadnezzar) and often ephemeral state-building. However, this impression is misleading, and is based partly on an uncritical reading of primary sources, partly on the desire to find in Egypt solid evidence of an unbroken civilizing path linking antiquity with the contemporary world, especially as Egypt was the setting of biblical and classical stories that helped forge the identity of the Western world. In fact, whereas ancient Mesopotamia, Anatolia and Iran have delivered hundreds of thousands of administrative documents to modern researchers, analogous texts are much rarer in ancient Egypt. Furthermore, many pharaonic documents were discovered in tombs and temples and, consequently, their contents are focused mainly on the activities of kings, officials, priests and official institutions. Even more unhelpfully, many of these texts are geographically and chronologically isolated pieces of information rather than exhaustive series of documents, which in turn makes it difficult to make generalizations. Private archives, as well as documents from urban settlements, are also conspicuously scarce, adding to our lack of knowledge about the role played by crucial sectors of the Egyptian society beyond the ruling elite (peasants, traders, urban craftsmen, local chiefs). Finally, the apparent ideal of rational order, efficiency, moral values and clear division of tasks emanating from the official sources is contradicted by other texts in which versatility, overlapping functions and departments, royal favour, clientelism, influence and corruption were commonplace.

It is important to note that the enduring image of an idealized and unique Egypt is also due to a crucial gap – in fact, an absence of dialogue between Egyptology and social sciences (Baines 2011; Bussmann 2015). The reluctance of many Egyptologists to use social or political theory, or to engage with archaeology or anthropology, has led to a kind of self-satisfied 'splendid isolationism' that finds its counterpart in the inability for many historians, anthropologists and archaeologists to penetrate the apparently arcane world of ancient Egypt – a world alien in many cases to current debates in history and social sciences, and whose intellectual concerns seem limited to philology, rituals, religion, art and factual history, having little to offer to comparative research. The resultant dearth of intellectual engagement across specialisms is rendered even more painful in light of the recent renewal of discussions on the emergence and characteristics of ancient and modern states (Routledge 2014). Since the 1960s, for many years archaeologists thought it plausible to build up solid narratives about the origin, typology and development of early states on the sole basis of archaeological evidence. However, this route reached a dead end in the late 1990s, as it proved impossible to trace a narrow neo-evolutionary path leading from tribe to state, when crucial concepts such as 'chiefdom' and 'complex chiefdom' remained vague, and when accounts of the transition from 'complex chiefdoms' to 'true' states proved elusive, if not inconclusive (Yoffee 2005; Chabal, Feinman & Skalník 2017). This may explain why more recent discussions in archaeology have shifted focus to the dramatic external driving forces of historical change, from societal 'collapse' (and regeneration) to 'climatic change' and 'catastrophic events' (2200 and 1170 BC respectively being the most popular currently). Egyptian contributions to such debates have been marginal and rather crude, other than those from researchers engaged in a productive dialogue with social sciences (for example, Baines & Yoffee 1998; Lehner 2000; Trigger 2003; Warburton 2016; Wenke 2009).

Yet the alleged 'modernity' of the pharaonic state placed ancient Egypt in an ideal position to plug the gap between two main trends in social sciences, one derived from ancient history, archaeology and anthropology, the other from modern history and political philosophy, especially because both trends have followed parallel paths in their respective analysis and conceptualization of the nature of statehood and on the emergence of states, despite little communication between them. A handful of social scientists, such as Max Weber, Shmuel Eisenstadt and Michael Mann, have made a significant effort to integrate the ancient 'oriental' world in their studies, but their contributions have barely influenced Egyptology at all. Inversely, the extraordinarily abundant evidence about the emergence and organization of, and crises in, a great diversity of state forms in classical antiquity and the ancient Near East (city-states, empires, ethnic nations, territorial states, etc.: see Yoffee 2005 and 2015a) has had barely any impact on current thinking about the emergence of the modern state. It is almost as if this European creation were so unique that it owed nothing to its precedents, still less to 'oriental' ones – or as if its main characteristics (division of powers, individuality, property, disintegration of communities, weight of law, exclusive sovereignty over a territory, etc.) constituted the achieved (and exclusive) expression of rationality. Furthermore, the modern state was considered *the* universal model of statehood, the one that indicated the path other polities could follow, and the standard by which 'modernity' could be judged. Underpinning these assumptions was the idea that the emergence of capitalism, industrialization, individuality and 'true' states was an unparalleled European achievement, an exception in history that marked the divergence of the modern Western world not only from its classical and medieval precedents (the Roman Republic, Greek democracy, medieval city councils, etc.), but also from the ancient and modern tributary states that existed in the Near East and in South-East and East Asia. The implications of this interpretation, in which notions such as state, progress, modernity and rationality were inextricably linked, remain influential and their impact visible, for instance, in the recent popularity of neo-institutional approaches in ancient and modern history (North, Wallis & Weingast 2009; Scheidel 2017). In any case, state theory and political philosophy have shown little interest in the study of ancient non-Western states as they diverged markedly from (and had, apparently, a very reduced heuristic potential to explain) the historical trajectory followed by the West.

However, the gradual consolidation of East Asia as the centre of economic and geopolitical power and, as a consequence, an increasing discomfort with traditional eurocentric narratives, explain the recent renewed interest in comparative research, in global history and in the history of alternative paths towards statehood and 'modernity'. In the case of China, this interest justifies the vast mobilization of archaeological research focused on studying the roots of Chinese civilization, its first political structures and their dynamics over millennia. Among the most spectacular finds are the discovery of historical and administrative texts that help understand the political circumstances that led to the consolidation of the Qin empire (221–206 BC), not to mention the ways in which rulers presented themselves and thought about the polities they governed (Pines 2015a). Paradoxically, if Confucianism was invoked in the past to justify the alleged conformism that had blocked the development of capitalism and progress in China, nowadays it is considered a major catalyst for economic development and efficient rule given its emphasis on submission to authority, frugality, loyalty and respect for law, a sort of parallel of the Protestant ethic that, according to Max Weber, contributed to the birth of capitalism. A similar interest revolves around ancient Indian state 'treatises' and their surprisingly 'modern' views on the exercise of royal power and the organization of tax systems, administration, international relations and good, efficient rule (Arjomand 2001). Also based on Indian evidence, some authors have recently shown the shortcomings of the very idea of 'oriental despotism', founded on arbitrary rule and predatory taxation, as it served, in fact, to legitimize the exorbitant taxes levied by British officials after the conquest of India, although this had (allegedly) also been collected hitherto by Mughal rulers. From a different perspective, other studies emphasize that, far from being stagnant political structures, tributary states such as the Ottoman empire and modern China implemented their own original pathways towards 'modernity' and, in doing so, they managed to preserve social and economic practices and customs as efficient as those based on contractual procedures and law in the Western world (Islamoğlu & Perdue 2009). Ultimately, recent comparative research tends to minimize the gap between the West and the East, reduced in these perspectives to a short period between 1750 and 1950 AD. From an economic point of view, other studies reveal that areas dominated by tributary states such as seventeenth- to eighteenth-century AD China, South Asia and Southeast Asia were characterized by a dense network of trade relations, complex manufacturing production systems and sophisticated financial practices in a context of regional economic specializations. As we can see, commercial capitalism was not a characteristic exclusive to the modern West. It had been already operating in the Islamic world and in Asia centuries before it appeared in the cities of medieval Italy and northern Europe, so the trope of Western 'exceptionalism' appears difficult to justify (Banaji 2018; Tedesco 2018). Finally, recent studies go one step further and suggest that capitalism already existed in other parts of the world well before its final triumph in the West and that, contrary to common assumptions about its economic efficiency, rational organization and managerial superiority, it actually led to inequality and to the decline of the societies in which it appeared (Van Bavel 2016).

In my opinion, these historiographical trends may help reconsider the concept of the 'tributary state' and recalibrate its heuristic potential (Haldon 1993; Banaji 2010; da Graca & Zingarelli 2015). Once liberated from the traditional role ascribed to tributary states as the negative 'Other' in the narratives that celebrated the irresistible rise of the West and the success of its vibrant liberal capitalist societies, those states now appear in a new light. They emerge as dynamic *and enduring* political organizations in which power was negotiated and in which formal and informal authorities challenged (and limited) the authority of kings. In these tributary states, religion supplanted the role of *civic* communities for two main reasons. First, it provided social order thanks to the primary 'ICT-pack' discussed in the Introduction. And this divinely sanctioned order was non-negotiable (it derived from the gods) and, consequently, it rendered politics superfluous, considering politics as social groups defined by distinctive identities and interests, that promoted collective deliberations about long-term goals and that reached provisional agreements (or ended up in conflict) depending on their respective balance of power within a civic community. Second, at the same time, tributary states were perfectly compatible with the private economy, markets and sets of rules that regulated transactions and social relations, often in the absence of formal laws or of any intervention from 'public' powers. So, the 'ancient' and 'oriental' city cannot be reduced to the role of a mere ceremonial stage for rulers, to a parasitical centre of consumption and accumulation of wealth (mainly taxes) that had little to offer in return to an otherwise impoverished and almost autarchic rural population. Quite the contrary: the city's manufacturing and commercial activities were facilitated by credit, joint ventures and investments in specific sectors that for some time paved the way for commercial capitalism, for economic specialization within international spheres of trade and for modest economic growth (Banaji 2018). Furthermore, even though an extraordinary diversity of political entities have been labelled 'tributary states', they share nonetheless distinctive configurations of power that should encourage comparative research. For example, the idea that tributary states blocked the emergence of powerful landed aristocracies, whose main basis of revenue and wealth was independent of the income granted by the state, is challenged by the Persian tradition and its wealthy regional nobility, from pre-Achaemenid Elam to the Sasanian and Safavid empires. In other cases, such as the Vijayanagara empire, royal power (including taxation and monumental buildings) was far from homogeneous over the territory supposedly under its authority. Border areas separating tributary and feudal states (as in medieval Spain) also offer fertile ground for comparative analysis about crucial questions such as taxation, territorial organization, the structure of the ruling class, the resilience of peasant communities, the impact of trade and specialized manufacturing, etc. on the kingdom's economy. Finally, recent trends in global history tend to qualify the alleged 'great divergence' of the West (including economic growth, the impact of technological innovation or the rise in living standards: Kron forthcoming) while stressing autonomous paths towards economic growth and economic performance in other areas of the world, particularly in Eastern Asia. In some cases, they open new avenues of research on topics such as the persistence of a subsistence economy despite widespread commercialization, one that was able to sustain an extremely high level of market growth without bringing inevitably capitalist socio-economic relations.

In the light of these considerations, neo-institutionalist analyses of pre-modern states and economies, taking modern Western states as their model, appear rather problematic (Inomata 2016). The idea that institutions such as law, markets, capitalist relations, property, contracts, individuality and rational decision-making – specifically *in the forms they took in western Europe following the Renaissance* – are the most common ways of reducing transaction costs, and that they mark the universal route to economic growth, efficiency and universal prosperity, seems debatable at best. To begin with, these social and economic relations emerged in a very particular historical context. It was a period during which diverse actors offered rival interpretations of sovereignty, legitimate authority and fair taxation (particularly after the Wars of Religion during the sixteenth and seventeenth centuries). Taken together with the extension of social relations based on property (and the disintegration of communal property), continuous warfare, etc., these conditions led to a precarious construction of civic communities, all of which were searching for an acceptable equilibrium they would never be able to achieve in the long term. So, provisional arrangements prevailed in the construction of institutions whose very foundations were subject to continuous negotiation. Yet other – non-Western – societies developed informal sets of institutions rooted in a dense network of social relations that proved their efficiency in procuring economic security and in stimulating extensive trade networks, economic growth and social prosperity. Furthermore, the very idea that Western institutions are unique in their achievement of rational operations, as if they were neutral and ahistorical, is simply false. Institutions are the unstable result of power relations, struggles, alliances and negotiations between different actors, partially framed by and expressed in traditions, partly capable of modifying such traditions and the older balance of power they encoded in order to cope with new realities. Institutions are rooted in history and in politics and it would be too simplistic to analyse them in the light of modern Western concepts and forms of organization (from law to property) as if they were the expression of natural and universally valid human qualities and attitudes that spanned the millennia unchanged, irrespective of the society and time that engendered them (Bryant 2006; Narotzky & Manzano 2014; Manzano 2015; Sánchez León & Izquierdo Martín 2002; Zarakol 2018). The same can be posited about the state. As Jessop claims, 'instead of looking at the state as a substantial, unified thing or unitary subject [...] *state power* is a contingent expression of a changing balance of forces that seek to advance their respective interests inside, through, and against the state system' (Jessop 2016: 54).

To conclude, the role played by ancient Egypt in recent discussions about statehood and the nature of the state is very limited, despite the increasing interest in the organization, structure and dynamics of non-Western states, ancient and modern, and the growing importance of comparative research in these topics.

Rethinking ancient states: The Egyptian example

This new approach to the analysis of ancient states and statehood, far removed from well-established views about the universality of Western concepts and historical trajectories, is fast gaining traction. Its consequences are manifold. While, for example, rigid typologies inspired by traditional archaeological and anthropological thought have lost much of their former appeal, we see a shift towards sophisticated methods and theories borrowed from social sciences, all of which make it possible to glean richer and more nuanced insights from selected case studies (from single sites to entire regions and periods). The result is the accumulation of an impressive mass of information that helps us understand ancient societies and their mutual interactions in their own terms. Researchers are being forced to rethink basic concepts and models of social interaction, of management of resources and of creation of landscapes. This in turn facilitates the formulation of questions about the origin, modalities and historical dynamics of ancient states; the capturing of a diversity that cannot be reduced to a mere arena for the application of models of historical change elaborated elsewhere; and, consequently, the stimulation of disciplinary dialogue and comparative research. The Mari archives, for instance, have modified older views about nomad populations and revealed their political autonomy, scope of interests and capacity to force states to negotiate if vital routes of trade and communication were to remain open. The site at Tell Leilan, in northern Mesopotamia, reveals that, in the early second millennium BC, kingdoms in this area initially comprised people in the main, and places in a secondary capacity, as they were often geographically non-contiguous and intersected with zones controlled by nomadic populations, by other states or by independent villages and regions. Thus concepts such as 'sovereignty' and 'border(s)' appear problematic when it comes to defining the intensity of royal power over such a patchwork of peoples and territories (Ristvet 2008; Smith 2005). Furthermore, the actual exercise of royal authority over a kingdom was actually patchy at times, despite the claims to supreme rule expressed in royal ideology. This was the case for the northern Mesopotamian kingdom carved out by Shamshi-Adad I and which included Assyria, the strategic caravan city of Mari and the plain east of the Tigris. Shamshi-Adad managed to conquer a substantial territory and installed his sons as kings of the cities of Ekallatum and Mari. However, the correspondence between Shamshi-Adad and his sons portrays a desperately chaotic organization of the kingdom, replete with ad hoc measures necessary to forge a semblance of cohesion. This unique documentation shows the actual implementation of authority as the three leaders of an early empire disclosed, deliberated and discussed their strategies and tactics in some detail (Eidem 2014). Finally, textual and archaeological evidence shows areas that escaped the control of any central power or state (peoples living in autonomous villages and in marshy or mountainous environments). Substantial settlements reveal the existence of heterarchical forms of power, in which the absence of centralized political and religious institutions probably points to collective (but not necessarily egalitarian) forms of decision-making (i.e. councils of elders, city assemblies) and ritual activities (i.e. ancestor cults) that provided cohesion and identity to the entire community (Otto 2012; Feinman & Nicholas 2016).

Many more examples could be given and, as is the case already with regard to ancient economies, the potential and wealth of information of the societies of the ancient Near East should provide a more complex and nuanced basis for current debates in social sciences. This is why recent comparative research between two or more ancient political formations combines the analyses of key concepts with the use of the methods and conceptual framework of social sciences. Infrastructural power, taxation, statehood, the formation of the elite, the shaping of ethnic and religious identities, etc., are just a few expressions of this shift (see, for example, Bang & Bayly 2011; Liverani 2013; Monson & Scheidel 2015; Lavan, Payne & Weisweiler 2016; Ando & Richardson 2017; Düring & Stek 2018). Another is the increasing number of comparative analyses about selected case studies, probably the most influential being those on ancient Rome and China (Scheidel 2015), the specific traits of tributary states and, ultimately, the comparative historical trajectories of societies that pointed either to precocious forms of (commercial) capitalism and sustained economic growth or to alternative, idiosyncratic paths towards 'modernity'. Some incipient research reveals the possibilities for comparative studies between pharaonic Egypt and ancient China, the two most enduring pre-modern political formations (Baines 2014; Yoffee 2015b).

In fact, pharaonic Egypt provides a unique opportunity to study the transformations of a political formation that claimed continuity and adhered to an ideal of kingship over three millennia. More specifically, it is only in the last two decades or so that research has gradually departed from uncritical interpretations of the Egyptian state, based mainly on the ideological values it produced and the ideal order it allegedly embodied. Instead, the focus is moving increasingly to the reality of and limits on the exercise of authority, to the networks of power sustained by the ruling elite and its main institutions (temples, the royal palace, etc.), to the formation and transformations of the dominant social sectors, to the very possibilities of politics in a supposedly highly centralized monarchical order, to the fluctuating relations and balance of power between the centre and the provinces, etc. According to this perspective, the work inspired by Gundlach (2006 and 2009) and Baines, among others, and developed by Quirke (1991), Eyre (1999 and 2004), Kanawati (2003), Spence (2007), Raedler (2004 and 2006), Shirley (2010) and Moreno García (2013a) centred on a particular pharaoh, institution or period (Gnirs 1996; O'Connor & Cline 1998; Cline & O'Connor 2012; Dodson 2012), and the increasing use of the methods of social sciences in the study of the diverse articulations of power, prove particularly illuminating. Another very promising area of study concerns the influence of geopolitics on the distinctive historical trajectories followed by the Egyptian state(s), from unification to collapse, from the emergence of many rival political entities to the final crystallization of state power in the areas connected to a changing international environment. The role played by different regions, the influence of ecology (such as the deltaic conditions prevalent in Lower Egypt, or the local availability of pasture land and the presence of mobile populations in Middle Egypt), access to key resources and routes, the influence of Nubia and so on, may help explain how and why different combinations of regions were integrated at last into one or several larger states in the Nile Valley. Such factors tell us why, for instance, the political system prevailing in Lower Egypt in most periods of history seems more akin to the Levant (small polities in which supremacy of one of them was short-lived); why Upper Egypt (at least its southernmost section), on the contrary, constituted a more homogeneous political space; and why, consequently, political unity was one possibility (among others) but turned out to be the one that prevailed for longer periods of time than in any other area of the ancient Near East. In the end, Egypt shared many characteristics with other societies of the ancient world, but it also displayed particularities as well as idiosyncratic historical trajectories that may reveal how articulations of power proved to be more stable there than elsewhere. These idiosyncrasies can only enrich our knowledge of tributary states and, more generally, the organization of power in early states.

2

Integrating Spaces

A patchwork of regions and ecotopes

Ancient Egypt consisted mostly of a narrow strip of fertile land over 870 km long (stretching from Memphis to Elephantine), and surrounded by one of the harshest desert environments on earth. The valley then opened into a delta crossed by several nilotic branches, some of them less stable than others, in a marsh landscape spotted by *gezira* ('turtlebacks'), mounds of sand unaffected by the annual flood and on which crops were planted and herds kept. Marshes and wadis spotted Upper and Middle Egypt, and their humid conditions produced a diversified landscape made up of pasture land, bushlands and seasonal waterways. These conditions explain why ancient Egypt was a patchwork of regions, across which were marked differences in ecology, demography and settlement patterns. Their varied integration into trade networks and routes (influenced by geopolitical factors), the local availability of resources (including political ones), the density of settlements and population as well as the balance between diverse lifestyles (based on agriculture or on pastoralism, fishing, waterfowling and different combinations thereof), marked the particular historical trajectory of each region and its integration into the monarchy. Far from the apparent uniformity suggested both by its oasis-like appearance and cartography, characterized by both well-defined borders and an homogeneous implementation of the pharaohs' authority (Smith 2005), Egypt included quite divergent areas. Lower Egypt (the Delta) was an unevenly settled region, with close links to the Levant and where power frequently took on a 'confederate' aspect, in that it was organized around one principal kingdom and several smaller ones. Upper Egypt, by contrast, appears to have been more easily centralized, to the point that the area between Abydos and Elephantine appears as a well-defined territorial entity by the third millennium BC. Cultivable land was far less abundant in this narrow strip of the valley, but the presence of marshes, wadis and the many routes leading to the oases of the Western Desert, facilitated the arrival of nomadic peoples ('Libyans', Nubians) while trade flourished there. Its three major nodes of power were Elephantine itself (the traditional gateway to inner Africa), the area around Thebes/Coptos (which connected the Nile Valley to the Red Sea) and Abydos/Thinis (the departure point for routes toward the oases of the Western Desert). Finally, Middle Egypt (particularly the area between Asyut and Bersheh) often exerted a strong political influence during Egyptian history, sometimes opposed, sometimes allied, to the state's rulers (Moreno García 2017). It was a sparsely populated area with abundant areas of marsh and pasture, the latter ideal for cattle-grazing. Recent geoarchaeological research also shows that the course of the Nile moved over the millennia, towards the east in general, thus producing a changing landscape of waterways, sand islands, marshes, pasture, bushlands and shifting alluvial plains quite different from the homogeneous landscape visible today. Let us not forget, however, the influence of external actors. The arid conditions of north-eastern Africa meant that savanna and grazing land bordering the Nile Valley were very limited (basically confined to wadis, the oases of the Western Desert and some areas of the Mediterranean coast between the Delta and Cyrenaica). Pastoral peoples were therefore of little relevance demographically, although they were influential actors in many other regions of the Near East. However, 'Libyans' (in fact, peoples living west of the Nile Valley) were more than simple marauders and played an important role, still to be determined in modern research, as traders handling alternative commercial routes to the Nile. Nubia, occasionally a major African power, influenced the internal affairs of Egypt sporadically, and even limited the geopolitical role of Egypt as privileged mediator between inner Africa, the northern Indian Ocean and the Mediterranean. So, far from being a 'despotic' centralized state,

Egypt was the playground for different configurations of power and territorial integration, all of which determined its historical dynamics and its variable capacity to capture resources and control land and peoples.

In such diversified landscape, the Nile not only played a key role in guaranteeing the subsistence and lifestyles of the populations living on its margins, but also provided an essential means of communication and transport. However, navigating it was far from simple. The seasonal shift of dominant winds, not to mention the presence of changing sandbanks (especially after the annual flood), made transport difficult, while the considerable distance between Elephantine, in southernmost Egypt, and the Mediterranean (about 1,000 km) hampered the communication of messages and instructions, as well as the mobilization of resources. The deserts provided alternative routes along which goods and people could circulate, and opened up the possibility of travellers and traders bypassing the Nile route, and the control imposed by

Figure 2.1 Egyptian landscape showing the sharp contrast between the flood plain and the adjacent desert.

pharaonic authorities, altogether. Nonetheless, as dromedaries were introduced only relatively late in Egyptian history, donkeys were required to traverse the desert tracks, which limited the ability of desert populations and caravans to escape the control of pharaohs; checkpoints at selected locations monitored the circulation of goods and people, and taxed the riches circulating across these areas. It should be noted, however, that such control was possible only through the collaboration of local people, who were frequently employed as guides and guards or escorts.

Networking in a fluvial environment

Three aspects marked the articulation and integration of spaces in *early* Egypt. The first is the complementary use of diverse areas and ecosystems by the populations living in the Nile Valley, the wadis and the surrounding steppes. Seasonal migrations were common between hunting and fishing areas, pasture land, etc., both in the Nile Valley and in the Western Desert and, according to the titles held by some officials, mobile populations crossed into and moved through the Nile Valley. In other cases, nomadic people lived *inside* Egypt, particularly fishermen, bird hunters and cattle-herders. Settling them into sedentary habitats was a goal pursued by Egyptian authorities but, in other cases, the itinerant peoples preserved their distinctive lifestyles down the centuries, as was the case in the Eastern Delta with the *sekhetiu* 'countrymen' of the early second millennium BC or the Greco-Roman *boukoloi*. The circulation of people across extensive tracts of land was a distinctive mark of early Egypt that never disappeared fully afterwards. The second aspect is that a low demographic density, coupled with the persistence of nomadic lifestyles in marshy and bushland areas (particularly in Lower and Middle Egypt), favoured those dispersed habitats and economic activities that were based more on networks than on a landscape of dense urban life with intensive agricultural activities. The third aspect is that the geographical location of the Nile

Valley made it a privileged transit area between the Red Sea, northeastern Africa, the Mediterranean and the Levant. (The strip of oases across the Libyan desert played a similar role, but to a lesser extent.) The circulation of riches and fluidity of contacts in a loosely occupied territory seem thus to prevail over intensive uses of spaces and resources (agriculture, urbanism, etc.), while pastoralism remained an important economic activity that marked the origins of pharaonic civilization. This may explain why control over mobile wealth (cattle and, secondarily, gold) was crucial in the organization of the early royal taxation system, to the point that the biannual census of cattle became the standard event by which years were dated in the third millennium BC ('the year of the x-th occasion of the count of the cattle'). In some cases, the counting of gold was occasionally celebrated in the annals of the archaic kings ('fourth year: first time for counting gold'), sometimes at the same time as the assessment of fields (or the countryside), also on a biannual basis ('year 13: seventh time for counting gold and fields/countryside'). In turn, cities remained surprisingly modest (judging from the archaeological evidence) and hardly played a major role as transformation and craft production centres that supported market-oriented activities, until the second millennium BC (Moeller 2016).

In these circumstances, funerary monuments remained distinctive landscape markers from the Neolithic to the early second millennium BC. I refer here not to huge temples or 'public' structures, such as those found in ancient Mesopotamia, but rather to distinctive mound burials (mastabas, later pyramids) erected in places with high symbolic importance. This is why early kings built mastabas in key centres of their kingdom, such as Abydos (the ancestral burial place of the first pharaohs and their predecessors) and Memphis. Other members of the royal family also built monumental mastabas near important sites, including Naqada, Abydos and Elkab. Later on, around 2600 BC, kings built small step pyramids in Upper Egypt (none have yet been discovered in Lower Egypt), but their actual function is still debated. They could well have marked the symbolic presence of the monarchy at significant locations within the kingdom and it is even possible that each one of them was the core of an economic unit. Other documents confirm the importance of networks in the early implementation of royal authority in the country. Hundreds of stone vessels buried as offerings in the corridors of the step pyramid of King Djoser (2686–2668 BC) were inscribed with the names of the institutions and officials that presented them. They thus provide invaluable information about the administrative organization of the kingdom and reveal the existence of a network of royal agricultural centres (replete with cattle, extensive fields and workers) scattered all over the country, the 'big *ḥwt*' being by far the most common of these. The *ḥwt* was a prestigious building, a kind of tower that served as the centre of an agricultural and productive unit which included fields, workers and cattle, and which also played the role of storage facility and even defensive structure. Royal plantations (mostly vineyards, particularly in the Western Delta), specialized workshops or storage facilities (such as the '*ḥwt* of flax', the '*ḥwt* of gold', and so on), as well as the 'houses' of individuals, completed the picture. It seems that the territorial organization of the kingdom was dual, based partly on agricultural and production centres founded by the crown, and partly on 'houses' of local potentates whose links with the royal administration are poorly understood (local magnates? Agents of the king?). In any case, the monarchy recognized the authority of these potentates as leaders in their own areas of influence. Cities played apparently no significant role in this administrative pattern. A practical illustration of how this system operated comes from Elkab, where a complex was equipped with storage facilities and processing areas for agricultural produce. Moreover, recovered administrative seals mention several high-ranking officials whose activities are also known from other locations, extending from Abydos in the north to Elephantine in the south, and who were involved mainly in the management of ploughs and granaries. The geographical scope of their activities, and the nature of their responsibilities, confirm the role played by the crown in the organization of networks of agricultural, storage, processing and supply centres. Finally, hundreds of seal stamps found at Elephantine and dating from around 2650 BC, reveal that the control of gold was a major concern for the monarchy and that many people (both men and women) were involved in trading activities there. A fragment of an inscription even refers to 'the desert which produces gold'. In all, the circulation of wealth across the Nile Valley stimulated an early organization of power based on networks whose nodes were royal foundations involved in production and supply activities for expeditions, officials on the move, etc. In this model cities played a very minor role, to the point that when local elites became more visible in the archaeological record thanks to their temples and decorated tombs, the urban centres (if any) associated with them remain in many cases rather elusive throughout the third millennium BC. Perhaps, in some cases, because their physical traces have been destroyed or not yet discovered. The pharaonic model of the early state differs substantially from that prevailing in the Near East at that time, and probably owes much to its pastoral roots (Moreno García 2013b).

From 2600 BC, private officials' inscriptions as well as the royal annals reveal a substantial change. Former 'houses' – which in some cases include entire localities – were replaced by royal centres of the crown as sizeable organizational hubs in the countryside. The territorial organization of the country was systematically reclassified at that point, leading to the formal integration of local potentates in the administrative structure and courtly life of the kingdom. King Snofru encouraged the foundation of many ḥwt-centres and the inscriptions of some of his officials who were involved in the control of the provinces confirm this pattern. The relevance of this network was such that the decoration of royal funerary temples and private tombs included a new motif, the procession of personifications of royal ḥwt and localities bringing offerings to the deceased. Sometime later, from around 2500 BC, temples appeared as another major pole of territorial organization, judging from the massive donations of land granted by kings and from their role as providers of manpower and supplies for expeditions. Land donations to provincial temples made kings 'present' in the countryside, but they also provided local potentates (who controlled these temples) with increased means to assert their economic and symbolic predominance in their home sphere.

This policy reached a peak in 2350–2180 BC. The *ḥwt* network covered all Egypt and these centres were distributed evenly across Upper and Lower Egypt. Temples and *ḥwt* were thus the landmarks of a network of economic and production hubs that constituted 'islands of (royal) authority' and which imposed order on an extensive, if sparsely populated, territory, where cities remained the exception rather than the rule. Temples and *ḥwt* also constituted powerful tools via which the ruling class could penetrate into a rural world dominated by provincial potentates. Similar networks operated in Memphis (the capital) itself: administrative documents show that a network of institutions including the palace, some state departments and other temples in Memphis, supplied the funerary temples of kings with the foodstuff, cattle, textiles, ritual objects and so on used in their everyday activities.

Despite their undoubted importance, temples and *ḥwt* were only two of the main components of the Egyptian landscape. Many dual expressions from the third millennium BC evoke *ḥwt* and *nwt* ('settlements', ranging in size from hamlets and villages to towns and cities, even agricultural domains) as the main habitats in Egypt, and several *nwt* formed a district under the authority of a *ḥwt*. However, it is striking that – as noted above – cities played a modest role in the articulation of power in this early phase of Egyptian history. Judging both from the epigraphic and archaeological evidence, cities happened to be rather small when compared, for instance, to their contemporary Mesopotamian and Syrian equivalents, thus pointing to a different path of organization of the country in the Nile Valley (Moreno García 2013b).

Elusive cities?

The very end of the third millennium BC was a period of significant change in the structure of settlement in the Nile Valley, as the crown's *ḥwt* virtually disappeared, cities emerged for the first time as nodes of territorial organization and social identity and harbour or port areas (*dmj*) became distinctive poles of economic activity as markets and trading centres, to the point that the word *dmj* became gradually a synonym of town, 'city'. *Dmj*-cities/harbours even became major targets in the military operations undertaken by the regional powers competing for power at that time, as is recorded in the fragmentary biographical inscription from the tomb of Iti-ibi of Asyut. Finally, another word, *wḥyt* ('village'), appeared for the first time in some inscriptions to designate a kind of settlement whose members were bound by kinship ties (in fact, *wḥyt* also meant 'tribe'). So when vizier Rekhmire (who lived around 1450–1400 BC) had the main units of the fiscal structure of the kingdom portrayed on the walls of his tomb, he chose to feature a procession of eighty offering-bearers who represented cities of Upper Egypt, from Asyut in the north to Elephantine in the south. According to the texts that accompany the bearers, each city delivered taxes in gold, silver, cattle and other goods. The importance of precious metals is corroborated by the bearers themselves, who carry baskets loaded with rings and necklaces of gold and silver. As had been the case fifteen centuries earlier, gold, precious metals and cattle constituted the basis of the royal tax system. Another innovation related to the emergence of cities as territorial and administrative units was that each city controlled a *w* or 'district', which replaced the *ḥwt* as the centre of a group of villages. Finally, titles and biographical records from this period mention 'governors' (*haty-a*) of specific cities. Taken together, these elements reveal that a crucial change had led to the abandonment of the previous state-organized network of institutional centres in favour of a structure of organic settlements. Cities apparently assumed functions formerly devolved on *ḥwt*, specifically their role as collecting and supply centres and the administrative nodes of rural districts. It is also possible that this move towards a decentralization of functions and the increasing autonomy of settlements was accompanied by some form of urban (self?-)government, judging from the title of 'member of the council (*qnbt*) of the district (*w*)', dating from the early second millennium BC. Nonetheless, the composition of these councils is unknown: perhaps they comprised urban notables, a mix of dignitaries and local potentates? Maybe their functions were similar to the 'councils' (*djadjat*) formed by village chiefs and agents of the crown that administrated the agricultural domains granted by the kings to local temples in the late third millennium BC. About 1550 BC viziers instructed 'district councillors' to report on the state of their districts and, at the same time, some records suggest that city-dwellers acted as a collective body in legal lawsuits, like 'the people of Elephantine', owners of serfs, described in Berlin Papyrus 10470 or the witnesses presented collectively as 'the people of the town (*nwt/dmj*)' in British Museum (BM) Papyrus 10335 and Berlin Papyrus 9785.

If the end of the monarchy at around 2160 BC – and its replacement by the emergence of rival regional powers competing for wealth and supremacy – was the outcome of the increase in trade activities across the Nile Valley since 2350 BC, then it is possible that the development of cities (and their harbour facilities) made redundant the *ḥwt* network as providers of logistical support and supplies along the Nile. At the same time, this crucial change suggests that the organization of trade was far from being a royal monopoly, as trade continued to flourish after the collapse of the monarchy. It was at exactly this point that, when no unified monarchy ruled over Egypt, city-size increased dramatically: for example, Edfu expanded from eight to fifteen ha; a large residential 'middle-class' neighbourhood was built at Dendera; and a new neighbourhood was also erected at Elephantine. 'Middle-class' residences, equipped with storage facilities, have also been found at Abydos; the relatively small quantities of seals recovered there, and the lack of repeated seal designs, suggest that they do not represent institutionally connected administrative activities, but rather the administration of lower-level households. Finally, cities thrived in Middle Egypt (Asyut and Bersheh) as well as in the Western Delta (Barnugi, Kom el-Hisn, Abu Ghalib), in this case linked to the trade route that connected the Mediterranean to Middle Egypt through the western branch of the Nile (Moeller 2016).

Trade, economic prosperity and the emergence of cities seem to go hand in hand. At the same time, this was a period in which cities became ideologically relevant as source of legitimation and identity, in the absence of a single monarchy. Thus, the approval of an official's actions by his city became a popular expression in many inscriptions ('one beloved by his city'). Protecting or enriching one's town were also popular motifs, and similar epithets remained fashionable in later inscriptions commissioned by the elite, particularly in the provinces. Even ritual texts from the early second millennium BC incorporated the new role of cities in their descriptions of households of the deceased, and expanded to include a person's relatives and immediate social network as well as *nwtjw* and *dmjw* ('fellow-citizens' – literally people from the *nwt/dmj*-city). Urban audiences thus became significant for reasons of ideology and legitimacy in the early second millennium BC. Their rise in importance meant they could pose risks to rulers, which may explain why, in some passages from *The Teaching for King Merykara*, the incendiary speeches of demagogues and agitators disturbed the peace of cities and swept urban dwellers into rebellion. New terms appeared at this time, such as 'man-of-the-city' (citizen?) and 'living-one-of-the-city' (officer of the city troops), and point to the growing importance of towns and townsmen as providers of military support to provincial leaders. In fact, it is quite probable that the use of city troops during the upheaval that followed the Old Kingdom implied some kind of recognition towards (and perhaps approval of) urban dwellers, especially in the inscriptions from Hatnub, Asyut, etc. In this context, economic autonomy and personal initiative became highly prized values, as indicated by the motif of the autonomous individual (*nedjes*, 'the modest/humble one'), who is able to earn his own living, to build up a personal patrimony by his own actions, and to transfer that to his descendants without any royal intervention. Women also participated in this societal shift. The new title 'mistress of the house' designated an adult, independent woman who was able to manage all aspects of a household – with, or without a male owner – or take part in some other business activity. In fact, the analysis of women's seals found in Middle Egypt reveals traces of wear and usage which show that they were not made exclusively for funerary purposes. Seals and sealing ended up being used routinely in everyday transactions and contracts, such as the purchase of land and houses and the hiring of specialized priests, and the echoes of this practice emerge in contemporary ritual texts. Thus sealing practices were much more frequent in the *Coffin Texts* (dating from the very late third millennium BC onwards) than they had been in the earlier *Pyramid Texts*. The extent of sealing, and the use of sealed documents, point to a greater scope of transactions and economic initiative in which formal agreement and authentication were required.

In this more decentralized context, a question appears: were *ḥwt* the nodes from which at least some cities emerge? 'The *ḥwt* at the crossroad of Khety' (Khety being a royal name) could be found near to Tell el-Daba, in the Eastern Delta, and it seems plausible that a *ḥwt* founded by a king within this important strategic area would ultimately develop into a city that became one of the major trade hubs of the Eastern Mediterranean in the Middle Bronze Age (Goedicke 2002). An early Middle Kingdom administrative document enumerates the various kinds of textile items delivered to an overseer of the seal during his journey to the locality of Per-Ikhekh; he received them from a warehouse, a working centre and a locality or royal centre named 'The *ḥwt* of (king) Khety' (Moreno García 2013b). The names of other Egyptian cities were formed with the element *ḥwt*, so it seems plausible that some of them developed from an original royal foundation. In any case, if previous formulaic expressions included the words *ḥwt* and *nwt*, later 'juridical' expressions featuring the formula 'in the city and in the countryside' served to evoke all the possessions of an individual. Later on, from 1550 onward, formulaic expressions refer to *dmj*, *nwt* and *wḥyt*-villages as the three main types of settlement in Egypt.

Not surprisingly, as harbours and quays were also market places, terms such as *dmj* ('city') and *mryt* ('quay') became, in some cases, synonymous with markets. Thus Sarenput I, governor of the caravan and port city of Elephantine around 1950 BC, included among his duties control over river trade, ports, markets and foreign commodities arriving into Egypt. He was 'overseer of all tribute at the entrance of the foreign countries in the form of royal ornaments, to whom the tribute of the Medya-country was brought as contribution of the rulers of the foreign countries', as well as 'one who rejoices over the quay/market-place, the overseer of the great ships of the Royal Domain, who supplies the Double Treasury, the superior of the ports in the province of Elephantine (so that) what navigates and what moors was under his authority'. A similar claim figures in a brief literary text that celebrates markets in the city of Pi-Ramesses: 'Pleasant is the place of distribution/market-place with its money/silver there, mainly the vine tendrils (?) and business/commerce (*t-m-k-r-i-t*). The chiefs of every foreign country come in order to descend with their products.' Several scenes discovered in tombs dating from the third and second millennium BC show busy harbour areas full of people selling and buying, a role in which women excelled. Furthermore, several archives from the second half of the second millennium BC record the deliveries of textiles, wine, fruits, food and so on made by individuals along the river routes to groups of boats dispatched by temples and institutions in search of specialized (mostly perishable) goods. In some cases, such deliveries concerned textiles and cloth, in other cases dates, fruits and vegetables, produced in small plantations by affluent landowners able to afford the costly irrigation devices that made their cultivation possible. Literary texts from this period also celebrate the wealth of the horticultural landscape that surrounded cities. Unfortunately, we lack detailed evidence of the scope of the transactions involved, but in any case cities and their harbour areas emerge as active centres of river-based trade and barter, places that were frequented by traders who also lent to individuals. In fact, inscriptions and papyri from 1500 BC onwards reveal that quays and landing stages were not only fluvial facilities but also sites in which taxes were levied, and on some occasions they were provided with income to fulfil their administrative and economic duties (Moreno García forthcoming).

The commercial role of at least some pharaonic cities is evident in the cases of Elephantine and Tell el-Daba/Avaris. In some cases, their impact on the distribution of power was such that they became the core of emerging polities. The emergence of Heracleopolis Magna in the late third millennium BC seems connected to its role as 'gateway' for foreign goods – particularly myrrh and aromatic plants – arriving into the Nile Valley. Its decline shortly afterwards was perhaps the consequence of a shift in this trading activity to the benefit of Bersheh, whose leaders bore the unique epithet 'he who loves myrrh' and controlled the surrounding deserts, from which caravans of foreign traders came with their goods (flocks of sheep and goats from Libya, the mineral galena from Asiatics, and so on). Asyut also emerged in the very late third and early second millennia BC as a fluvial trade node and crossroads of desert routes, whereas harbours (*dmj*) close to Bersheh were celebrated in texts of the second and first millennia BC (Djehutihotep mentions the transport of a colossal statue to the harbour 'of this town/city [*nwt*]', while the Victory Stela of Piankhi refers to the quay of the Hare province: Moreno García forthcoming). It is also tempting to link the fortune of Thebes, a rather obscure city until the late third millennium BC, to the creation of the Red Sea port of Mersa/Wadi Gawasis, departure point of naval expeditions to the southern Red Sea and its resources in incense, precious metals and other commodities. Most importantly, the decline of the political and economic importance of Thebes towards the end of the Late Bronze Age, was concomitant with the emergence of a land route connecting south-western Arabia and the Mediterranean, thus bypassing the maritime trade route traditionally controlled by Egypt. At the same time, the last centuries of the second millennium BC saw the expansion of Mediterranean trade and the consolidation of Lower Egypt as the main commercial hub and economic centre of Egypt, around the cities of Avaris/Pi-Ramesses, Sais, Naucratis and, later, Alexandria.

Yet the monarchy retained a considerable capacity for developing infrastructure, as specialized settlements reveal, ranging from the fortresses/trade centres aiming to focalize and control trade in Nubia (Middle Bronze Age) and the Western Delta (Ramesside period), to funerary 'cities' close to royal pyramids (such as Ilahun), from workers' camps and maritime facilities (Tell el-Daba, Wadi el-Jarf) to massive temples that organized economic and managerial activities in Nubia and Egypt. But the increasing importance of cities and temples, plus the disappearance of networks of crown centres such as *ḥwt*, suggest nevertheless a more decentralized territorial organization. It was indeed around 1600 BC that temples definitively emerged as major administrative and economic agencies; these were also organized in networks and established intricate administrative patterns of mutual responsibilities in order to exploit their assets, which were scattered across the Nile Valley. There were two main consequences of these changes. First, the increasing role of cities and temples suggests a more dense occupation of the territory and that agriculture and sedentary activities became dominant from the beginning of the second millennium BC. The impact of this move on royal ideology and the symbolic role of kings should not be underestimated as cities and their local cults (cf. the concept of city-god) became powerful tools in forging identities. Kings made themselves 'present' in the local sphere through donations to royal statues cults, the decoration of local temples and a mix of syncretic and new 'national' cults able to provide some kind of community sense acceptable for all Egyptians (Moreno García 2013b; Moeller 2016). It is worth noting that royal tombs and funerary complexes alone were unable to fulfil this role. Second, until quite recently urban Egyptian archaeology focused on ceremonial settlements founded by the monarchy ('pyramid cities', royal capitals, specialized settlements like Deir el-Medina, the Nubian fortresses). Their orthogonal and hierarchical layout, and their dependence on royal favour, in all probability shared little with 'organic' cities, which would have been subject to cycles of growth and decline more dependent on economic and geopolitical factors (as well as natural ones, like shifts in the course of the Nile). That is why recent findings relating to residential neighbourhoods dating back to the late third millennium BC at Dendera or Abydos, as noted above, and inhabited by a 'middle class', confirm emerging social patterns of this period that had been merely hinted at to date from texts and objects (Moeller 2016). The 'middle class' towerhouses discovered in several localities of the Delta, dating from the Saite and subsequent periods, confirm the economic dynamism of

Lower Egypt, which until quite recently was visible only through the lens of temple building and donations of land.

Finally, the ambiguous term *nwt* ('settlement', 'locality') also referred to villages. While archaeological evidence about 'organic' villages still remains scarce, administrative texts provide some glimpses into their organization and structure. It appears that villages were separated by areas of bushland, marsh and pasture, particularly in Middle Egypt, and that the landscape of the Nile Valley was far from being a continuous succession of arable fields. Land was abundant and had the potential to support alternative lifestyles, based on pastoral, fishing and nomadic subsistence patterns. Their importance was arguably larger than that suggested by official sources, which were more focused on sedentary activities and agriculture. Thus, some inscriptions from the very end of the third millennium BC refer to nomadic herders and to the initiatives taken by some provincial governors to settle them in towns/villages. Archaeology has also revealed that, during this period, many settlements along the Eastern branch of the Nile in the Delta were abandoned, a process concomitant with the appearance in this area of people called *sekhetiu*, 'countrymen', who apparently led an autonomous existence and were not thoroughly integrated in the monarchy (they managed to avoid being taxed, in particular). Later on, the Ramesside inscription of Nebre, commander of the fortress/trade centre of Zawiyet Umm el-Rakham, on the Libyan coast, boasted about procuring local indigenous peoples by means of the promise of a dignified lifestyle – 'he made [the Libyans] possessors of settlements, so that they would plant trees, so that they would work many vineyards and [. . .] in the countryside' – and he describes the fortress as 'the Town of Ramesses II [. . .] which he built for these Libyan people, who had been living on the desert like jackals'. In any case, mobile settlers penetrated and settled in the Nile Valley, leaving their mark in its settlement pattern. It is not by chance that the development of extensive pastoralism in Egypt during the very late third millennium BC ran parallel to the emergence of new terms such as *mnmnt*, 'cattle on the move', and *whyt*, 'clanic village, tribe', particularly in Middle Egypt, a region frequented by Libyan sheep- and cattle-herders. Finally, the area of Fayum was also crossed by foreign populations who, in some cases, preserved their own distinctive enclosure-settlements, such as *wnt* and *sgr* (Moreno García 2017).

Royal tombs, temples and ceremonial landscapes

Temples remain some of the most conspicuous and monumental expressions of pharaonic culture. Along with religion, rituals and beliefs in the afterlife, they also represent some of the most (if not *the* most) popular aspects of ancient Egypt. However, monumental stone temples were a relatively late development in Egyptian history and the story of their social, political, economic and cultural role is inseparable from the transformations of both royal ideology and of the actual executive power of the king over the millennia. The relation between temples and monarchy was thus a dynamic one that helps us understand how kings built their authority and justified it in reference to society and the wider cosmos.

Early royal tombs consisted of large tumuli that aimed to indicate a landscape of power. The cultural roots of these monuments probably lie in the pastoral lifestyles and neolithic foundations of pharaonic society, when funerary tumuli and necropolises marked the territories frequented and claimed by a social group. Once the monarchy was consolidated, tumuli (mastabas first, pyramids later) still expressed the symbolic role of the king as core of a territory (the kingdom) as well as head of an extended kin group (encompassing the ruling elite) whose tombs surrounded that of its master. Temples, on the other hand, were rather modest constructions (especially provincial ones), and it was not until 2600 BC that this situation changed definitively. However, early Egyptian temples had nothing to do with the massive contemporary Mesopotamian sanctuaries and their extensive productive and administrative activities. However, after a peak characterized by the gigantic tumuli/pyramids built by pharaohs Snofru, Khufu (Cheops) and Khafra (Chephren), between 2613 and 2532 BC, large pyramids were abandoned, royal tombs – while still impressive – decreased in size, and local temples emerge in the epigraphical and monumental record as key cult and economic institutions that helped forge (local) identities. Not only did they receive considerable land donations from the crown, but they also became a powerful tool used by kings to integrate the local elites into the administrative organization of the kingdom.

This change was in line with the attendant expansion of bureaucracy, especially in the provinces, and with the incorporation into the high administration of dignitaries who were not necessarily members of the wider royal family. The titles they bore also reveal the implementation of an increasingly specialized bureaucratic structure. Taken together, all these changes point to a shift in the way the kingdom was organized and the monarchy conceived, with crucial effects on the actual exercise of power and on the executive capacity of pharaohs to implement a personalized centralized authority, based on a reduced group of officials close to them. It seems then that the attempts of the 'great builder' pharaohs (at least Snofru and Khufu) to achieve a considerable centralization of power, resources and, particularly, elites, coupled with a thorough territorial reorganization of the kingdom, was a short-lived experience that ultimately failed. Thereafter, the mobilization of resources and administrative skills was possible only through the combined efforts of local powers and an increase in the size of the administration. This may explain the development of provincial temples (power bases of provincial potentates), the attempts of the monarchy to intervene in their affairs (through donations of land and the building of chapels provided with royal statues), the association of palatial and provincial officials with royal cults in the funerary temple of the king, the emergence of the cult of Osiris (closely associated with the ancestral burial place of the monarchy, at Abydos, and with the royal ideals of order and regeneration) together with the increasing importance of *maat* (order, justice) in priestly and administrative titles, and the construction of decorated tombs in the provinces for the local elites. Unlike the pyramids dedicated to individual kings at Memphis, the cult of Osiris became a sort of 'universal' cult, accessible to non-elite people and focused on ceremonies and pilgrimages that helped create a sense of community. Pilgrimages and important religious feasts probably helped strengthen these links. In other words, kings lost part of their symbolic and executive centrality and recognized the weight and contributions of local powers. So the old ideal of an extended family surrounding the Memphite tumuli of their royal patron lost most of its sense, particularly in regions far from the capital (Moreno García 2010a; Bussmann 2015 and 2016).

The symbolic shift between royal tombs and temples increased in the second millennium BC. From 1500 BC, royal tombs remained hidden in isolated desert areas (the Valley of the Kings) while temples became colossal constructions as well as the most important economic and managerial institutions of the country. However, they were neither independent institutions nor rivals of the crown. The cult of Amun (the god of Thebes, the province that reunified Egypt in 2150 and 1550 BC) was the most important of them and its endowment made it the wealthiest institution in Egypt, but kings monitored carefully the appointment of High Priests of Amun. How and why temples reached such a prominent position seems related to the relative weakness of kingship. Reunification meant negotiation with local powers, the integration of local authorities with their own agendas and interests, and arbitrations between factions of the palace and of the elite. So, behind the facade of a monolithic authority, the power of kingship becomes more fragile and dependent on negotiation and politics. Episodes such as co-regencies in the early second millennium BC, the rise of military men to kingship (Horemheb, Ramesses I, etc.), the development of solar 'imperial' cults (like that promoted by Akhenaten), and conflict between potential heirs to the throne, not to mention conspiracies and regicide, point to a monarchy whose roots lay in politics and shifting alliances, rather than autocracy. In a theocratic world where legitimacy depended on divine support rather than on modern concepts such as sovereignty or nationhood, temples provided institutional security: their assets were supposed to be eternal and, as the property of gods, any attack on them was deemed impious and questioned the authority of the aggressor. They were also crucial institutions in the articulation of the territory, as local nobles, potentates, rural elites, chiefs of villages and people of status (scribes, military personnel, etc.) became priests and thus integrated into the monarchy, as temples were privileged points of contact between the crown and provincial society. Finally, temples managed substantial wealth, principally agricultural land which, in the case of the most important sanctuaries, was spread over vast distances. Their managerial capacity meant that they also administered the landed assets of other institutions (the crown, other temples) located within their vicinity, in a kind of indirect management that cut costs for the owner institution. This gave rise to an intricate administrative structure and to complex patterns in which 'divine households' had interests in several provinces and incorporated people from different social backgrounds and geographical areas. The success of such an indirect administrative structure depended partly on the mobilization of fleets and scribes in order to monitor and collect wealth scattered across long distances, and partly on the participation of 'rural entrepreneurs' who exploited land and other goods in the name of the owner sanctuary (Moreno García 2016b). However, cults remained fiercely local and attempts to create a 'national' religion foundered, and were reduced to the emergence of syncretic cults between local deities and 'universal' gods. The failure of the cult promoted by Akhenaten to achieve this goal, or the overly abstract nature of 'solar' cults points to the difficulty in creating a national religion (Baines 2000). Temples continued to mark the landscape and to forge local identities. The final shift of the core of the country from the Theban area to the Eastern Delta, far from the Domain of Amun, was followed by the foundation or expansion of temples in the Delta. In the fragmented political landscape of the Delta, temples became repositories of cultural tradition and poles of agricultural expansion, and validated the quality of silver in circulation. Temples also provided institutional security: land donations to them, and guaranteeing the quality of silver used in economic transaction in a society that cultivated new values based on money and business, meant that they procured security. In some cases, kings themselves built their tombs inside temple precincts (Agut-Labordère & Gorre 2014; Moreno García 2016b). The increasingly subsidiary ideological role of kings is also evident in the relatively ephemeral nature of their palaces, to the point that, with some notable exceptions, little is known about them. They were mostly built from fragile materials (brick) and, as was the case with late royal tombs, they convey a sense of frailty in the face of the 'eternal' nature of temples and tombs, which were constructed in the main from durable materials. Temples' massive enclosures also conveyed a sense of majesty, of overwhelming authority, restricted access and a distancing from common people. In fact, most Egyptians had no access to temples. More than potentially defensive buildings, temples convey a sense of power reserved for an elite, in which popular participation in public ceremonies (both religious and 'civil') was rarely a priority. It seems that massive ceremonial gatherings may have taken place only very occasionally (feasts, perhaps parades; see Baines 2006). Such a restricted concept of authority, in which 'civil' counterpowers had no voice or place, plus the absence of powerful civic organizations, may also explain why plazas and large spaces intended for social gatherings were largely absent in Egyptian cities (for a comparative perspective, see Manzano 2015). It might thus be posited that the increasingly oligarchical nature of power after 1550 BC was expressed in the construction of massive temples managed by an elite who earned income from them. This also means that some of the social trends that emerged around 2150 BC, based on a 'middle class' and on autonomous producers, came to an end when royal power was reorganized again around 1550 BC. Temples assimilated local elites and associated them closely to a monarchy that itself was being rebuilt. Such social sectors obtained riches and prestige from the opportunities offered by the new kings (imperial tribute, positions in the army, priesthoods, royal administration). But they paid a price – they lost their potential to influence and act as a social force. Their aspirations and ambitions were now mediated through *royal* institutions, not their own, which often resulted in factional fighting *inside* the apparatuses of the state, not outside them. Temple monumentality in the Late Bronze Age probably marks a significant change, namely the closing-up of the possibilities that had opened up when the monarchy collapsed in 2160 BC.

3

Managing Resources

The pharaonic state managed several kinds of resources, some of them material (taxes, manpower, raw and luxury materials), and others immaterial (information, dominant cultural values, legitimacy, allegiance and obedience). Both types formed the very basis of the monarchy and provided the means necessary to enforce its authority and to guarantee the reproduction of the ruling class: the collection, selective distribution and expenditure of revenue, the building of monuments, the provision of order and security, the affirmation of legitimate and moral rule through religious and cultural values. Obviously, this was a *desideratum*, an ideal constantly challenged by the potential appearance of alternative poles of accumulation of wealth, information, force and legitimacy. Their more conspicuous manifestations were the lavish display of private wealth in the form of monumental tombs, chapels and temples; the cult of 'deified' ancestors; the existence of extensive patronage networks centred on potentates; corruption and the capture of income due to the state; imprecise limits between public duties and private interests in the activities of the ruling elite; the existence of a powerful provincial nobility as well as families entrenched in senior administrative and court positions, etc. The monarchy thus had to negotiate with such potential foci of trouble and find satisfactory arrangements with them (not always successful, as the recurrent periods of crisis of the monarchy reveal), from co-option to the forced exile of rivals, from integration to coexistence and utter erosion of local powers. However, the pharaonic monarchy diverges from other political formations of the ancient Near East in its *apparent* capacity to produce considerable political stability in the long term or, to put it in other words, to prevent the emergence of durable challenges to its authority. Yet it was the *manner* in which the state managed the resources at its disposal to achieve this astonishing goal that was a crucial factor in its success (Moreno García 2013a; Jursa & Moreno García 2015).

Managing income: Taxation and its limits

Two myths have accompanied modern reconstructions about the Egyptian past. The first is that of an efficient, all-encompassing royal administration, organized in 'departments' (Granary, Treasury, House of Life, House of Weapons, Chamber of the Documents, etc.) that controlled and centralized much (if not all) of the resources of the kingdom. The second is that of a homogeneous provincial administration, with officials appointed to represent the authority of the king and execute his orders, from levying taxes and directing manpower to the development of public works. The roots of this modern perception of ancient Egypt can be traced back to the nineteenth century AD, when the consolidation of national states in Europe, America and Japan, along with their attempts to expand their authority and managerial competences, crystallized in a new perception of what a modern state was and were transposed anachronistically to the past. Thus the long lists of administrative titles in the monuments of Egyptian officials, accompanied by claims about their efficiency and good administration, seem to recall 'normal' governmental practices that could be imputed to any 'advanced' society, ancient or modern. They were thus accepted at face value, as if they constituted another prestigious precedent of Western states – *ex oriente lux*. Such interpretation was reinforced by the assumption that ancient Egypt was a despotic 'oriental' state, dominated by a stifling bureaucracy whose only aim was to levy taxes from an otherwise stagnant and exploited peasantry. However, these interpretations were based more on prejudices than on a careful evaluation of the coercive and taxation capacities of ancient states. The administrative reality hidden behind terms like Granary, Treasury, and others still remains rather elusive, and we do not know if they really centralized and controlled specific resources of the kingdom or if, on the contrary, their goal was rather more modest and specialized. As for the limits of their respective areas of competences, in many cases they are hard to determine.

To begin with, the basic units of taxation are not always clear. Administrative documents from several periods reveal control over households and settlements founded by the crown, detailing the number of people living in them and tasks performed by the heads of the households or their proxies (such as members of their family, clients or subordinates). The general impression is that the priority was to evaluate and mobilize manpower and, perhaps, to obtain specialized items such as textiles (judging from documents from Gurob and Elephantine), rather than collecting agricultural produce and revenue from common people. Substantial amounts of agricultural produce were acquired through other means, such as the foundation of specialized royal agricultural centres close to strategic areas (quarries, garrisons, crossroads, harbours), and even the construction of temples, provided with considerable landed assets as well as workforce in a variety of forms, from seasonal forced work to leasing, serf-like workers, etc. This may explain why the basic fiscal structure of the state comprised networks of royal production centres and agricultural land, temples and so on, that produced, collected and stocked agricultural goods that would later be transported by ship to specific departments (such as the Granary). Boats would collect goods – mainly perishable and low-profit items such as wine, fruit, dates, fresh vegetables, and even textiles – from suppliers, but there is still some uncertainty about whether some of these operations should be interpreted as trading activities or a type of tax.

In any case, the amount of goods at the disposal of the crown was staggering. The Harris I Papyrus, as well as other contemporary documents, enumerate enormous amounts of grain, land, people, fresh produce, offerings and cult items granted by the king to several sanctuaries in Egypt. Temples appear thus as essential nodes of the fiscal system of the crown as well as autonomous agencies of production.

They were subject to taxation and their resources used as payment for these taxes when the crown estimated it necessary. So, when pharaoh Neferirkare endowed his own funerary temple with offerings and personnel, these were gathered from several institutions, including the royal palace and the temple of Ptah at Memphis. And when Weni enumerated the institutions that were required to contribute towards a large army, overseers of temples paid up too. The interplay between crown and temples produced in many instances intricate webs of relations. Kings endowed temples with land and workers and also trusted them with the administration and cultivation of royal land. In other cases, temples benefited from specific donations made by kings, such as revenue from fisheries, mining, etc. As autonomous productive centres, temples managed their own affairs, employed merchants to commercialize part of their production and were thus able to pay to the crown substantial amounts of silver. Pharaoh Akhenaten, for instance, collected silver and other goods from temples. At the same time, kings granted temple land to (among others) officials, soldiers and local potentates, thus helping to consolidate and expand the influence of the crown in the local sphere and to secure support from local authorities. However, clarifying the rights over this land was no easy matter, as beneficiaries bought, sold and transferred these legal obligations to other people.

Another fiscal contribution made by the temples took the form of manpower, and its use by the state oscillated between donation, taxation and appropriation (if needed). As royal decrees of the late third millennium BC reveal, provincial agents of the king compiled lists of people who could work for the crown, from priests to peasant labourers, and temples would be obliged to comply. In fact the only way they could avoid these obligations would be to obtain a (revocable) exemption decree from the pharaoh (Jursa & Moreno García 2015).

Temples were only part of the picture, though, as other institutions helped create a fiscal 'landscape' that changed over time depending on the collecting and enforcing capacity of the kingdom. During the early phases of the Egyptian monarchy (late fourth and third millennium

BC), the crown founded many agricultural and production centres all across the country. In some cases these were devoted to the production of specialized goods, such as wine or cattle; in the case of the latter, certain areas and herds would be expected to deliver a specified quota of animals to the crown. Other centres (particularly the *ḥwt*) produced and stocked foodstuffs and supplies delivered to expeditionary groups and agents of the crown passing through the locality. It appears that each of these centres controlled a small district, comprising several villages. As noted above, this system was complemented by temples, recipients of considerable royal donations of land but liable to taxation and the rendering up of goods on demand. As we can see, this early fiscal system was characterized by the crown's direct involvement in the production and management of some of the kingdom's basic resources, which could indicate difficulties in the collection of taxes directly from producers. From this perspective, it may be significant that the main tax objective of the monarchy in the third millennium BC was to control cattle (also gold); in other words, mobile wealth. This system disappeared around 2000 BC, and the *ḥwt* were not reintroduced after the reconstruction of the monarchy. Instead, towns and cities carried the main burden of taxation, especially with regard to the delivery of workforce, while local leaders – who ranged from provincial lords to local chiefs and dignitaries – also provided workers from their own 'domains', households and districts. It was then that another institution expanded, particularly around 1800 BC: the *ḥnrt*, a kind of work camp. Later on, from 1550 BC, temples emerge as major hubs of economic management and mobilization, not only of their own resources but also of royal land, via what appears to be an indirect managerial system in which temples and private rural 'entrepreneurs' managed and cultivated crown property. Harbours were also regarded as fiscal units, because goods were stocked there and put at the disposal of the king's agents; in some cases the harbours were even provided with their own land (Moreno García 2013b).

With regard to other units of taxation, it is difficult to detect a homogeneous fiscal pattern, which confirms that taxes were levied on a relatively ad hoc basis, in sharp contrast to the apparent 'rationality' and 'all-encompassing' ideals suggested by official titles. Private inscriptions reveal that administrators received entire villages as reward for their activities, but it is far from clear what the villagers contributed to the state. Many inscriptions from different periods mention villages as providers of workforce for state projects (working temple or crown land, building temples and tombs, etc.), even when the villages and domains formed part of officials' remuneration. Texts dating back to the early second millennium BC – administrative papyri, rock inscriptions, stone marks made inside kings' pyramids – describe in detail the local organization of workers, their conscription, and the role played by the governors of villages and localities in their recruitment. Local potentates and officials also provided people from their own households and districts, and in some cases the name of an official had a toponymic value, as it referred to the territory he controlled. In fact, 'mayors' played a key role in mediating the mobilization of goods and manpower for the king from the districts and localities they ruled. In some cases, inscriptions from the late third and early second millennium BC record the number of workers recruited for royal expeditions from specific localities and the presence of 'mayors'. This is the case for inscription G 61 in the quarries of Wadi Hammamat, which mentions 17,000 conscripts and twenty mayors, working out at 850 workers per mayor, an average also cited in other texts. So Imeny, provincial leader of Beni Hasan, led contingents of 400 and 600 conscripts from his province to military and quarrying expeditions; an inscription from Hatnub mentions 500, 600 and 500 workers, respectively, from three localities, while the steward Henu set out from the 'garrisons' of the Theban province with an army of 3,000 men (Lichtheim 1988: 53). Another inscription from Wadi Hammamat mentions the participation of the 'mayor' of the town of Edfu 'together with his town', as well as ten 'mayors' from the province of Thinis. Documents from the second half of the second millennium BC, such as the edicts issued by Horemheb and at Nauri, mention royal agents who seized manpower from villages and forced village governors to deliver goods at the mooring posts, to cultivate crown land or to work for the temples (Jursa & Moreno García 2015). Finally, when Princess Nitocris was sent from Sais to Thebes in 656 BC:

> messengers sailed upstream to the south to arrange for provisions ahead of her [...] Every mayor was responsible for his (= the harbour master) provisions, having been furnished with every good thing, comprising bread, beer, oxen, fowl, leeks, dates, vegetables, and every good thing. One would then yield to the next until she arrived at Thebes.
>
> Ritner 2009: 579

Other goods rendered up by towns and cities included precious metals, specialized items such as textiles as well as grain and cattle according to the famous taxation scene depicted in the tomb of the vizier Rekhmire (who lived in the second half of the fifteenth century BC), that enumerates about eighty towns and cities in southern Egypt

Figure 3.1 Royal pyramid at Dahshur, built from poor-quality materials. A sign of a weakened tax system in the early second millennium BC?

along with the taxes levied from them, and to similar documents. According to the *Duties of the Vizier*, viziers were in charge of taxes ('it is he who fixes all fixed dues as supplies for recipients'; 'the mayors, governors of domains and every subject report their income to him') and of some agricultural planning, as well as perhaps a general evaluation of the areas under cultivation ('it is he who dispatches mayors and governors of domains at ploughing and harvest'). He also surveyed the boundaries of (institutional?) fields – ('it is he who dispatches the multitude of bureaucrats of the register (?) to calculate the expenditure of the Lord. District records are to be in his bureau for hearings on any fields. It is he who sets the boundaries for every district, every garden plot, every temple estate (?), every sealed land (?)') – and checked cattle quotas and herd lists ('it is he who makes the allotment (?) of income for the cattle-raising estates', 'it is he who makes lists of every herd of which lists are made'). In addition, he was in charge of ships (although it is unclear whether he was responsible for their cargo or condition: 'to him report is made by every council of the start of ships and end of ships') (Katary 2011; Jursa & Moreno García 2015).

The provinces' conspicuous place in the ideal representation of administration and the governmental structure of the kingdom contrasts with the paucity of actual information regarding their fiscal contributions. The recent discovery of administrative papyri at Wadi el-Jarf shows that some provinces delivered agricultural produce on a rotating basis. However, the absence of further parallels points perhaps to the ephemeral nature of this system, which was implemented during the reign of Khufu but abandoned later. When the inscriptions of provincial leaders become more informative, as in the cases of Qar of Edfu and Imeny of Beni Hasan, they show that raising cattle was one of their main fiscal responsibilities. Other inscriptions from the very late third millennium BC also confirm that administrators submitted cattle censuses to the royal administration.

From the evidence we have about the crown's fiscal capacities, a tripartite system emerges. First, agricultural produce was obtained mainly directly, through agricultural domains and production centres established by the crown, temples or other institutions. This system produced a fiscal geography organized in networks and provided with facilities such as harbours, etc. Second, the crown's principal fiscal concern was to control and mobilize workforces. Third, control over mobile wealth suggests that many economic activities were carried out independently of any state initiative, and that in some cases they involved the accumulation of precious metals subsequently taxed by the state. The fact that cities paid taxes in precious metals, as did temples, wealthy peasants, traders and fishermen, suggests that private 'business' was far more important than royal documents indicate, and goods could be exchanged at markets for silver and gold, which would be subsequently taxed by the king. This might also explain the importance of traders as mediators in the economic activities of temples and the crown, even though they could well have 'laundered' precious metal stolen from temples and royal tombs.

Bearing in mind that Egypt is situated at a crossroads between northeastern Africa and the Near East, it will come as no surprise that customs and taxes levied on the circulation of goods (both arriving into Egypt, or being exported) represented another source of income for the king. The Turin Royal Canon (dating from the thirteenth century BC) reveals, for instance, that a single overseer of natron delivered to the crown, as his annual tax in the Late Bronze Age, an astonishing amount of 91 kg of gold. Natron was certainly a strategic item in the manufacture of glass, an industry that flourished then as the archaeological evidence, such as the cargo of the Uluburun shipwreck, shows. However, other – much more modest – goods probably represented the bulk of Egyptian exports abroad, as indicated by the discovery of abundant remains of Nile perch in the Levant and Anatolia. The *Story of Wenamun* reveals that Egyptian fish, hides, lentils, papyri, linen and grain were sent abroad, while the depreciation of the value of silver during the Late Bronze Age (from a silver:copper ratio of 1:100 to just 1:60) is probably linked to the exports of huge amounts of grain to the Hittite Empire in exchange for silver, thus opening the intriguing possibility that Egypt had already become an international exporting power well before the Greco-Roman period. Customs fees may have represented a considerable source of income for the crown, including those taxes levied in the Nile harbours. If the Turin Royal Canon mentions taxes paid at several fortresses that monitored the entrance into Egypt, Sarenput I, governor of the caravan and harbour city of Elephantine around 1950 BC, included among his duties control over river trade, harbours, markets and foreign commodities arriving into Egypt in his role of 'overseer of all tribute at the entrance of the foreign countries in the form of royal ornaments, to whom the tribute of the Medya-country was brought as contribution of the rulers of the foreign countries', as well as 'one who rejoices over the quay/market-place, the overseer of the great ships of the Royal Domain, who supplies the Double Treasury, the superior of the harbours in the province of Elephantine (so that) what navigates and what moors was under his authority'. A similar claim figures in a brief literary text that celebrates markets in the city of Pi-Ramesses: 'Pleasant is the place of distribution/market-place with its money/silver there, mainly the vine tendrils (?) and business/commerce (*t-m-k-r-i-t*). The chiefs of every foreign country come in order to descend with their products' (Moreno García forthcoming). Several references from the first half of the first millennium BC refer to taxes levied by harbour-masters on merchants: '[who are] under the authority of the elders of the portal who are before the merchants' (Ritner 2009: 356); '[in order to protect] and exempt the door-keepers [of the estate] of Amun, and [the] sailors of the sacred barge of the estate of Amun likewise in order to prevent them from paying departure tax for their ships on the river at any harbor of any city [forever (?)]' (Ritner 2009: 358); 'oil for the estate of Amun-Re-the-Lion-at-the-South upon the riverbank/market under the supervision of the harbor masters' (Ritner 2009: 356). Finally, a harbour-master and governor of Heracleopolis also passed orders to the mayors who provided supplies to Princess Nitocris on her journey south to Thebes (Ritner 2009: 579). These examples reveal that harbours were not only active markets and trade centres, but also ideal places to levy and collect taxes, thus resulting in a potential source of income not only for the monarchy but also for local leaders.

As customs monitored part of the wealth arriving into Egypt, it was not by chance that the provinces ruled by leaders charged with controlling foreign tribute during the late third and early second millennium BC became the most active political players of their time. Some of these provinces seem linked to trade with the Red Sea (Thebes), others with the arrival of goods from the deserts and, perhaps, also from the Red Sea through Ayn Sukhna (Bersheh, Beni Hasan). The wealth accumulated by such potentates can be measured by the extraordinary tombs, almost royal in scale, they built for themselves in provinces considered as 'gateways' into Egypt. So, rulers with vested interests in foreign trade might use their influence at court to shape Egypt's foreign policy. The implications are considerable. Whenever taxes and contributions filled the coffers of the king, this flow of wealth had the potential to induce undesirable and, in the long term, dangerous effects for the stability of the whole system. Corruption, the appropriation of taxes and/or illegitimate seizure of state income, tax exemptions to institutions and individuals, not to mention insufficient taxation, were all sources of destabilization in the balance of power between regions, between the palace and the provinces and between different sectors of the elite. And not only because these practices limited the resources and income at the disposal of the monarchy, but also because they could easily crystallize into the excessive accumulation of wealth in private hands and lead to the emergence of other potential foci of power. Ultimately, then, tax collection appears to be less a technical issue than a political one. Hence, many officials boasted about their efficacy as tax collectors in comparison to their peers or predecessors: when Weni was appointed Overseer of Upper Egypt, for example, he claimed to have levied twice as much taxation revenue as had been usual before his time, while an official proclaimed on the stela he erected at Bilgai that:

> I am an effective official for his lord, fulfilling harvest and tax obligations, (such that) my excess of harvest and taxes was ten times greater than my assessment of harvest and taxes: 4632 amphorae of wine was [my] quota of people's labor, (but) I had them (the amphorae) delivered as 30,000, an excess of 25,638. Nedjem, who used to be high steward, did not [approach (?)] me at all in any task which I undertook: 70 amphorae of honey was my assessment of honey, – I delivered them

(the amphorae) as 700, [an excess] of 630; 70,000 [sacks] of grain was my yearly harvest assessment, – I delivered them (the sacks) as 140,000, an excess of 70,000.

Frood 2007: 180

The bombastic tone aside, these examples are typical of the scribal culture and of the *topos* of the efficient official, and suggest that the amount of taxes levied depended on the zeal of officials, on political considerations and on specific needs of the monarchy (such as war, exceptional building programmes or buying political support from powerful factions and potentates). Such claims could also indicate that the evaluation of the wealth and resources of the kingdom was rather rudimentary (workforces being perhaps an exception): rather than carefully checking and updating lists of resources and taxes, tax collectors might have considered 'local potentialities' that could be exploited at a variable rate depending on individual circumstances, negotiation tactics, or even the resistance of local leaders. This may explain why 'assessments' and 'quotas' figure so prominently in the documentary record, as if they represented an acceptable minimum susceptible of expansion in case of need.

Other evidence supports the idea of a certain fiscal unpredictability. Royal decrees tried to put an end to illegitimate seizures of goods, especially the illegal diversion of revenue and resources – such as temple land or private funerary foundations – that had been granted previously to an institution or an individual. The enactment of consecutive decrees, seeking to enforce or to confirm previously issued rulings, reveals that the actual implementation of royal orders was difficult, especially given the absence of 'laws' that might provide clear, normative guides for bureaucrats' everyday activities and competences. In other cases, privileges favoured certain institutions with temporary tax exemption. Inefficient allocation and mobilization of resources also hampered the redistributive capacity of the crown, as revealed by one of the earliest known letters ever, which complained about the non-delivery of equipment promised to a team of workers. Similar concerns affected the community of craftsmen and artists at Deir el-Medina, when delays in the delivery of the rations by the administrative powers-that-be provoked strikes and interruptions to work. Both cases reveal the limitations of the administrative system, because conflicts erupted in the vicinity of the capital (Memphis and Thebes) and the vizier himself was addressed directly by the workers and their foremen.

Another problem related to the fiscal capacity of the monarchy is the emergence of a 'middle class' in some periods of Egyptian history (Mazé 2017). The end of the third and the early second millennium BC was one of them. On the one hand, archaeology reveals the existence of houses owned by moderately wealthy people, equipped with storage facilities (such as silos) whose capacity exceeded the needs of a nuclear family. On the other hand, some owners of high-quality possessions (inscribed stelae, decorated coffins, statues, etc.) were not members of the royal staff and the administration, but had managed to obtain them despite being outside the circuits of rewards and remunerations granted by the king and traditionally reserved for officials. Furthermore (and as noted in Chapter 2), the frequency of the title 'lady of the house' and the abundant use of seals by women suggest that some ladies developed their own business in a period when texts mention an increasing use of sealed documents in private transactions. Seals of this type from Abu Ghalib, a settlement in the Western Delta, reveal domestic activities, probably developed by women, connected to the storage of grain in houses, sealing boxes and, in some cases, papyri, and probably textile production, judging from the spinning bowls also found at this site (Moreno García forthcoming). Another element highly celebrated in the sources of this period is the importance of patronage networks; these provided resources and protection and helped connect diverse social groups without any intervention of the royal administration. Heqanakhte, a prosperous tenant from the early second millennium BC, is a good example of such a 'middle class' and of the economic basis of its prosperity (Allen 2002). The letters he addressed to his subordinates contain very precise instructions about the management of his land and the allocation of resources to members of his household. What emerges from them is that his agricultural choices were guided by purely private interests, as he sought to obtain the best possible returns. Moreover, his strategies of leasing land from wealthy neighbours, and lending grain to many people near where he lived, show that he used his wealth to create a network of social relations in which he reinforced his status as neighbourhood patron and member of a local sub-elite. So how should we interpret the emergence of this 'middle class'? One possibility is that the concentration of wealth in private hands, when fluvial trade and intense commercial activities between Nubia and the Mediterranean flourished, was possible because the crown was less efficient at capturing and taxing such wealth than it had been previously. The political consequences are obvious, as indicated by the enormous tombs built around 1950–1850 BC by some provincial officials who controlled foreign commerce: these massive constructions suggest the bureaucrats' astonishing capacity to hang on to substantial wealth for their own advantage. Their power, and capacity to influence the affairs of the kingdom (including control over precious commodities, such as myrrh), reveal the limits of a monarchy that finally crumbled just a few decades later. The emergence of rich and powerful provincial potentates, thanks to their control of flows of wealth that had (apparently) escaped the monarchy, had an enormous political impact in the end, as it contributed to the collapse of the state and of the monarchy itself (Moreno García 2017).

Another point to consider is the impact of taxation on promoting economic activity. State employees received rations and, judging from inscriptions found in quarries, these rations (which could be viewed as salaries) may have represented a considerable source of income for a substantial part of the population. Furthermore, it is also possible that this type of redistributed wealth stimulated economic activities in areas where garrisons and trade hubs had been founded by the crown. Marked storage vessels – that is, items bearing the marks of the institutions that delivered them – found at political and economic centres from 2000–1800 BC (Lisht/Itj-tawy, Dahshur, Hawara and Karnak) and in peripheral areas (harbours, quarries, fortresses and caravan centres such as Abu Ziyar, Ayn Sukhna, Mersa/Wadi Gawasis, Askut, Qasr el-Sagha and

Figure 3.2 Djoser's step pyramid at Saqqara, a sign of the lavish investment of resources in royal monuments around 2650 BC.

Gebel el-Asr) show the importance of storage jars in the government's distribution of supplies across a steadily expanding territory, and that those supplies facilitated a diversification of economic interests. As for the huge Egyptian containers found in Nubian settlements in the early second millennium BC, these reveal the fluidity of trade between the pastoral populations of northern Nubia and Egypt, which are barely documented at all in the written records. In the case of the Egyptian fortresses built in Nubia during this period, the substantial settlements that grew outside their walls (and the protection they provided) suggest that trade was the main reason for the construction of such substantial buildings, as some papyri and inscriptions from this region confirm. The economic centres built by the crown in the late third millennium BC (like the *ḥwt*) played a similar role. An inscribed dish from Elephantine mentions a *ḥwt* governor who delivered foodstuffs to the agents of the crown sent from the palace but, at the same time, who also delivered rations to a considerable number of female weavers, as if the *ḥwt* were involved not only in grain and cattle production but also in the production of textiles. In fact, expeditions – and the organization of their logistics – probably favoured business. The inscriptions from the mining centre of Serabit el-Khadim, in Sinai, mention people ('countrymen', etc.) and donkeys, as if the former provided some of the pack animals used by the expeditions. A rock inscription from around 1938 BC at Wadi Korosko in Nubia, an important route to some gold fields in the Eastern Desert, mentions a group of people from the same household that included two women (one originating from Kom el-Hisn and the other from Sais, in the Western Delta). The men are referred to as *khenes*, a term that refers to 'friends'. In fact, neither the leader of the group nor its individual members are given any title at all, military or 'civil'. The presence of women further reinforces the idea of a group of 'civilians' who were perhaps involved in logistical or scouting activities for a royal expedition and/or in trading (Moreno García forthcoming). The recent discovery at the Ramesside garrison city of Beith Shean, in Israel, of three small silver hoards found in the twentieth dynasty levels is of particular interest, as it points to the 'monetary' use of silver objects delivered as wages to Egyptian officials or mercenaries, and subsequently spent. Inversely, according to his inscription, an Egyptian soldier from Edfu, Haankhef, received twenty-six pieces of gold for his military service, which he subsequently spent on buying three fields for him, his wife and his children. Supplying military garrisons certainly stimulated trading activities, as illustrated by the forty-six silver bars distributed by a fortress commander to several ship captains in order to purchase fish, among other goods.

Finally, the conquest of foreign territories was accompanied by the imposition of tribute in the form of taxes and prestige items (slaves, cattle, horses, cereals, metals, timber, ivory, chariots, etc.). Harbours and supply hubs would also be used to provision armies, messengers, diplomats and Egyptian officials in transit. So, local resources were evaluated and taxed, as was the case for the farms founded in the Jezreel Valley, which produced 207,300 sacks of wheat (probably per year). Workers also arrived into Egypt as tribute – and as prisoners. Settled in temples as weavers and on the land as peasants, they contributed to the expansion of cereal production and cattle raising, thereby increasing the sanctuaries' income (partly in grain, partly in silver) (Liverani 2001: 141–202). The Harris I Papyrus, for example, records that only a part of the taxes paid by cultivators to the temples amounted to the considerable sum of a ton of silver. That enormous quantities of precious metals thus stored 'unproductively' in temples and tombs were occasionally robbed and 'laundered', thanks to the complicity of their own personnel and merchants, constitutes indirect proof of the role played by markets, tribute and precious metals stored in temples as incentives of economic activities.

State expenditure

It seems improbable that the royal administration promoted a large-scale policy of hydraulic works (canals, dams, etc.) in order to improve and extend irrigated areas. The surviving evidence refers occasionally to the excavation of canals, especially for transport purposes. However, the Ramesside Wilbour Papyrus, and its detailed description of more than 2,500 plots of land and their boundary marks in the Fayum and the adjacent areas to the south, hardly mentions any canals among them. As for the redistribution policy usually credited to pharaohs, there is no real proof for it, other than rhetorical claims about the delivery of food to people in periods of shortage. In fact, the state delivered food only in exchange for work and activities it had ordered. It seems thus that the main expenditures were on court provisions, followed by the remuneration owed to officials and administrators. In some cases, particularly during the third millennium BC, the resources allocated to the 'children of the king' (a phrase which could apply not only to the children of reigning kings but also to offspring of the wider royal family) were managed by a specific administrative office, and it seems that their property was scattered across different provinces. Furthermore, the royal palace consumed great quantities of foodstuffs and commodities, as the bakery papyri from the reign of Seti I or the St Petersburg Papyrus 1116A, with its accounts of deliveries to the granaries of the palace, reveal (Ezzamel 2012: 306–40).

Few documents describe the scale of regular remunerations paid to scribes and agents of the administration. Officials in the service of the king were usually rewarded with land, manpower, and 'houses', benefits that could be confiscated easily in the case of any subsequent serious misconduct. The formula '(his) house, field, people and all property' and its variants described such grants, yet the ownership of entire villages was thus transferred (Moreno García 2013c). One of the most informative sources is a rock inscription from the Middle Kingdom carved at Wadi Hammamat (around 1950 BC). It reveals the following proportion of income: Chief of expedition – 200 loaves of bread; 'mayors', the head of a team of stonemasons, and chiefs of Tens of Upper Egypt (a category of high-ranking officials in charge of manpower, usually connected to the royal family) – 100; Overseer of the Great Council, Overseer of the Treasury – fifty; scribes and middle-rank officials – thirty; craftsmen – twenty; seal bearers, warriors – fifteen; conscript workers – ten (Ezzamel 2012: 248–70). An administrative papyrus composed about 200 years later (Boulaq Papyrus 18) records the daily allowances of the members of the royal family and of senior officials associated with the court. The allotments included twenty loaves for the king's wife and the chiefs of Tens of Upper Egypt, ten loaves for high-ranking officials and for each of the king's children, and five loaves for mid-ranking officials. According to this papyrus, the ruling elite that ran the country during this period comprised a rather reduced number of people (about thirty), all connected through marriage links and with the extended royal family (Ezzamel 2012: 193–218; Spalinger 2015). In any case, the ratio seems quite similar in both documents: members of the highest elite (including the royal family) received about twice as much income as the most senior officials and four times more than middle-rank administrators. The ratio is quite similar to that described in the annual levy of oxen delivered to a sanctuary at Heracleopolis: high-ranking officials handed over ten oxen (but the General of Heracleopolis gave sixty), high priests and administrators of the temple between six and ten, two assistants of the general eight each, two administrators of a fortress gave five and six respectively, while twenty-five localities handed over between one and four oxen. Finally, some collectives of specialized workers (copper-smiths, gardeners, military personnel, stonemasons, potters, builders, etc.) handed over an ox each (Ritner 2009: 180–86). Land was another source of wealth, and it was not unusual for the elite to receive extensive land assets from the king (Ibi, governor of Deir el-Gebrawy: 55.9 ha; Mentuhotep, High-Steward of Amenhotep III, transferred 118.5 ha of land to a statue of the king, but 60.6 ha had been given previously to Mentuhotep by the pharaoh: Moreno García 2013b). Setting aside extraordinary rewards, royal gifts, etc., we can gather that the state paid off standard salaries according to a well-defined hierarchy of revenue. Judging from some comparative evidence analysed by Scheidel (in a study on Han China and the second century AD Roman empire), the state spent roughly about 15 per cent of its annual revenue in salaries paid to civil servants.

Military expenses were limited until the second half of the second millennium BC. Until then, permanent forces seem rather limited and armies mostly consisted of expeditionary forces recruited as required or, as was the case in the early second millennium BC, for the construction of an exceptional chain of fortresses in Nubia (some of which were used only seasonally) supported by garrisons. However, changes in warfare and weaponry from 1550 BC, as well as repeated military campaigns and confrontations with other major powers of the Near East, meant that substantial resources were now employed in metal-based activities, such as production of war chariots and swords, not to mention of a fleet of warships. Maintaining a cavalry force also required abundant pasture areas (at least 7.5 ha for a pair of horses, according to Ramesside documents) as well as specialists and the provision of special types of hard wood that would be used in the manufacture of chariot parts. Judging from Late Bronze Age documents, soldiers and veterans – including foreign mercenaries – were paid with land, and military colonies were founded in areas like Fayum. These activities certainly had a considerable impact in the organization of crafts, the supply of raw materials, etc., and it is perfectly possible that they involved not only state-sponsored workshops but also skilled 'independent' craftsmen, from leather-workers to metalworkers and shipbuilders. Papyri from the early second millennium BC record administrative orders regarding the shipment of wood and other materials to the dockyard of Coptos, along with 3,756 workers, in order to build a fleet on the shore of the Red Sea. Unexpected requests from military personnel on assignment were a concern that emerges in documents from different periods (Jursa & Moreno García 2015: 152–53). The burden of military expenses grew in the first millennium BC, particularly when kings recruited thousands of mercenaries and built war fleets to lead operations in the Mediterranean. While grants of land served to remunerate military personnel, grain exports probably also helped secure the resources needed to finance these activities.

In both cases (remuneration of military personnel and administrators), temples were crucial providers of income for the agents of the state, including (but not limited to) priests. So, some state expenditure was diverted to autonomous institutions, especially when remunerations and salaries consisted mainly of land. The various uses of temple land – from plots attached to a royal statue to a mix of land and prebends, and so on – cast some light on the complex relations between the monarchy and the sanctuaries. A good example of direct allotments of land appears in the inscriptions of Ahmose, son of Ebana, a veteran who fought under the first kings of the New Kingdom and whose deeds were rewarded with slaves (nine men and ten women cited in his tomb) and extensive estates: two of five arouras (1 aroura = 0.27 ha) in his home city of Elkab, and sixty arouras near Hadja. Plots of land of this type would remain in the hands of his descendants for generations. Mose's inscription traces the history of one such land grant, awarded by Ahmose to Mose's ancestor, the ship-master Neshi, veteran of the wars against the Hyksos, and the litigation that ensued among his heirs over the control of the undivided estate down to the reign of Ramesses II. In other cases soldiers were granted similar plots of land, as in the case of the Wilbour Papyrus, when smallholders of all occupations cultivated heritable plots on temple land, typically three or five arouras in size. Officials and cultivators also obtained temple land as rewards, not as salaries, and this particular category of fields fell under the supervision of the vizier. Finally, temples also received land from individuals: Berlin Papyrus 3047, a lawsuit from the reign of Ramesses II, details the transfer of privately held land to the management of a temple. According to this document, a certain Neferabet was the representative of a group of co-heirs that held an estate of more than 140 arouras, and he transferred it to the temple of the goddess Mut in what appears not as a transaction between two private parties but rather a transfer of shares to temple management for the benefit of both the temple of Mut and Neferabet himself. With the transfer, Neferabet could obtain a good income from the property as an absentee landlord while safeguarding the land by establishing a 'tie of dependence' with the temple (the managing institution). In this way, both parties obtained income under advantageous conditions (Katary 2012). Penniut, a leading official in Nubia, made an endowment for a statue of King Ramesses VI. The text in his tomb enumerates the fields rented to endow the statue-cult, the total surface of which amounted to 4.1 ha. Furthermore, Penniut added another parcel of land of 1.65 ha from his own property to ensure provision of a regular sacrifice (Frood 2007: 215–16). In return, he was rewarded with a symbolic gift of two silver vessels of unguent, in what appears as a strategy to strengthen his contacts with the pharaoh.

Another substantial area of state expenses lay in building and maintaining fortresses as well as organizing the logistics for expeditions sent to quarries, mines, harbours, the desert areas, etc. (for the construction of wells, approach roads, diverse types of facilities and so on). The impact of these activities on state expenditure was probably considerable for many ordinary Egyptians, at least in periods of centralization of power, but had nothing to do with the alleged redistribution economy so often ascribed to the pharaonic monarchy. Expeditions to quarries gathered in some cases up to 20,000 men, mostly villagers and conscript workers who received salaries (rations) in exchange for their work. However, this service also deprived their households of the main breadwinner during their period of duty – if they returned at all. Not by chance, officials heading up expeditions boasted about returning with no losses when, in reality, losses could be rather significant, up to 10 per cent of the total contingent in the reign of Ramesses IV. This may explain why prisoners and soldiers were employed in strenuous work, such as extracting minerals or clearing scrubland so that it could be cultivated. It seems that one man in a hundred could be mobilized for military service in the Middle Kingdom, but that number went up to one in ten during the reign of Ramesses III. The organization of conscripts in groups of tens might explain the title of the official known as the Great of Tens of Upper Egypt (mentioned briefly above), who would be involved in the recruitment of men for expeditions, both military and 'civil'. Work camps and workers' 'towns' discovered at several sites, and dating from different periods, attest to the importance of this system and to the logistics necessary to feed, equip, accommodate and transport substantial numbers of people.

What was the cost and the economic impact of building projects? Scheidel estimates that it rose to about 13 per cent of the annual 'budget' of the Roman Empire in the first centuries AD. In the case of ancient Egypt, however, it is much more difficult to calculate. Leaving aside the logistics needed in the provision of building materials (bricks, blocks of stone, etc.) and equipment, such programmes certainly had an impact on the economic life of towns and cities: they provided jobs, promoted craftsmanship and opened up opportunities for specialized activities (collecting firewood, making ropes and leather, etc.). The use of compulsory workers supplied by towns and settlements is well attested, as is the foundation of settlements like Deir el-Medina, the village that hosted the artisans (nearly 120) who built and decorated the royal tombs of the New Kingdom and who were paid and supplied by the state. However, as of the third millennium BC, artisans also satisfied a private demand for luxury items in exchange for wages, when officials boasted about paying out of their own pockets for the artisans who built their tombs. A late third millennium BC carpenter from Akhmim, for instance, declared that he had manufactured 180 coffins for the people of his province. So it seems rather probable that the great building programmes also engaged artisans, specialists, skilled and seasonal workers, etc., who worked for wages and not as part of a workforce employed exclusively by institutions. As metals were used to pay craftsmen, the huge amounts of precious metals brought as tribute into Egypt may have contributed towards the financing of building programmes and stimulated the economic life of towns (Goelet 2015). Furthermore, imperial expansion from 1500 BC onwards also boosted the workforce (via prisoners of war, tribute, slaves, specialists) by at least 150,000 people, who were then assigned to temples and put to work cultivating large tracts of land and producing textiles. These workers facilitated the expansion of a system of agricultural production based on workers attached to the fields in which they laboured and who delivered fixed quotas of grain (15,360 litres of grain per year) from standard plots (5.5 ha). This system declined at the beginning of the first millennium BC, when the empire collapsed. Thanks to their increased economic capacities, temples became great consumers and their expenditures stimulated specialized agricultural and craft activities in their local areas.

A final word concerns an indirect source of 'expenditure': corruption (Vernus 1993). Documents such as those outlining the so-called 'Elephantine scandal' describe the theft of just over 5,000 sacks of grain from the temple of Elephantine, over a period of several years, by a captain of a ship employed by this institution and assisted in his nefarious activities by its priests. In other cases, corruption consisted of the annexation of state land, as in the example described in Rylands Papyrus 9, whereby the priests of a provincial temple illegally seized part of the crown land on a Nile island including cultivable land, woodland and sandy areas. Abuses of authority by officials inspired literary works such as *The Eloquent Peasant*, while bribery helped 'buy' support in feuds and lawsuits. In other instances, soldiers and state personnel requested extra workers, private or temple property or whatever they needed through requisitions, appropriation or basic theft. The edicts of Dahshur of Pepi I, Nauri or Horemheb are good examples of these practices. The other side of these practices is that people might use them against their opponents, as was the case in the affair of the robbery of the royal tombs, when one faction accused the other of being involved in the plundering of tombs. However, high-ranking officials often came out well from these situations, even when they had appeared in court. A letter from the late third millennium BC shows the disappointment of two Elephantine dignitaries about the behaviour of a senior official who had committed robbery, because he was not 'one who is living off his own possessions', and yet who came through the trial unscathed. While the burden on the state is impossible to evaluate, these cases nonetheless show that any claim about thorough bureaucratic control over the wealth of the country was more ideal than real. We receive the impression that both the taxation system and tax records were less than rigorous, and left ample room for corruption of all types and for officials' personal enrichment through 'illegal' practices. As the protagonist of *The Teaching of Amenemope* (a scribe and overseer of fields and grain in the Ramesside period) exhorted:

> do not move the markers on the borders of fields, nor shift the position of the measuring-cord. Do not be greedy for a cubit of land, nor encroach on the boundaries of a widow... do not move the scales, nor alter the weights nor diminish the fractions of the measure. Do not desire a measure of the fields, nor neglect those of the treasury... beware of disguising the measure, so as to falsify its fractions. Do not force it to overflow, nor let its belly be empty. Measure according to its true size, your hand clearing exactly. Do not make a bushel of twice its size [...] Do not accept a farmer's dues and then assess him so as to injure him. Do not conspire with the measurer, so as to defraud the share of the (royal) Residence.

It seems that the state sometimes resorted to these extreme measures. Thus the robbery of royal tombs and temples at the end of the second millennium BC seems to represent exceptional circumstances (a rebellion in Nubia) that demanded extra income in order to raise an army.

4

Co-opting Leaders

The stability of the monarchy depended on the capacity of kings to tie together, co-opt and integrate into the structures of government four different groups of people: the extensive royal family (including its secondary branches), a potential source of trouble and rivalries; senior dignitaries and provincial nobles, many of whom descended from powerful families with their own interests, connections and political agendas that could eventually crystallize in factions; more junior officials who owed their position, wealth and income to the king and whose loyalty should have been more solid (although they too were linked to powerful patrons); and, finally, 'informal leaders' – people whose power was based on social position, wealth, traditional authority, influence and connections that did not depend on any official position. This group included village chiefs, wealthy peasants, merchants, urban notables, etc. Maintaining a robust equilibrium between and within these sectors was no easy task, especially when special circumstances altered the balance of power between them, or when one sector was promoted and the influence of others declined. For instance, as of 1550 BC, imperial expansion – and the rise of the army as a prominent institution – offered new opportunities for administrative careers, promotion and income. Moreover, some of these actors might have felt that, under particular conditions, their interests no longer coincided with those of the monarchy. In such cases, political fragmentation ensued from the collapse of the monarchy and local polities emerged, seeking a new balance of power more favourable to their aims and strategies – which ultimately would be to gain and maintain the ascendant. In the absence of a 'civil society', of 'citizens' or of a 'public opinion' capable of having an impact on political decisions, power remained in the hands of a relatively small group of people who were influential enough to limit the alleged absolutism of royal authority.

Far from being autocratic rulers, pharaohs had to cope with and arbitrate among factions and interests and create the material and symbolic means necessary to rally to their cause potentates from different social backgrounds (court, provinces, etc.). Distribution of wealth, honours and rank was one such means of attraction, as were strategic marriages, the display of royal favour and continuous interference in the internal affairs of powerful families. In this way, political ability constituted the very basis of royal authority (Gundlach & Klug 2006; Moreno García 2013a; Agut-Labordère & Moreno García 2016).

But what of the potentates? What were the foundations of their power? And were these foundations strong enough to transform them into potentially autonomous actors, capable of limiting royal authority effectively and institutionally? World history presents many examples of notable individuals or groups who counterbalanced the power of kings or who transformed rulers into mere symbolic authorities, deprived of any substantial executive power. Two aspects are crucial here: the formation, extent and transmission of the elite's patrimony; and the elite's capacity (or that of significant sectors within it) to define collective interests and to enforce them through political action. The formation and composition of the patrimony held by the elite remains elusive. Officials, for instance, boasted in their inscriptions about the awards and income granted by the king, but only very reluctantly did they mention private acquisition of wealth or the inheritance of family assets. Transfers of land between individuals are well known, as are the possession and transmission of temple land held privately (leases, acquisition of rights on fields, etc.). However, it is extremely difficult to ascertain whether such sources of income were genuinely significant or if, on the contrary, income granted by the king represented the bulk of the elite's wealth. Hapidjefa, a governor of Asyut who lived in the early second millennium BC, distinguished carefully between 'the house of the father' (the patrimonial assets of his family) and 'the house of the governor' (the income derived from his own position as governor). In any case, there is no trace of a significant class of aristocratic landowners whose private wealth, and ability to capture and transfer state assets within their wider family for the long term, could transform them into a sort of feudal class. While provincial potentates are prominent in the epigraphic and archaeological record from a very early date, there is no indication that they thought of themselves as a group with shared interests, even less that they acted politically as a 'lobby' with specific demands and collective goals.

These two aspects reveal three things. First, that the consolidation of a feudal class or, simply, of a group of noble people able to own privately or to acquire substantial wealth, and who could transfer it within their family for generations, seems negligible. Second, that kings retained a considerable ability to forge the ruling elite, to intervene in their affairs and to prevent the emergence of powerful local autonomous actors for most of Egyptian history. Third, that in the absence of a true aristocracy and of corporative urban bodies (associations of craftsmen, of traders, etc.) that could support collective interests and demands and defend them through political negotiation, the monarchy never had to cope with institutionalized political counterpowers (for instance, a league of cities, a parliament, a tribal confederation, etc.). In fact, the fate of the ruling elite was closely linked to that of the monarchy, the only exception being the long period between 2200 and 1550 BC when regional actors, mainly based in Middle Egypt, maintained substantial freedom of action. From this perspective, it is significant that the main decision-making executive 'institutions' were informal, short-lived and revolved around the king. Councils of (high-ranking) dignitaries and palatial factions certainly advised the king and influenced his decisions, yet in both cases the prominence of their members was fragile, as it depended on royal favour and on the overt competition between peers, thus providing the king with an ideal tool to disrupt any potential solidarity between potentates and to preserve his central role as arbitrator.

The court and the royal family

The very concept of royal family is quite complex in an Egyptian context. It included not only the parents, spouse(s) and children of the reigning king, but also the 'sons of the king' – probably the descendants of former kings and/or members of secondary branches of the (extended) royal family. Furthermore, the private area of the palace in which queens and princes lived (sometimes referred to as the 'Inner Palace'), retained a considerable political importance. Young princes were educated there together with selected children from the kingdom's most eminent families, both from the provinces and the capital, thus helping create a ruling elite closely linked to the monarchy, a link forged further through marriages. The Inner Palace was also the perfect environment in which to produce and spread a common set of values, from etiquette to high culture and official (high) language. At the same time, the Inner Palace was the ideal setting for political intrigue and conspiracy. As kings took several spouses, all the daughters of powerful families, more than one child might have a reasonable expectation to ascend the throne, and political factions would have aimed to enhance their position and influence by supporting one candidate or another. In the end, this system reveals the oligarchical and highly personalized nature of power in ancient Egypt and shows the limits of political practice there, more particularly its 'informal' aspect, far away from the public ceremonies, promotions and grants of titles that marked official court life. Conspiracies, culminating occasionally in the murder of the king (as with Amemenhat I and Ramesses III), as well as the killings of (overly powerful) favourites (such as chancellor Bay), are good examples of such shadowy exercises of power, many of which involved courtiers, high-ranking dignitaries, priests, military personnel and, of course, the sons and spouses of the king. In other cases, foreign influence left its mark in this secluded palatial environment. The diplomatic correspondence of the New Kingdom mentions foreign messengers with access to the Inner Palace who met princesses sent there from abroad. In other cases, ambitious Egyptians and foreigners alike found in the Inner Palace and the court a propitious arena for their ambitions, a place where crucial support as well as promotion to eminent positions might be expected thanks to their connections with queens and prominent dignitaries. The 'Zannanza affair' – in which a recently widowed Egyptian queen asked the Hittite king to send one of his sons to marry her in around 1325 BC – reveals the existence of informal channels of communication between royal courts, even of palatial factions (pro-Hittite, in this particular case) enjoying the support of foreign powers, which proved influential enough to leave their mark on Egypt's foreign policy. Finally, the oligarchical nature of power emerges clearly at certain periods, as occurred from 1800 and 1000 BC onwards, when kingship circulated among a number of important families in an irregular fashion or when kings entrusted crucial positions to members of their own kin (Quirke 1991).

The Outer Palace was the set of 'formal' expressions of politics. Being a highly personalized environment, royal favour, administrative skills, knowledge of formal codes (from etiquette to eloquence) and proximity to the king (such as that enjoyed by barbers around 2400 BC), made this sector of the palace another crucial decision-making arena. This was expressed most strongly in the Chamber of Dignitaries, sometimes evoked in a literary *topos* (*Königsnovelle*), where the king asked his dignitaries for advice, and where their disappointing, pusillanimous responses prompted the pharaoh to take, in sharp contrast, audacious measures. In any case, the Chamber of Dignitaries appeared for the first time around the end of the third millennium BC as a consultative institution that advised the king. The biographical inscriptions of many of its officials reveal the qualities most appreciated in this institution: being calm, providing good advice, talking properly and eloquently and excelling at making suggestions. Not by chance, it was slightly later that the first 'literary' compositions, which aimed to instruct scribes and officials, emphasized precisely these same qualities as well as respect for hierarchy and one's superiors (Coulon 1999 and 2010). Little is known about the composition of the Chamber of Dignitaries. It apparently hosted only a very small number of officials (perhaps about ten) and included the vizier, overseers of crucial institutions (the Double Treasury, the Sealer, etc.) and people trusted by the king – although these were not necessarily holders of official responsibilities. That is why some officials simply presented themselves in their monuments as 'children of the *kap*' (*kap* being the private sectors of the palace), as this title sufficed to express the rank of its holder and his close links to the royal family.

The role of the royal family as holders of senior administrative positions varied over time. In the early Old Kingdom (2613–2503 BC), many officials bore the title of 'son of king' while not necessarily being related by blood to the monarch. The title expressed nevertheless an ideal of government, in which executive power was limited to the royal family as well as to high-ranking officials who were considered part of an ideal extended family centred around the king. The enormous pyramids built at this time, surrounded by the tombs of the highest elite, symbolize this ideal. However, this system fell into abeyance from 2500 BC, when the administration became more diversified, was organized in specific departments and offices and when the ranks of the administration expanded. The image of the 'extended royal family' was no longer appropriate, great pyramids were thus no longer necessary and new means emerged to enhance the status of the elite: these included rank-indicating titles, the greater visibility of provincial leaders, and marriage alliances between kings and powerful families. In other cases, co-regencies helped transfer royal authority within a specific branch of the royal family; this could have been particularly helpful in unstable political environments, when kings had to face rebellions and the ambitions of powerful sectors of the elite. Inversely, there were instances when royal sons remained in the background and their executive was modest: indeed the great majority of Ramesses II's roughly fifty sons and fifty daughters displayed no major administrative or official responsibility. In stormy political contexts kings could also be tempted to establish their own sons at the head of all prominent national offices, as in the case of Osorkon II. So the formal political role played by the royal family oscillated between personal participation in executive power and a secondary position in a highly bureaucratic system. Kings themselves rarely escaped these constraints as they faced rebellions that occasionally led either to complete political powerlessness or to the emergence of rival kingdoms in Egypt.

Regional leaders

Regional leaders were crucial for the stability of the monarchy. They represented the indispensable link between the court and the provincial society and it was through their collaboration that the monarchy could implement its measures at the local level, from the collection of taxes to provision of manpower. However, regional leaders are not always easy to detect in the archaeological record, and their participation in the administrative structure of the kingdom has sometimes led to confusion. Thus, behind the consideration of these regional leaders as 'provincial governors' or *nomarchs* lies an anachronistic interpretation based on Greco-Roman evidence and on modern concepts about the state. The truth is that regional leaders played a far more complex role than that of (supposedly) appointed delegates of the king. Moreover, it is difficult to discern a homogeneous pattern of provincial administration that was operative all over Egypt. To the contrary, deep differences distinguished Upper and Lower Egypt and, in the case of the provinces of Upper Egypt (by far the best documented area), they also show a great diversity of political and administrative situations. It also becomes apparent that the archaeological visibility of provincial leaders depended on their access to (and display of) the prestigious cultural productions of the palatial sphere (decorated tombs, inscribed monuments, etc.). This might explain why in some periods they are difficult to detect, despite occasional references to their collaboration with the monarchy and their full integration into the highest sphere of power. In other cases, a title such as 'great chief of a province' (erroneously equated to 'provincial governor') took on different meanings in 2300, 1900 or 1450 BC respectively and was used very selectively after 2000 BC.

The importance of regional leaders is apparent from the earliest periods, when huge tombs in some provinces symbolized the integration of their elites within the monarchy. Later on, the hundreds of inscribed stone vessels found in the pyramid of King Djoser (who lived around 2680 BC) show a two-fold administrative pattern, based on royal production centres and on 'houses' of officials and local potentates. Other texts, from 2500 BC onwards, provide another clue, as temples scattered all over the country represented another pole of authority. In their role of 'acquaintances of the king', 'great chiefs of a province' and other functions, the fact is that powerful families controlled the main provincial institutions – temples and royal production centres. Sometimes such families are exceptionally well documented for eight generations or more and, as was the case for Elkab or Meir at different periods of their history, they took great pride in evoking long genealogies. Ancestry was coveted, to the point that prestigious forebears were venerated and their cult (and the ceremonies and offerings related to it) helped strengthen the cohesion of the local elite. A similar sense of strong provincial identity is also visible in the deification of local magnates at Asyut and Qaw. Moreover, in some cases full provinces or entire districts were named after one of their leaders, as indicated by the label of 'The House of Khuu' in the late third millennium BC, that designated Edfu and neighbouring areas; it was also not unknown for the 'domains' of dignitaries and local potentates (holders of administrative positions or not) to represent territorial units. That is why the names of local leaders were occasionally listed as toponyms in administrative texts, for example to record the geographical provenance of teams of workers.

But what of the relations between local leaders? Khnumhotep II of Beni Hasan, himself one of a provincial family of 'great chiefs', claims that he married the daughter of the 'great chief' of a neighbouring province. In Ramesside times, Wenennefer of Abydos, born into a family that dominated the local highest priesthood of Osiris for generations, married a lady from a powerful family at Asyut. Not surprisingly, both examples show that local leaders sought to maintain and strengthen their power through marriage alliances with other influential families. Two aspects should be stressed about the interests and strategies of these families, however. First, the interests of the nobles buried in a particular province were in no way limited to that province. Officials from Elephantine cultivated land at Gebelein and buried officials there, for example, while a 'great chief' from Beni Hasan is known from the dedicatory stela he left at Dendera. In some exceptional cases, a 'great chief' might have held this function in two different provinces. Second – but in a similar vein – the existence of decorated tombs in a particular province should not make us think that their owners were based only in that province. In fact, it cannot be ruled out that members of a powerful local family might choose to be buried in different provinces within the territory under its influence over the course of time. This could explain the sudden (and ephemeral) presence of decorated tombs in one province, and then in a neighbouring location. Inversely, when several elite families coexisted in a single province, each one might have used its own cemetery there. Only the titles of their members and occasional references to their family connections reveal that they belonged to different kin groups, who held often distinctive ranks and responsibilities. This may explain why the sources from the late third millennium BC refer to 'chiefs' in a single province, but only one of them bore the title of 'great chief', probably to distinguish the dominant family among the local elite, or the family that was the privileged mediator between the royal palace and the local society (Moreno García 2013a).

The integration of regional leaders into the official structures of power followed different paths. Close links with the royal family were by far the most important, and provincial leaders might have fulfilled distinguished missions for the monarchy even when they left no monumental trace of their existence in their own provinces. This is the case for two 'acquaintances of the king', from the otherwise poorly documented provinces 17 of Upper Egypt and 14 of Lower Egypt, who are known only from the inscriptions they left in Nubia when they commanded great military expeditions around 2600–2500 BC (Strudwick 2005: 150). Likewise, the papyri from the funerary temple of King Neferirkare record dignitaries from the Delta among the cult personnel of that particular institution, while other sources from this period (including tombs) only very rarely mention officials from this region. In fact, royal funerary temples were far more than cult centres;

they also became sources of income for the provincial elite as well as providers of privileged links with the court, the royal family and distinguished nobles from the capital. Yet kings were in no way absent from provincial temples. As these sanctuaries were in many cases the principal bases of power for eminent local families, kings employed several means to extend their influence there. Royal donations of land, building royal chapels within provincial temples and the creation of ritual offices, provided with income, were the most usual routes. Local nobles also created and endowed cults centred around statues of the king, thus emphasizing their proximity to the monarchy and enhancing their local prestige. The education of provincial children at court, in the company of the princes, and marriages between kings and local noble ladies also favoured these contacts, which reinforced the basis of royal power and enabled its expansion outside the prevailing groups of power at court. In return, when provincial ladies became queens, their own families and allies were raised to prominent positions in the kingdom. Queens Ankhkhenespepi (two women with the same name were married to Pepi I and Merenre respectively) and Queen Tiyi (spouse of Amenhotep III), based at Abydos and Akhmim respectively, are good examples of this policy.

Close contacts between the court and the nobility (palace-based and provincial) explain why they all shared the same (high) culture, including the standard official language and artistic codes displayed on their monuments. But such contacts also served the strategies of eminent local families seeking to preserve and enhance their power. Tjeti-Kaihep, who lived around 2260 BC, entered the service of the king when he was a young man. A member of the most powerful family at Akhmim, his family controlled the positions of 'great chiefs' and 'overseer of priests' for at least eight generations. Since Tjeti-Kaihep was the youngest child, his elder brother inherited the title of 'great chief' and Tjeti-Kaihep was sent to Memphis, where he held very senior positions that point to a career that should probably have culminated with the role of vizier. However, Tjeti-Kaihep returned to his home province, where he too became great chief and overseer of priests. Tjeti's unexpected return to Akhmim was probably due to his elder brother's premature death and, in the absence of an heir, he chose to maintain his family's control over its traditional power base rather than pursue a high-ranking career in the capital. Finally, if the positions of great chief and overseer of priests remained in the hands of the dominant branch of the local ruling family (in which Tjeti-Kaihep was born), a secondary branch of the same family held titles related to the central administration. So, control over the local power-bases plus holding influential positions at the court define this family's strategy. Such dual approach helped integrate local magnates into the monarchy and also shaped a local elite that was eager to collaborate with the monarchy and attach itself to the values of palace culture. At the same time it provided influence and income to local families far beyond the limits of their provinces. Similar cases at Beni Hasan (around 1900–1830 BC) and Edfu and Elkab (around 1550 BC) reveal the remarkable position local dominant families enjoyed for many generations, as they continued to provide senior officials to the royal administration. Indeed their control over their respective provinces was not incompatible with their participation in state affairs or in court life.

What these examples reveal is that local nobles enjoyed considerable autonomy, and were able to follow their own agendas and strategies while serving kings, thereby creating their own webs of influence at provincial, regional and 'national' levels. Wenennefer of Abydos, the high priest of Osiris who lived during the reign of Ramesses II, is a good illustration of these practices. While his family controlled the highest priesthood at Abydos for hundreds of years, he also displayed family and 'inter-peer' connections with many other high-ranking contemporaries, including the holders of prestigious priestly roles and eminent dignitaries of the king's court of Ramesses II; he referred to these men – who included two viziers and the high priest of Onuris at Thinis, to name but a few – as his 'brothers'. Wenennefer's wife also came from a long line of overseers of the Granary at Asyut. Erecting statues dedicated to prominent members of the court, including the king himself, was a privileged way of displaying and strengthening such connections. In fact, he erected many royal statues, endowing them with offerings as well as with substantial amounts of land, a policy which recalls similar methods from other members of the Ramesside elite like Penniut of Aniba (northern Nubia). So, the 'political' and marriage alliances established by Wenennefer included powerful families from other provinces, high-ranking members of the court and the king himself, a strategy that maintained control over the local priesthood, the true basis of power for him and his family. As a result, Wenennefer could proudly boast of being a 'great chief in Abydos'. Thus, the political influence of some provincial leaders in the affairs of the kingdom was considerable, as the state ruled through these leaders while they in turn 'used' the state to their own ends. For example, the mayors of the town of Wah-Sut, a specialized settlement founded by Pharaoh Senusret III around 1850 BC to accommodate the staff of his mortuary complex at Abydos, came from Bersheh and Qaw respectively. Nobles from another provincial centre, Beni Hasan, fulfilled missions related to trade expeditions and diplomacy with foreign territories, while nobles from Bersheh took on the role of overseeing trade in myrrh (which formerly had been controlled by Heracleopolis, Thebes' rival) once they joined the Theban kingdom, as if their support to their new masters came at the price of managing the buying and selling of this precious commodity. Of course, such influence could nourish political ambitions and rebellion. This may explain the hostility towards the Theban kings Antef V, Kamose and Ahmose shown by three rebels, two of whom were called Teti (from the cities of Coptos and Nefrusi respectively) and Teti-an (hailing from Nubia, perhaps), all of whom had rallied other 'malcontents' from, presumably, northern Egypt. Amenemhat I also faced rebels in Middle Egypt supported by Nubians and Asian peoples, as if such rebels relied on foreign support.

A final point concerns potential rivalries among provincial leaders and the (geo)political implications thereof. The end of the monarchy at around 2160 BC was probably due to Egypt's increasing integration into the international trade networks of the Early-Middle Bronze Age, mainly as provider of gold, incense and exotic items (hides, ivory). As trade goods circulated between Nubia and the Mediterranean through a network of logistical centres controlled by local nobles, wealth began to accumulate in the provinces. This process may have stimulated local autonomous policies, thus breaking the traditional commonality of interests between the king and the provincial nobles. Two main poles emerged then, one centred at Thebes and probably related to the creation of the port of Mersa/Wadi Gawasis, on the Red Sea. The other pole lay in the area of Asyut, Bersheh and Beni Hasan, which had connections to the Mediterranean and Nubia. From each pole emerged the rival kingdoms of Heracleopolis and Thebes respectively. Similar conflicts arose again during the Middle Bronze Age, when the area of Asyut, Bersheh and Beni Hasan supported the Hyksos kingdom in the north against its Theban rivals. Further geopolitical changes may have also left their mark in the provincial sphere. The increasing importance of Mediterranean trade may explain why the balance of power inside Egypt swung definitively towards Lower Egypt in the second half of the second millennium BC, when Pi-Ramesses became one of the capitals of Egypt. But before this major shift took place, two phenomena point to a last attempt from the leaders of Middle Egypt to preserve their traditional political influence. It was in the period 1479–1400 BC that the title of 'great chief' of a province reappeared, borne by potentates from Bersheh and Qaw, not to speak of the title 'great chief of Upper Egypt', adopted by a potentate from the Fayum. Slightly later (1390–1336 BC), the family of Queen Tiyi, from Akhmim, rose to a prominent political position and Pharaoh Akhenaten established his short-lived capital at Tell el-Amarna (near Bersheh). Should these events be interpreted as the latest effort to revive Middle Egypt? As the area between Asyut and Beni Hasan had traditionally controlled fluvial trade, one may infer that rivalry over control of trade along the Nile and other routes, as well as shifts in the balance of power between Egyptian regions as well as the expansion of trade in the Eastern Mediterranean, underpin the political machinations and rivalries noted in some provinces.

Immaterial roots of power

A common theme in numerous biographical inscriptions is that officials and nobles progressed in their careers thanks to their administrative and organizational skills. The successful achievement of their duties and missions was celebrated at court, in the presence of dignitaries and the royal family, and these men were rewarded with honours, precious gifts and the public praise of their qualities. Other merits included observance of etiquette, morality and eloquence. However, behind the façade of a meritocracy, other factors were at play. Weni of Abydos, for instance, has been traditionally considered the archetype of a dignitary promoted because of his prudence, capability and administrative skill, as his own autobiography claims. However, new epigraphic evidence from his tomb reveals quite a different story, as he came from a high-ranking family of viziers, and was well connected with two queens who also came from Abydos. Thus his exceptionally successful career was based not only on his own qualities and the political opportunities exploited in his early career (conspiracies, dismissal of senior officials), but also on his influential family background. Furthermore, in the competitive environment of the court, where contacts and integration in powerful networks of patronage were crucial, the support of high-ranking officials was as essential as royal favour. Sometimes officials did record these aspects in their autobiographies, as when Simut-Kyky or Hezi claimed that they had neither protector nor backer and that the advancement in their careers was the consequence of their qualities, thus admitting tacitly that these practices were common.

Genealogies confirm the importance of a favourable background. In periods of crisis and during the collapse of the monarchy, when this institution could no longer legitimize the authority claimed by officials, ancestry was invoked to prove the rightful claims of a family to a position or to justify its dominant position. Provincial potentates from Elkab and Meir left lengthy genealogies in which they and their ancestors appeared as the 'natural' rulers of their territory. In other cases, priests from the early first millennium BC inscribed on their monuments the names of their ancestors, going back for dozens of generations in the more detailed examples. The message was simple: their position should not and could not be challenged as they were the legitimate holders of the roles they occupied. There are also instances in which ancestry went back further, when a governor claimed that he was the grandson of governors. In this vein, there were other ways to express the power and exclusivity of a family of officials. On the one hand, sanctuaries erected in memory of an ancestor became a symbolic node that expressed the power and legitimacy of the local ruling elite, as was the case with the sanctuary of Heqaib at Elephantine. On the other hand, clusters of tombs belonging to a single family embodied the power and rank of their owners and their close links to kings. The visual impact of the resulting landscapes was considerable, as demonstrated by the ranges of rock tombs in many sites across Upper Egypt, and in complexes formed by mastabas (such as Senedjemib at Giza) or rock tombs (such as Princess Sheretnebty's at Abusir).

Family connections were crucial in the reproduction of the ruling elite, and played a much more important role than the alleged meritocratic values so praised in biographies. This may explain why the scribal culture of Egyptian officials departed from the Mandarin system prevailing in ancient China. Nobles and important dignitaries sent their sons to the royal palace. They were educated there in the company of royal children and prepared to become the ruling elite of the kingdom, forming a pool of well-connected and high-ranking young men who would be the closest friends and colleagues of future kings. This system later extended to conquered territories in the late second millennium BC, when princes from subject regions arrived into Egypt as hostages to be educated at the court. Royal favour appears thus as the crucial element to be promoted, taking precedence over competence or administrative skills, even over a well-defined *cursus honorum*. The troubled times that accompanied the advent of Pharaoh Teti and his descendants to the throne (2345 BC) are a good example, as crucial functions (vizier, overseer of Upper Egypt, etc.) were held by a surprisingly large number of officials (some of them very young) in a relatively short span of time. Perhaps meritocracy was more important among middle- and low-ranking officials, but the extensive patronage networks to which they belonged, controlled by senior dignitaries, meant ultimately that the right contacts were essential for their careers, and exchanged for loyalty, discretion and support to their patrons. Sometimes officials celebrated cultural values based on knowledge of literary texts, the scribal tradition and the veneration of previous masters, as indicated in the brief inscriptions they left in the tombs of ancient scholars and – alleged – authors of wisdom texts. However, integration in patronage networks was always essential, even if it was an aspect deliberately played down in texts that proclaimed the moral superiority and advantageous work conditions achieved by scribes by virtue only of their managerial and writing skills.

This leads to a crucial question: was there a true 'bureaucratic class', repository of a *raison d'état* and of an administrative logic that would result eventually in the emergence of autonomous spheres of decision-making? Did its values, interests and strategic goals go beyond those of the immediate familial and professional interests of their members, even

Figure 4.1   Scribes represented the ruling class at the service of kings.

to the point of challenging those of the nobility? In fact, despite the emphasis placed on merit and service to the king, not to speak of the popular image of Egypt as a highly centralized and bureaucratic state, the reality was far different. Certainly, the monarchy needed specialized keepers and managers of information, but their role appears instrumental and subordinate to the king and the nobility, both provincial and palace-based. Ancient Egyptians were quite aware of this fact. *The Teaching for (King) Merykara*, a sort of treatise on royal power, stated plainly that the king should respect officials but, at the same time, it also advised that he should enrich his great men so that they enacted the laws of the king. The text went on to state that 'great is the great man whose great men are great', so the best way for kings to assert their authority was being 'lords of an entourage' as well as 'rich in officials' (who must fear kings nevertheless) and in not damaging the officials in their seats of office. In short, hierarchy and the balance of power between dignitaries and 'great ones' should be respected. Bureaucratic values, and scribal culture, however, are absent from this piece of realpolitik. Furthermore, bureaucracy appears hardly distinguishable from other spheres of power, such as priesthood or military functions, as it was far from uncommon for those officials who engaged in 'managerial' and scribal activities to also hold responsibilities in these other spheres. So, the stability of the monarchy relied more on guaranteeing a *sustainable* balance of power between nobles and palatial factions than in the creation of a corps of specialized bureaucrats who were increasingly detached and opposed to other staff. And while there is no trace of a 'bureaucratic class', raised to prominent positions from service to the king alone, and based on meritocracy instead of inherited social position and wealth, there was no true aristocracy either, even in the case of the most powerful provincial families: most of their income and rank also depended on their service to kings. There was certainly an ideal of justice and harmony (*maat*), but it derived from respect for the eternal order of things and society embodied by the king and his assistants, not from bureaucratic domination based on normative regulation of authority, impersonal forms of exercise of political power, and seemingly rational *homo politicus*. The contrast

Figure 4.2 Officials depicted themselves on costly prestigious monuments. Here, we see one shown as a receiver of funerary offerings.

between proclaimed values and realities of power is nowhere more evident than in the cases where exceptional circumstances put officials at a crossroads: should they develop a promising individual bureaucratic career or prioritize firmly maintaining the traditional sources of their families' authority? Given the prevalent oligarchical nature of power, an official like the above-mentioned Tjeti-Kaihep had few doubts: facing a conundrum of this kind he chose to return to his province instead of achieving top rank at the palace.

Temples as providers of social connections and institutional stability

Temples played a crucial role as bases of power and providers of authority and income for people of status (mostly nobles, rural potentates, dignitaries, royal staff, etc.). Their origins are not easy to trace. In most cases their early incarnations were as modest sanctuaries for local cults, lacking the monumental dimensions and ornamental sophistication typical of the temples built from 1550 BC onwards. In other cases, kings founded and expanded already existing sanctuaries and, in fact, this activity – together with the provision of statues, ritual equipment and economic resources – was proudly evoked as a prominent duty of pharaohs in their inscriptions and annals. In a world in which law had little relevance to the regulation of human relations, legitimacy and authority derived ultimately from gods, so direct access to those gods and acting as intermediaries between the divine and the human sphere were essential political arenas. Pharaohs were perfectly aware of this issue. When pyramids failed in their role of main symbolic expressions of an extended-kin ideology, one centred on pharaohs and their funerary 'tumuli', kings had to cope with an inescapable reality, namely that as the administration of the state became more and more complex, other foci of power developed far away from the royal palace and kings had to try to integrate these into the governmental structure of power. Temples and royal funerary monuments in and around capital cities barely served to mark the symbolic attachment to the state of officials and rural population living far away in the provinces. So, the small pyramids built in several provinces in the first half of the twenty-sixth century BC, at around the same time as the massive pyramids erected near Memphis, reveal that kings were conscious of *also* having to assert their presence at a great distance from the capital. But such distant areas were not symbolic empty spaces. Local sanctuaries and cults devoted to ancestors of powerful provincial lineages, etc., represented *other*, potentially *alternative* foci of loyalties, identities and legitimization.

The strategy followed by kings was two-fold and destined to endure for several millennia. On the one hand, kings participated in the daily life and organization of local temples. Donations of land and offerings, granting temple and religious titles and promoting 'national' cults (such as that of Osiris), became powerful tools that helped them interfere in the social structure of local priesthoods, to promote rivalry and division among their members (through selective promotions of some people to the detriment of other members or their kin) and to provide locals with privileged channels of communication with the monarchy. On the other hand, royal funerary monuments and temples consecrated to 'national' deities helped strengthen the links between kings and local nobles. New Kingdom pharaohs proclaimed in several inscriptions that they had built enormous temples, staffed with priests chosen from the nobles of the land. Royal funerary temples were in any case precarious institutions, as reigning kings did not hesitate to divert to their own funerary cults the resources and revenue established by their predecessors for *their* funerary foundations. In fact, the massive aspect of the most important temples from 1550 BC onwards, all endowed with enormous wealth, was concomitant with the reduction of royal tombs to a marginal, symbolic role. The geographical distribution of temples all across the kingdom, coupled with their gradual transformation into managerial agencies that assumed economic and administrative functions previously shared with the economic centres of the crown, meant that they became more effective in and functional to the interests of the crown as well as of those of the local elites.

In fact, temples provided income, contacts with the crown and institutional stability. It would be too simplistic to see in royal donations of land mere acts of piety. The considerable amounts of wealth put into the hands of local leaders via these, together with their official recognition as legitimate holders of ritual functions, helped strengthen their allegiance to the crown and the integration of local cults into the official pantheon and religious structure in which kings were, in the end, the only legitimate representatives of gods on earth. This move was reinforced when provincial temples included chapels and cults associated with royal statues provided with land and offerings and whose beneficiaries were, once more, dignitaries, nobles and agents of the crown (from scribes to military personnel). Inversely, nobles also created cults centred on royal statues and endowed with revenue (typically, the donor and his/her direct descendants administered and obtained rents from their donations), a strategy that sought to strengthen their links to the crown. Hence Neshor, a senior dignitary in charge of the customs at Naucratis and Elephantine, made several donations to the temples of these cities as well as to those of Mendes, Sais, Abydos and Hermopolis (Moreno García 2013c). The geographical range of his donations closely matches those made by, for instance, King Psammetichus I, which suggests that Neshor intended not only to safeguard his own patrimony by putting it under the protection of the sanctuaries most favoured by the king, but also to obtain prestige and social 'visibility' thanks to his close association with such institutions. And during those times when the monarchy weakened or collapsed, temples remained as repositories of institutional stability and reserves of wealth – they were (in theory) inviolable as they were under the protection of gods. In this way, the elite preserved part of their patrimony, had access to substantial economic assets and joined institutions that controlled extensive networks of patronage. This point is crucial: access to priesthood was fiercely controlled by local associations of priests, whose claims to certain positions were justified through extensive genealogies.

Under these conditions, temples were ideal tools via which kings could introduce themselves to their rural citizens and build extensive social networks to support their authority. The Wilbour Papyrus (1145 BC) provides a unique insight about this. Most of the temple tenures mentioned in this administrative record were in the hands of people of relatively modest status, a sort of local sub-elite made up of wealthy peasants, soldiers, priests, scribes, 'ladies' – that is, wealthy women who did not rely on the support of their male relatives – and so on. Moreover, many of the temples were located in what had been, hitherto, very sparely populated areas, so they played a crucial role in organizing social and economic life there and rallying the local power groups to the monarchy. Their importance in provincial life was further confirmed in periods when the monarchy stumbled, as was the case, for instance, at the beginning of the first millennium BC, when Prince Namlot recorded the restoration of daily cattle offerings to Harsaphes, god of

Heracleopolis, and provided a detailed inventory of the annual levy, specifying the assessment required of officials and 'cities, towns, and settlements of Heracleopolis' responsible for oxen deliveries to the temple (Ritner 2009: 180). Furthermore, about a hundred donation stelae from the first half of the first millennium BC confirm that such gifts had become indispensable to preserving the income and legitimacy of the elite when the monarchy could no longer fulfil this role.

Elites, their patrimony and the state

Little is known about the origins, composition and transmission of the private patrimony of the elite – especially in the case of potentates who did not work for the state – as they left hardly any documents about their activities, goals or opinions (such as letters, managerial accounts, etc.). As a result, our main source of information consists of documents (usually inscribed in tombs) produced by people of status, well-connected to the monarchy. Not surprisingly, these texts emphasize royal rewards and remunerations, proudly described by their beneficiaries. Other ideals much valued by the elite and frequently evoked by scribes and priests, refer to the deceased passing on their functions to their children. Two logical positions were at work here. On the one hand, it was important to keep a privileged social position within one's wider family as long as possible. On the other hand, it was imperative to secure and keep an income provided by the state in order to achieve such a goal. In both cases, the state and its institutions were crucial to accumulate wealth, prestige and status.

Metjen (who lived around 2580 BC) is one of the rare officials who described in detail the origin and composition of his patrimony. It included the position of scribe inherited from his father, a field of 13 ha inherited from his mother, several fields in diverse provinces (each one serving as remuneration for particular administrative functions), offerings derived from the cult of the mother of a king and land acquired privately, including an orchard of about 1 ha and a field of more than

50 ha (Strudwick 2005: 192). Another exceptional document, the will of Prince Nykaure (Strudwick 2005: 200), lists fourteen domains, scattered across several provinces of Upper Egypt and, principally, of the Delta, and transferred to his wife, son, daughters and other members of his kin. Many other inscriptions from the third millennium BC describe idealized situations in which officials list many domains, supposedly distributed all over Egypt. A somewhat different situation appears in the inscription of Ibi, a governor of the province of Deir el-Gebrawy. He obtained from the king a field of more than 50 ha as well as villages, cattle and dependants, 'not including the property of my father', which is not specified in his inscription (Strudwick 2005: 365). As for Hapidjefa of Asyut (discussed above), in the early second millennium BC, he distinguished carefully between his patrimonial property ('the house of the father') and the remuneration for his position of governor ('the house of the governor'); domains of this kind usually included not only provisions but also serfs, fields, specialized workers and a suitable residence. Similar conditions prevailed 1,000 years later, when Nakhtefmut, a priest of Amun, stated that his property was truly his because it derived from goods inherited from his parents, as well as from what he had acquired through his own initiative and from rewards granted by the king (Moreno García 2013c and 2013d). Hence, high-ranking officials made a formal distinction between their family household and the income provided by the state. Temple land and special allotments of land rewarded exceptional exploits and emphasized that the holder was a member of the core elite of the kingdom. Temples remained a prized source of revenue for the elite, and the rights over the plots thus obtained were bought and sold by the elite as a way of increasing their patrimony, as several inscriptions from the early first millennium BC reveal. Henuttawy, sister and wife of Smendes II, great priest of Amun, declared that she had bought some land, including 'fields of free men'; Princess Maatkare bought, when she was just a child, some property, and also acquired 'anything of any sort that the people of the land sold to her' and which was recorded as goods of 'free people'. Similarly Iuwelot, great priest of Amun and son of King Osorkon

I (924–889 BC), acquired a domain of 153 ha located in the domain of Amun but also attached to royal Domain and consisting of 'fields of free people'. Finally, another high priest of Amun, Menkheperre, bought a field from about two dozen individuals ('the free men of the town') (Moreno García 2016b). Besides temple land, some texts mention private acquisitions of other forms of wealth (fields, people, cattle, ships), usually from people in distress; in other cases, land was leased by individuals, but it is impossible to quantify the importance and extent of these practices in the composition of private fortunes.

However, dependence on state income was also a source of tension among beneficiaries and their relatives, and that friction gave the king opportunity to manipulate and reshape the elites. In a world dominated by extended family groups, promoting a particular official and providing him with substantial income stimulated individual strategies that clashed with the collective interests (and solidarity ties) of one's kin. Such tensions were particularly evident when officials sought to create a funerary cult for themselves, endowed with land and offerings granted by the king, and to then pass it on to their own children. In such cases it was common for the donors to formally forbid other members of their family (brothers, etc.) to usurp or to interfere in the management of the cult and its rents, which were reserved for their own descendants exclusively. But if service to the king promoted individualistic strategies, there are cases in which income granted to a family group ultimately led to conflicts among the descendants and/or with the actual managers of the gifts. Of course, the administration could also transfer property from one beneficiary to another and thus arbitrarily deprive former beneficiaries of the income they had enjoyed hitherto. Rivalries between officials, or the arrival of a newly appointed dignitary to a position of power, also ended up in some cases with the random seizure of the goods enjoyed by former holders of the position. In other cases, as happened in the Medamud endowment text, when the entire domain of a temple was reorganized, former beneficiaries of plots belonging to the sanctuary were to be compensated 'plot for plot, threshing-floor for threshing-floor'.

To conclude, from the perspective of the organization and structure of power in ancient Egypt, it is crucial to note that the state and its institutions were essential sources of revenue for the ruling elite and that the latter worked hard to acquire, manage and transmit (if possible) these assets to their descendants. There is certainly evidence pointing to the private acquisition of wealth. However, judging not only from official documents but also from private letters and inscriptions, it seems that private property and the possession of substantial independent economic assets never matched those provided by the state. Furthermore, economic strategies involving the mediation of institutions (such as donating part of one's possessions to a temple) helped to preserve them and avoid the uncertainties derived from inheritances, indebtedness, abuses, etc., that menaced private patrimonies. The absence of a true landed aristocracy is perhaps one of the key characteristics of the Egyptian state, as it prevented the emergence of a 'feudal class' that owned substantial independent (and inheritable) wealth, and were capable of challenging the power of the kings. Local nobles often had very few opportunities to accumulate a substantial patrimony of their own, confined as they were to a specific town or province. We must remember too that dignitaries and officials could be removed summarily from their position, and would then lose their land-based remunerations; these would typically be dispersed over several provinces (as outlined in the best documented cases) in order to prevent the concentration and consolidation of wealth and power in a given area.

5

Hidden Forces?

Invisible Actors and Their Impact on the State

The ruling elite of pharaonic Egypt never represented more than a very tiny minority of the population for most of Egyptian history. However, its overwhelming presence in the monumental and written record may give rise to a misleading impression about its actual power and influence, as if the official channels of authority and the control of prominent institutions it embodied (temples, the royal palace, the administration, etc.) were the *only* sources of power and influence. Yet many Egyptians could hardly afford the costly prestige items usually reserved for the elite, often elaborated in robust materials (stone, metals) that have helped secure both their survival and the over-representation of their owners in the archaeological record. So, influential or affluent people, whose power and wealth had nothing to do with official positions and functions (for instance, successful traders and craftsmen, wealthy peasants, etc.) may remain underestimated in number and difficult to detect, except when they chose to depict themselves behind a respectable appearance (for instance, as holders of priesthoods, courtiers, etc.) that concealed their true sources of authority. In any case, their relative elusiveness was perfectly compatible with their social prominence as heads of parallel networks of influence and wealth that put into their hands, at least potentially, the capacity to shape the operational capacities of the state – even to direct its strategic choices. In this chapter I aim to explore three possible cases of such a scenario, as well as the barriers encountered by the individuals involved.

Elusive guilds in an urban setting?

A vast body of literature, mostly inspired by the work of Max Weber, has contrasted the characteristics of the 'Western city' to those of the 'Oriental city'. While the former was the realm of a vigorous urban economy based on trade, arts and crafts, with an active bourgeoisie, the regular use of regulations and law, and well-established guilds and institutions that enjoyed considerable autonomy in the organization of local government and the direction of local affairs, the second was not. In 'Western cities', the weight of guilds of craftsmen, financiers and merchants was crucial in the emergence of a sort of counterpower potent enough to influence and even oppose the decisions taken by kings, bishops and nobles. On the contrary, these forms of organization were absent in the 'Oriental city', as their initiatives suffocated under the pressure of arbitrary despotic authorities barely constrained by law. Moreover, contrary to the organic development of the 'Western city', 'Oriental cities' were mostly administrative and tax collecting centres where central powers displayed their authority through monumental constructions and through religious, civil and military ceremonies.

Nonetheless, this contrast has been strongly rebutted in recent times. Cuneiform archives, for instance, reveal that some characteristics attributed to the 'Western city' were also to be found in the ancient Near East, at least in some cities and during certain periods. For example, the economic activities of the merchants of Larsa and Kanesh, the distinctive urban neighbourhoods in which they lived, their involvement in operations that were partly independent, partly at the service of institutions (royal palace, temples), and the presence of foreign traders grouped in distinctive districts and who were part of trade diasporas (as in the case of the merchants from the Indus Valley living in Mesopotamia in Ur III times), prove their prominent role in urban life. Finally, Mesopotamian sources across all periods mention urban self-governing institutions enjoying some degree of autonomy (Otto 2012). However, the role played by traders, craftsmen, etc., in the organization and government of urban life and its institutions in ancient Egypt, not to mention their ability (if any) to negotiate with the state and its representatives, is still up for discussion. However, references to 'people of the city', to slaves owned by cities, to taxes paid by cities, even to local 'councils' (*qnbt*) that treated with the vizier on administrative affairs, suggest that some form of urban collective government and political organization was present there too.

An Egyptian inscription from the middle of the second millennium BC, when Egypt followed an expansionist policy towards Nubia and the Levant, mentions four main social categories: warriors; low-ranking priests (*wab*); 'producers' (*hem-nesut*, literally 'servant of the king') and craftsmen (*hemu*). While information about warriors and priests is plentiful in the sources of this period, little is known about the organization of craftsmen, especially those working in urban settings. Certainly, the famous community of artists settled at Deir el-Medina has provided an exceptional wealth of data about their lives and everyday occupations, but the very specialized nature of the site, and of the working conditions of its inhabitants, makes it problematic to consider them 'typical' craftsmen. Deir el-Medina was founded in the desert by the crown, and its personnel were employed almost exclusively in the construction and decoration of the royal tombs (there is also evidence that they ran, in parallel, lucrative activities for private clients). The survival of the artists and their families depended on rations/wages delivered by the state, which monitored and organized their activities. It could well be that in an urban environment, where their activities would not have been so squarely focussed on the state's requirements, craftsmen may have found many opportunities to develop their skills, to accumulate wealth and to create autonomous corporate bodies. As early as the third millennium BC, officials boasted about having their tombs decorated on their own account, when they paid craftsmen for their services.

Craftsmen were frequently organized in workshops, and very often specialized in the production of quality objects for the elite. Whereas the output of some of these workshops was put under the direct supervision of crown officials, many others were located in the provinces and are recognizable by their distinctive styles and features. Yet evidence about professional guilds is ambiguous. On the one hand, particular skills and knowledge specific to some crafts were considered 'secret'; it could be that joining a professional guild was dependent on candidates' passing a final oral examination. On the other hand, craftsmen were organized in associations that provided mutual help and support for their members, for instance, for the families of dead members. The fact that in a list of personnel from the city of Ilahun, widowed and orphaned female family members were not only described in terms of their relationships to the head of the household but also as 'wards of the necropolis workers', suggests that an early form of trade associations existed and enjoyed some official recognition. Seshenu, a Middle Kingdom senior sculptor and overseer of the temple, dedicated an altar at the funerary temple of King Snofru at Dahshur. Nevertheless, the inscription recorded the piety not only of Seshenu, but also that of about fifteen other men of lesser status, mainly minor priests and a sculptor. Judging from their maternal filiation, they were not members of Seshenu's family. Therefore, the monument seems to have been erected by a small community of priests and artisans reporting to Seshenu, whose superior status was thus enhanced. Evidence from around 1750 BC shows that craftsmen were organized in 'sections/trades/guilds' (*waret*), each one headed by an 'overseer of the section', but we do not know how the overseers, artists and artisans worked together. We have references in private inscriptions and papyri from this period to a 'section overseer' of furniture carving, of gold workers, of builders, of jewellers, of laundrymen, of coppersmiths, of sculptors, of draughtsmen, of leather workers and of glaze workers (Miniaci et al. 2018). Yet we also do not know whether such 'sections' were autonomous organizations of craftsmen, able to influence the political and economic life of cities and towns through their collective demands and aspirations (Moreno García 2013a). Perhaps this was the case, judging from an inventory of the annual levy upon officials and localities in the area of Heracleopolis for deliveries of oxen to a temple in this city, as it mentions collectives of specialized workers (coppersmiths, gardeners, warriors, stonemasons, potters, builders, etc.) that also contributed oxen (Ritner 2009: 180–86). Note that craftsmen *did* get access to institutional land, for instance as agents in charge of the cultivation of land granted by the king to other people, as in the case of the craftsman Khayiri, who was responsible for the lady Nubnefer's land, cited in the famous lawsuit of a certain Mose. In other cases, craftsmen, such as those from Deir el-Medina, also owned small pieces of land and donkeys, rented the services of female slaves, worked on commissions for private clients and were involved in a 'market' (*mryt*) in the Valley of the Kings. With regard to their political role, an inscription from Sayala in Nubia (end of the third millennium BC) states that Irunetjeru, an overseer of artisans, was the father of the governor of Hieracompolis, while their mobility is mentioned in a Ramesside text that lists several specialist craftsmen administratively dependent on the domain of a king near Memphis, but who were working or residing in other areas of Lower Egypt.

How were traders organized in urban areas? Turin Papyrus 1887 (dating from around 1150 BC), for instance, describes the procedure followed to select a priest for the temple of Khnum at Elephantine. Several candidates proposed by the body of priests to the vizier (as representative of the king) were presented to the god, who then elected one of them by oracular decision. But one of the priests expressed his contempt for a candidate as he was not of priestly lineage: 'if only we had three other priests, so that we might induce the god to throw out this son of this merchant!' Such contempt towards traders may explain why they were (apparently) excluded from the prestigious offices reserved for traditional elites, such as priests, 'mayors' and military leaders, and why traces of them in the monumental record are so scanty. A list of houses located in and around the temple of Ramesses III at Medinet Habu reveals that their inhabitants were officials, administrative personnel, priests, craftsmen and people related to the production and supply of foodstuffs (peasants, gardeners, bee-keepers, fishermen); there is no mention of merchants. They seem to be have been prohibited from settling in temple areas and from receiving temple income and temple land, in sharp contrast with the scribes, noblemen and soldiers often recruited as priests. In other instances, priests and mayors were eligible for local courts of justice, but traders (including wealthy ones) again seem not to have been deemed suitable for this office. However, things may have been quite different in the urban residential zones located outside temple areas. Timber accounts from around 1280 BC enumerate the owners of private houses in certain districts of Memphis. There, army officers and naval and dockyard personnel shared these zones with a variety of scribes, priests and merchants – even gardeners. About six centuries later, an inscription reveals that two merchants built their tombs in a section of a necropolis used by priests and artisans. And when precious metals stolen from temples and royal tombs in the eleventh century BC were to be 'laundered', priests, officials and military personnel had no qualms about asking merchants for their help (Moreno García 2016a).

Evidence about merchants' guilds is even scarcer, but some evidence may indicate that merchants were organized collectively and appointed a representative to deal with authorities and institutions. Boulaq Papyrus XI contains accounts of the sale of small quantities of goods, principally beef and wine. The majority of the transactions appear to be debits entered against the names of various traders who, in some cases, paid for their purchases in gold. These transactions seem to involve retailers making purchases from a wholesaler. Another document mentioning the same traders (CGC Papyrus 58081) shows that they co-operated among themselves and that when a quantity of goods and/or precious metals was due to one of them, another person could receive it in his name. A decree issued by King Seti I (1294–1279 BC) mentions – among the personnel employed by the temple and protected by the sovereign – the barge-crews conveying tribute, foreign merchants, gold-processors and dockyard workers. Some centuries later, a donation made by Prince Osorkon to the domain of the god Amun was put under the authority of 'the elders of the portal who are before the merchants', that is, temple personnel who dealt with traders at the entrances to the temple's enclosures (Ritner 2009: 356–57); similarly King Taharqa donated to the god Amun '23 *hin* of oil in the course of the month at the harbour of Memphis [from] the superiors of the merchants' (Ritner 2009: 515). These 'superiors of the merchants', documented since the Late Bronze Age, were not necessarily officials but could well have been merchants who represented their colleagues when dealing with an institution or an official and when paying taxes. In fact, such taxes were common in the ports along the Nile; supervised by officials (Ritner 2009: 356, 358), their control might have been particularly rigorous in the harbours located on Egypt's borders that would have been frequented by traders operating abroad. Sarenput I, governor of the caravan and harbour city of Elephantine around 1950 BC, included among his duties control over river trade, harbours, markets and foreign commodities arriving into Egypt, while the Great Edict of Horemheb refers to taxes collected from houses and ships. Later on, from about 600 BC, the entire area between Memphis and Elephantine was entrusted to a harbour master based at Heracleopolis, and who undertook a range of financial duties as revenue accountant for Middle and Upper Egypt. Finally, the epigraphy of this period testifies to an unprecedented development of customs administration, corresponding closely with the growth in trade activities in the Mediterranean area and the Near East. The top administrators who managed the customs administration at this time held the title of 'overseer of the gate of foreign countries', reminiscent of similar titles already noted in the third millennium BC. Negotiations and dealings between traders (represented by a 'superior') and port and custom authorities may have prompted the merchants to organize themselves collectively.

Nonetheless, all this evidence is inconclusive. In other regions of the ancient Near East where information about the organization of traders is more abundant (such as Middle Bronze Age Kanesh and Late Bronze Age Ugarit), there are references to associations of merchants operating together in joint ventures, but firm proof of guilds is absent. It appears that, as in Egypt, traders were more organized in harbour areas, close to markets in the main cities, settled according to their geographical origins (as in the case of the Indus Valley merchants present in Mesopotamia in the late third millennium BC, noted above), and operating in particular urban areas and 'offices' in which different weight systems were used (for example, Tell Bazi, in Syria). In Egypt, a passage from a papyrus referring to the expedition of a ship involved in trade activities, and dispatched from Thebes to the *mryt* (market/harbour) of Memphis, mentions the 'account of trading' made 'in the language of Kharu [= Syria, Levant]'. Temples built to honour the gods Baal and Astarte existed at Memphis' port (Peru-Nefer), and St Petersburg Papyrus 1116 even mentions food delivered to Baal of Peru-Nefer as well as to the messengers of several Asian cities settled there, so it seems that the harbour/market at Memphis was indeed a meeting point for traders arrived from within Egypt and from abroad. The same is true for Pi-Ramesses, in the Eastern Delta, as its markets were frequented by foreign merchants: 'Pleasant is the place of distribution/market-place with its money/silver there, mainly the vine tendrils (?) and business/commerce (*t-m-k-r-i-t*). The chiefs of every foreign country come in order to descend with their products.' Egyptian merchants did operate in foreign territories, as demonstrated by the twenty Egyptian traders in Cyprus mentioned in the Amarna letters, or the Egyptian-owned ships moored at Byblos that were involved in wood-trading activities with Ullaza, in Lebanon. It is thus clear that special areas in the harbours of important cities (such as Memphis and Tell el-Daba) were settled with foreign merchants and 'messengers' involved in transactions and diplomatic and trading activities with Egyptian officials (Moreno García forthcoming). In some cases, both foreign and Egyptian messengers accumulated substantial wealth and status. Prince Simontu, one of the sons of Ramesses II, married the daughter of a Syrian ship-owner, while the *Story of Wenamun* refers to fleets of apparently wealthy private merchants who owned dozens of ships that operated between Egypt and the Levant, such as Werekter and the fifty ships in the harbour of Sidon that did business with his 'house'.

Hence, the scope and power of collective organizations of traders, not to mention their political influence, are difficult to gauge, but these merchants certainly enjoyed a respectable status, dealt with Egyptian authorities, acted collectively on some occasions and might have been a powerful faction in trade-oriented areas. For instance, those men and women from Elephantine who traded in Nubian gold at the beginning of the twenty-seventh century BC, represented a significant sector of the local population. As for caravan leaders from this city, they were in close contact with the crown in the late third millennium BC and they were the dominant social group then.

A final word concerns other 'professional' associations, such as those for priests. Setting aside their organization in *phyles* (or service groups) or the diverse categories of priests tasked with performing ritual services in temples, there is little information about other kinds of 'professional' groupings, particularly nation-wide. A stela from around 1750 BC records the names of a temple administrator and of an overseer respectively, followed by those of fifty people whose affiliations with the monument's owners are never indicated. These people included five temple overseers, seven administrators, an overseer of a palace chamber, a priest, two 'Asiatic' people, fifteen 'mistresses of the house' and other people, both male and female, whose names and titles are lost. Although the names seem to be those of people of a certain status, mostly related to the priestly sphere, it is difficult to pin down their relationship precisely. More information is available about junior ritualists organized in guilds, such as first-millennium BC *choachytes*, who made libations to, performed rituals for, mummies. Well documented thanks to their extensive rules, their guilds provided mutual benefits such as rituals and burials for their members, assistance at court and the opportunity to take part in temple processions. Members paid regular dues, attended monthly meetings in which wine or beer was consumed, offerings given to the gods and the kings, and fines levied for transgressions (Moreno García 2013a). Alongside their funerary services, *choachytes* also took part in joint ventures, particularly in collective leasing and cultivating temple land rented out by members of the temple's hierarchy. Otherwise, their links with the temples are unclear. Even when documents do record the particular business of individual *choachytes*, they focus on purely private interests: the acquisition of slaves, fields and shares of houses; loans; the purchase and sale of cattle; and the management of diverse income streams. Later sources reveal that guilds of funerary specialists delimited and preserved their remit zealously, as indicated when *choachytes* undertook not to encroach upon embalmers' sphere of activity ('not to put remedies [embalming materials] on the dead in our [= the choachyte's] workshop'; 'let no man at all bring an embalmer into the guild of Amenope but only a choachyte.')

In summary, it is evident that guilds and collective organizations of specialized trades existed in Egypt. However, their influence in the organization and government of cities seems very limited and there is no trace of any similar organization at the regional or 'national' level that was able to impose its agenda on the ruling elite, even less to become an influential lobbyist or active political player. In fact, the guilds' initiatives seem limited to the sphere of their specific professional competences. However, the fact that some traders operated quite autonomously abroad on a significant scale, leaves open the question of their potential influence on the foreign diplomacy pursued by Egypt. Not by chance, the volume and importance of their activities was significant enough for rulers to include in their diplomatic agreements regulations about the safe conduct of caravans and merchants abroad.

Wealthy peasants: Leaders of the rural world?

Far from being an undifferentiated mass of labourers existing at the very edge of subsistence, prevailing conditions among Egyptian peasants were much more nuanced. Affluent peasants, for instance, emerge as important actors in rural society, a sub-elite indispensable to kings and institutions as mediators, and eager to ascend the social ladder and to gain access to prestigious institutions (such as temples) – and to their coveted resources. As they rarely produced documents, most of the evidence about them originates from institutional administrative records. The Wilbour Papyrus, for instance, mentions considerable tracts of temple and crown land put under the administrative control of an official but in reality worked on by a 'cultivator'. Each cultivator was in charge of agricultural units of up to 30–50 ha, areas too large to be farmed effectively by a single peasant, which suggests that these cultivators would have made use of a variety of resources (manpower, animals, transport and storing facilities, etc.) to fulfil their duties. Some documents even reveal that in some areas individual cultivators delivered between 1,000 and 1,500 sacks of grain in a single delivery to their employer institutions. It would appear, then, that some cultivators operated as true agricultural 'entrepreneurs', that their interests would eventually grow to encompass a district and that the sizeable resources they managed exceeded those of simple peasants. As for their role as local sub-elites, a Ramesside lawsuit over the rights over a piece of land claimed by the heirs of the former beneficiary of the field includes statements made by several witnesses described as 'people of importance' (literally, 'great men') including 'ladies' and a 'cultivator', the latter a role that also featured in other juridical documents, such as the Adoption Papyrus. 'Ladies' and 'cultivators' are mentioned side by side in the Wilbour Papyrus as holders of plots (rewards?) of temple land. In other cases, 'free' tenants who cultivated temple land paid their taxes, in gold, direct to the royal treasury. Note too the cases in which a cultivator claimed to be the son of an important dignitary and brother of priests, or when a dignitary claimed, among his administrative duties, that he was 'cultivator of the fields of the king' (Moreno García 2010b and 2016b). It was also not unusual for some cultivators to buy themselves prestigious items (such as ritual objects and funerary figurines) owned usually only by the elite, or for them to want to join the staff of temples as a means to formalize their social status, a strategy combated vigorously at times by the authorities, as in the case of a cultivator at Elephantine who had become a priest illegally, but who was forced to be 'now (again) a cultivator among the people of poor condition' (Moreno García 2016b: 229).

Unfortunately, little is known about the origins of the landed assets of these affluent peasants. They were probably threefold: property inherited from the family; and fields bought from other people. One of the oldest continuous inscriptions preserved, that of Metjen (who lived around

2600 BC), records the acquisition of a field of 55 ha from numerous tenants. Hard times – or particularly difficult conditions in the cycles of peasant life (divisions of property, indebtedness, bad harvests, etc.) – favoured the acquisition of land. Several inscriptions from the late third millennium BC record private land purchases and people forced to sell their fields, even being reduced to serfdom because of the debts they had accumulated. The acquisition by a certain Ikeni of the fields surrounding a well also took place in a context of hard times for the owners. Owning temple land was another key way of accumulating wealth, as was joining patronage networks and enjoying the protection they afforded. The Wilbour Papyrus, for instance, reveals that almost 10 per cent of the tenants of temple land were 'cultivators', alongside military personnel, priests, 'ladies', dignitaries and other members of the local sub-elites. The same impression is given by early first millennium inscriptions, such as the Apanage stela, a document listing private holders of substantial temple land who sold their rights to their fields to a king's son. While it might be difficult to say that a true property market existed in ancient Egypt, it seems nevertheless that private purchases of land enabled some sectors of the peasantry to accumulate substantial landed assets.

From this perspective, the interests, strategies and wealth of some 'cultivators' made them prominent members of their communities and allowed them to lead an autonomous existence. The term *nemeh* (literally, 'orphan') came to designate, from the second half of the second millennium BC onwards, independent affluent peasants, able to cultivate temple land or even to own boats, according to the Great Edict of Horemheb. The fact that some cultivators were considered 'great men', and that literary texts from the first millennium BC describe their local power and influence, suggest that the condition of some wealthy peasants was similar to that of local potentates (also designated as 'great (ones)'), of true local authorities, particularly in troubled times, as was the case around 1190 BC: 'the land of Egypt was in the hands of chiefs (*wr*) and of rulers of towns' (Grandet 2004: 335). It also seems quite plausible that this was the social group from which village governors were chosen.

The only information available on their political and decision-taking influence pertains to those who also held other functions, such as scribes and priests. Heqanakhte, for instance, was a wealthy landowner who managed an extensive portfolio of landed assets and cattle, enjoyed considerable local influence and was well connected to a powerful patron and with the local gentry. The late second millennium BC scribe Thutmose is another example in which holding land, whether institutional or private, was a familial affair involving Thutmose and his son. He owned two categories of land, one which explicitly belonged to him and his son ('our own land'), the administrative status thereof being difficult to identify (were these privately held fields on temple land, or simply private property?), and the other which quite probably consisted of estates pertaining to temples or secular institutions. Holding those two types of field was a sign of social prestige that confirmed Thutmose's high rank but, as with Heqanakhte, the administrative or juridical nature of these fields was a secondary concern: his main goal was managing the land so as to obtain the best agricultural yield. Both Heqanakhte and Thutmose behaved like managerial landlords, closely watching over all the details of agricultural operations, and they were certainly not absentee landlords, who delegated the management of their fields to subordinates preoccupied only with the revenue generated. Their interests extended over a district and, in the case of Thutmose, his letters refer to grain stored in magazines in several villages, thus suggesting that other cultivators living nearby worked the estate alongside household members. In fact, the men labouring in the fields were perceived as having the same level of importance as his son and his family, as if they were part of his household. Links with temples also emerge in one of his letters, in which Thutmose mentions chariot-pulling donkeys that, apparently, belonged to a temple (Antoine 2015). Other examples of affluent tenants, involved in diversified business, are the *choachytes* Djekhy (and his son) and Tsenhor (Moreno García 2016b: 242). All of these tenants accumulated priestly and/or administrative functions, alongside their agricultural affairs, and reveal a sector of society in which the lines between peasantry and officialdom had become blurred. Did they have access to modest priestly and administrative functions *because of* their agricultural wealth and local social prominence, or were these functions that provided them with landed assets? Such ambiguity is apparent in the case of a local potentate ('a great man') mentioned in a late literary text. He was also a priest in the local temple, a profitable source of income, as he obtained part of the agricultural income of the sanctuary because of his sacerdotal role. In addition, he worked some temple land as a cultivator in exchange for a share of the harvest; the considerable wealth thus amassed allowed him to pay wages to the personnel of the temple (considered as his clients) and he even married his sons and daughters to priests and potentates of another town (Moreno García 2016b: 237–38).

In their role of 'great men', wealthy peasants appear sometimes as witnesses in local courts. These institutions were not real courts of justice as we might recognize them but rather local councils formed by senior and/or respected members of their community in order to settle conflicts and exert authority in local affairs. In the case of the council in the Deir el-Medina area, the will of Lady Naunakhte shows that it had been composed by two local scribes, two officials and several members of the working community, from foremen and craftsmen to manual workers. As sources of local power and authority, such councils acted as intermediaries for the administration. The *Duties of the Vizier* records that it was the vizier who 'brings the district councillors; he who sends them; they report to him the business of their districts', while a scene found in the tomb of vizier Rekhmire depicts payments made to the bureau of the Vizier of Thebes by (local) governors, estate managers, district councillors and heralds, the scribes of district councillors and the scribes of their fields. As Eyre has pointed out, local councils must be visualized at all periods as the normal forum for both mediation and local dispute settlement, as well as the channel of communication between the local communities and the central authority of the state personified by the vizier (Eyre 2013: 327). Judging from the lawsuit of Mose, in which a cultivator, Horiherneferher, was one of the notables ('great people') of his village, and from the oracular decisions related to another cultivator, Patjauemdiamun, taken at several villages and involving many witnesses as well as his companions and the members of his personnel (British Museum Papyrus 10335), it seems quite plausible that wealthy and influential cultivators took part in these local councils, especially when their influence and interests extended over several villages. However, their ability to bring political influence to bear at a 'national' level seems negligible.

Pastoral populations, fishermen and foreigners

Contrary to the ideological claims of pharaonic inscriptions, foreigners and non-sedentary populations frequented the Nile Valley, settling there and leaving their mark on Egyptian society. Borders were not unbridgeable barriers but, rather, areas of contact. Archaeological finds reveal, in fact, a burgeoning world of interaction, collaboration and occasional conflict, to the point that foreigners and nomadic peoples were crucial to developing trade activities abroad, to exploiting regional resources and to influencing the political choices of Egyptian rulers, such as interventions in the Western Desert (Dakhla, later Siwa), Nubia and the Levant. Such collaboration is particularly visible at mining sites, harbours and trade centres, and in areas of pasture.

Herders, for instance, crossed the Delta and Middle Egypt and their presence in these areas has been interpreted as aggression by hostile groups eager to introduce themselves into rich pasture areas replete with abundant water resources. 'Libyans', for instance (in fact, populations living west of the Nile Valley), used grazing areas and were a constant presence there. Their presence had become established as of the late third millennium BC. It was then that local nobles – and later, pharaohs – were particularly interested in cattle and livestock raising for fiscal reasons, and many inscriptions refer to herd inventories and to the provision of cattle and herders to provincial officials in order to develop local resources. This interest is linked to changes in pastoral organization and itinerant herding, when hair-coated sheep with corkscrew horns were replaced by wool-fleeced breeds with down-curving horns, introduced from Asia, a change probably related to the increasing importance of wool production, and with new developments in textile manufacture. At the same time, a new term appeared, *mnmnt* ('cattle on the move'), in contrast to *iawt*, which refers to 'penned' animals, with the first mentions attested in Beni Hasan (in the tombs of Imeny and Khnumhotep II) and Deir el-Gebrawy (the tomb of Henqu), both in Middle Egypt. Also in this period and in this very area, at Bersheh, a new term emerged, *wḥyt*, usually translated as '(clan) village', even 'tribe', depending on the context. Finally, the tombs of Middle Egypt contain unusual scenes depicting Libyans driving and presenting cattle, while textile-related activities became quite popular in the local iconography, particularly spinning, weaving (using looms) and dyeing. Middle Egypt thus appears to be a crossroads of peoples and a privileged area for pastoral activities, which had a significant impact on the organization of its settlements (Moreno García 2017).

The importance of pastoral activities in Middle Egypt appears to be connected to changes in textile production and with increasing contacts between Egypt and the Levant, in which Middle Egypt's potentates played a crucial role as mediators. For example, early second millennium BC documents from the town of Ilahun mention women occupied in weaving activities involving wool, as well as officers who registered wool. Asiatic women were represented in figurines and in wall paintings in the tombs found at Beni Hasan and Meir, while references to the 'cattle of Retenu' (= Levant) are documented in some tombs at Meir and Bersheh. The discovery of monuments commissioned by officials from Middle Egypt in the Levant (including a scarab with the inscription 'administrator accountant of cattle' at Megiddo) points to their direct role in the external affairs of Egypt during this period. In fact, some leaders from Beni Hasan participated in expeditions to Punt and Lebanon. Similarly some tombs from this locality include in their wall decoration scenes of mythical animals of oriental inspiration, such as griffins, while wall paintings discovered at the palace of Tell el-Burak, in

Lebanon, seem inspired by similar scenes from Beni Hasan. In Bersheh, local leaders referred to myrrh in their inscriptions and displayed titles related to the control and supply of it and other precious unguents. The collaboration of Asiatics was essential in this trade and, in fact, Asiatics appear as an increasingly important element in Egyptian society as of the end of the third millennium, especially in Middle Egypt where they had a strong presence as traders, sailors, soldiers and craftsmen. They were depicted in the tombs of the local governors wearing colourful woollen clothes decorated with complex patterns, in sharp contrast to the white linen garments typical of Egyptians. The importance of foreign textiles (particularly those from the Aegean) was such that their patterns and motifs inspired the decoration of some monumental tombs in Middle Egypt, at Qaw, Meir and Asyut (Moreno García 2017).

As we can see, cattle, textiles and aromatic plants appear to be key marks of contact with Asia, probably alongside slaves and metals, as recorded in the inscriptions of Pharaoh Amenemhat II. The intensity of these contacts explains the emergence of Tell el-Daba as the main harbour in the Eastern Delta. Another fascinating aspect is that Eastern peoples preserved in some cases the memory of their origins and displayed it proudly on their otherwise Egyptian monuments, as they defined themselves as 'Asiatic' (*Aamu*).

Having in mind these facts, it is tempting to link the importance of specialized communities of foreigners in the Nile Valley with internal Egyptian political developments. The presence of Asiatics well connected with the Levant as a result of trade might explain why the Eastern Delta, Heracleopolis and Middle Egypt sometimes broke away from the kingdom and became the centre of independent political entities that co-existed for a while with other monarchies in Egypt (such as Thebes), as occurred during the late Early Bronze Age and in the late Middle Bronze Age or why, in other cases, Asiatics supported rivals to the ruling pharaohs, as revealed by some inscriptions from Beni Hasan and Hatnub and dating to around 2000 BC. At times, such polities were ruled by kings with Asiatic names. The famous Hyksos kings were, in fact, preceded in the Eastern Delta by monarchs with unequivocal Semitic names such as Yakbim, Ya'ammu or Qareh. Another king was Nehesi, whose name ('The Nubian'), and the fact of his being the son of a queen also bearing a Nubian name (Tati), point to contacts between the Eastern Delta and Nubia that would also be recorded by later sources. Trade was essential for these polities; the inscription of Kamose records the 'hundreds' of ships moored at the harbour of Tell el-Daba around 1550 BC. Centuries later, the Western Delta became once again the centre of trade networks crossing the Western Desert and linking Nubia to the Mediterranean, and in which Libyan populations played an active role. The importance of these networks (involving gold, ivory and, later, silphium) explains the chain of 'fortresses'/trade centres built by Ramesses II both in this area and as far away as Zawiyet Umm el-Rakham (300 km west of Alexandria). It might be possible that the Libyan populations' efforts to escape and bypass the surveillance of Egyptian authorities led to the growth of the oasis of Siwa as a major crossroads and trade hub, and to the development of a desert route to Cyrenaica. But Libyan pastoralists also struggled to use the pasture areas in the Delta during a period (Late Bronze Age) when this region became the centre of political and economic power of Egypt. Conflicts erupted and ended by settling Libyans as warriors and herders in the Delta and the Fayum. In any case, it is striking that when authorities from the Delta were emancipated from the control of pharaohs, they claimed a foreign ancestry rather than a purely pharaonic one: Hyksos kings defined themselves as 'rulers of foreign countries' while early first millennium BC kinglets in the Delta claimed to descend from (great) Libyan chiefs.

Nubians were another important element in Egyptian society, as noted above. Their presence in Egypt has been traditionally related to military activities, predominantly as mercenaries in Egyptian armies. However, the truth was more complex. Nubians crossed the southern border of Egypt and settled in the land of the pharaohs, in some cases as peddlers and herders, in others (for instance, at Edfu) as members of Egyptian mining expeditions sent to the Eastern Desert. There is also evidence that they traded across the routes of the Western Desert as well as at Tell el-Daba, judging by the pottery found there. In all these cases, their role can hardly be regarded as subsidiary to Egyptian authorities. More probably they were their partners and collaborators, especially when the central authority in Egypt collapsed and when agreements between regional Egyptian lords and Nubian polities culminated in alliances that enabled the circulation of goods from Nubia to the Mediterranean. In this light, the frequent presence of Nubian military contingents in the armies of Egyptian provincial nobles probably reflects these alliances, in which Nubians supported local lords and thus influenced the internal politics of the country.

That Asiatics and Nubians collaborated with Egyptian authorities also explains why some of them were raised to prominent positions in the Egyptian monarchy, particularly during the Late Bronze Age, when the expansion of Egypt in Nubia and the Levant was possible only through the support of (at least some of) the elites in these regions. It may also be possible that Egypt's foreign policy was guided partly by the interests of certain sectors of its elites, in close collaboration with certain echelons of privileged Levantine and Nubian societies. The inscription of vizier Khnumhotep (who lived around 1870–1830 BC) mentions Egyptians being involved in commercial activities and political affairs in the northern Levant, while traces of an Egyptian commercial diaspora may be discerned in the Levant during the Late Bronze Age. A son of Ramesses II married the daughter of a Syrian ship-owner, and people of Levantine background occupied important political positions in the Egyptian monarchy, such as chancellor Bay, who boasted about putting a king on the throne of Egypt and who was a major political influence at court during the reign of Pharaoh Siptah. Ben-Ia was an overseer of works as well as 'child of the *kap*' (= the inner palace) during the reigns of Hatshepsut and Thutmose III respectively. Born into a foreign family (his name was Semitic, and those of his parents, Irtenena and Tirkak, were not Egyptian), he was nevertheless buried in a tomb decorated in a typically Egyptian style. Another case is that of Maiherpri, a Nubian prince educated with the Egyptian royal princes, and buried in the Valley of the Kings. Conversely, Egyptians were also influential figures at foreign courts; Amenmose, known thanks to his Hittite seal, held a senior position at the Syrian court of Carchemish as assistant of Prince Tili-sarruma, to such an extent that he participated in the diplomatic contacts between the kingdoms integrated into the Hittite empire.

As we can see, then, foreigners played an important role in Egyptian society, and while their impact is understandably more visible in the person of high-ranking dignitaries and specialists (skilled craftsmen, interpreters, warriors, etc), they also marked pharaonic culture in such diverse areas as literature, fashion, etc. Their economic and cultural influence made them potential vectors for the circulation of new ideas and techniques, and even enabled them to forge links between Egypt and foreign regions that were not necessarily under Egyptian control. This was the case of populations with nomadic lifestyles, as their activities and contacts abroad (as herders, traders, warriors, etc.) paved the way for the expansion of states eager to capture the lucrative trade networks that these people had previously created. In other instances, nomadic lifestyles probably represented an alternative to sedentary ones, to the point that when the central authority and its ability to levy taxes weakened, rural populations might be tempted to return to more mobile and economically diversified modus vivendi (less easy to control and tax). Fishermen are just one example. The fact that they paid their taxes in silver to the administration meant that they converted their catches into metals through markets both in Egypt and outside its borders. Archaeological finds have revealed that fish from the Nile was exported to Asia throughout the Bronze Age, and that this activity escaped any royal monitoring. In other cases, itinerant pastoralism was regarded with suspicion and Egyptian officials did not hesitate to settle herders and nomadic populations in towns (as Henqu of Deir el-Gebrawy claimed in around 2200 BC). Indeed they tried to monitor (and tax?) the movement of herders, fishermen and wildfowl hunters, as well as Egyptian, Nubian and Libyan nomadic populations, as the titles of many officials show. Finally, fishermen and maritime populations also played an important role as vectors of exchanges independent of any royal intervention. Thus, while the circulation of goods, crops and animals between East Africa and the Indian subcontinent across the northern Indian Ocean was made possible by seafaring peoples, the circulation of aromatic plants and obsidian between the southern Red Sea and Egypt as of the Neolithic period may partly follow the same principle. The warrior tombs found in the Western Delta during the early Middle Bronze Age point to Levantine populations who were crucial for the diffusion of textile and metal-related technologies between the Eastern Mediterranean and Egypt, a period in which Nubian traders from the Pan-Grave culture are also well attested in Egypt. From the *sekhetiu* of the Middle Bronze Age to the *boukoloi* of the Greco-Roman period, these people – particularly those based in the marshy conditions of the Eastern Delta – maintained their autonomy for centuries.

6

Creating Authority

The Egyptian ideal of good rule was based on respect for hierarchy, appropriate moral behaviour from both officials and subjects and achievement of justice, under the authority of the pharaoh (Assmann 1990). According to this paradigm, the governmental apparatus and the administrative organization of the country followed a very precise division of functions and tasks. Texts such as *The Installation of the Vizier*, *The Duties of the Vizier* or some sections of the so-called *onomastica* (lists of words organized by category: living beings, localities, types of land, categories of people and officials, etc.) refer to an efficient bureaucratic machine in which kings' orders were accomplished promptly, instructions and information circulated fluidly between different categories of officials and authorities, subordinates reported to their superiors (and were punished when they failed in their duties) and procedures aimed to satisfy petitioners and guarantee justice. The monuments built by dignitaries, officials and members of the court featured lists of titles that convey an image of perfectly ordered functions and administrative departments. In reality, however, more prosaic texts are candid about the challenges of kingship and the everyday exercise of power: loyalty was linked to rewards, or to reasonable expectations of obtaining them from the king; the palace was a hotbed of intrigue, so much so that kings had to maintain a careful balance between different sectors of the elite (or between palace factions) in order to get the support they needed both for their own authority and for intended successors on the throne; rebellions erupted from time to time; powerful potentates were occasionally tempted to follow their own interests and political agendas (if necessary, in overt conflict with those of kings); and corruption and abuses were far from unknown (Eyre 2013: 55–77; Moreno García 2013a).

It goes without saying that similar conflicts between the ideals of good government and the crude exercise of power were common currency in many ancient states. But, at the same time, they point to fundamental issues about the extent and limits of the monarchy's executive power and the actual means by which it implemented and exercised its authority. In both instances, control over adequate resources (economic, symbolic, coercive) and over the distributive networks linking the king and his intended beneficiaries was crucial. This is why the mechanisms of raising taxes appear somewhat fluctuant and discretionary, depending on variables such as corruption, the actual capacity of tax collectors to levy taxes, the difference between assessment and actual revenue, etc. In the same vein, respect for the chain of command was also essential if orders were to be executed and abuses limited efficiently. However, the conflicting links between taxation, administrative duties and limits of executive power emerge when officials exceeded their authority (for instance, when they appropriated property and functions beyond their competences or without regard for moral standards), when they exacted unjust taxes, or when they fulfilled their orders at any cost – and by any means. Those tensions also became manifest when officials took arbitrary decisions in order to boost their own power and wealth, and to carve out autonomous spheres of control for themselves and their followers. Those texts that describe the 'ideal' – such as those noted above, as well as moral and literary tales (such as *The Eloquent Peasant*) – evoke in fact situations in which people whose rights and claims had been ignored struggled to be treated fairly by the authorities. Given the didactic intention of these compositions, it follows that justice prevailed in the end and that the government and its administration worked satisfactorily. But the fact that many administrative documents and letters refer to abuses perpetrated with total impunity points to a different reality, one in which official channels proved ineffective or were simply out of reach for ordinary people. In this reality, having a 'plan B' was the only way to get justice and protection and to achieve one's goals. So access to influential patrons, seeking protection from local leaders and even buying support if necessary all constituted informal avenues for the exercise of authority. To complicate matters, it was very common for dignitaries and agents of the crown to play both roles simultaneously, thus blurring any borders between the 'private' and 'public' sphere of their actions.

The sources of executive power

Decision-making – and the effective implementation of the resulting measures taken –can be analysed through three different lenses: how decisions were taken; the limits that determined the legitimacy of such decisions; and the manner in which they were implemented – and their effectiveness guaranteed – in the long term. The most important governmental decisions took the form of royal decrees and orders issued to solve a particular problem, to settle a matter or to define how the administration should act properly in a given situation. While pharaonic inscriptions usually present such decisions as expressions of the king's will, it seems that they were in fact the fruit of deliberation between the king and a small number of high-ranking dignitaries and influential courtiers. Hence, the Chamber of Dignitaries emerges in the sources of the very late third millennium BC as a place in which eloquence, discussion and proper presentation of facts and measures enabled officials not only to take decisions, but also to distinguish themselves in a very competitive environment (Coulon 1999). Some examples of this procedure appear, for instance, in discussions about the most appropriate options in a given political situation (as in the case of King Kamose, and the timing of military hostilities with the Hyksos), in tactical discussions preceding a battle (as when Ramesses II met his general staff just prior to the armed encounter at Qadesh), in restoration of monuments, etc. One of the best examples appears in the Berlin Leather Manuscript, when King Senusret I (1956–1911 BC) held a summit in the great hall with his courtiers and privy council officials, during which he outlined his plans to build a temple at Heliopolis. One of the officials present lauded the king's plan and in turn was entrusted with the building project because 'it is your counsel that carries out all the works that My Majesty desires to bring about'. In other cases, royal decrees and official orders and instructions sought to establish regulations and, quite often (and significantly), to eliminate abuses and restore order.

Once a decision was taken, it was communicated to the specific official or body of dignitaries charged with its execution. Usually a simple letter was enough, and many references describe the flow of messengers between the king, the vizier and the officials entrusted with a particular mission. In other instances no mediators intervened, and high-ranking officials were sent specifically to certain places to carry out a particular mission. That is why Ikherneferet reproduced on his stela the letter in which Pharaoh Senusret III ordered him to go to Abydos and 'build a monument for my father Osiris'. The reasons for his being so trusted were, according to the king, that 'you shall do things to

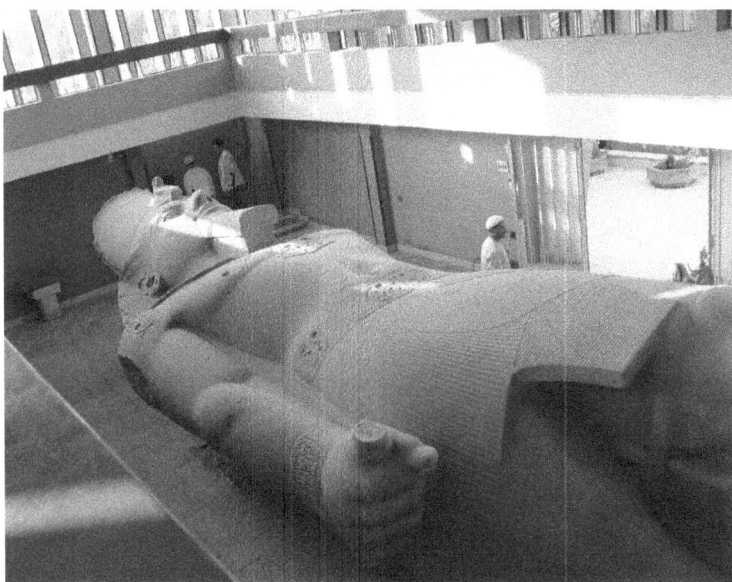

Figure 6.1 Colossal royal statue at Memphis, symbol of the pharaohs' power.

please the heart of My Majesty' and because 'you have become a child of My Majesty, the sole child of the palace. Indeed, My Majesty made you my friend when you were (still) a youngster of 26 years. My Majesty did this (because) I saw that you were excellent of plans and sharp of tongue' (Lichtheim 1988: 98–100). Setting aside the inscription's flowery style, several interesting aspects emerge from it, one being that the assignment followed a royal order and that it was entrusted to a high-ranking official closely related to the king, a member of his entourage, in what appears as a personal mission. This kind of procedure was quite common and shows that officials were assigned tasks that had little or nothing to do with their supposed skill set(s). That is why, in the case of Ikherneferet, royal favour and managerial skills were deemed far more important to carrying out the mission than heading a department charged with, say, royal works. The structure of power appears thus rather personal and closer to oligarchical rather than bureaucratic principles. Although *The Installation of the Vizier* puts in the king's mouth the idea that 'being vizier it is not sweet, it is bitter as gall. Lo, he is the copper that shields the gold of his master's house, he is not one who bends his face to magistrates and councillors, not one who makes of anyone his client', a tiny oligarchy of viziers and senior dignitaries were in some periods not mere servants of the king but true king-makers. The early eighteenth century BC was one such period, while Bay, the powerful chancellor of Pharaoh Siptah (1194–1188 BC), boasted in an inscription about his king-making abilities: 'he who put the king [on] the throne of his father.'

The volatile nature of making and enacting decisions is also evident when a mission was considered of particular importance (like promoting an official) or destined to be long term (for instance, endowing a temple with property). The royal decision would then be inscribed in stone and took the form of a royal order or 'decree' intended to facilitate a royal intervention. However, attempts to render royal decisions permanent were nuanced. Some royal decrees include clauses with exemptions (temporary or permanent) for measures enacted in previous decrees. In other cases, kings issued decrees aiming to redress injustices and to punish abuses perpetrated by officials. Finally, other decrees intended to redress illegal appropriations or to confirm measures that had been established by previous decrees but ignored afterwards. When considered together, these examples, issued at the highest level of the state, show that royal decisions were fragile, that their observance was far from guaranteed and that the officials in charge of their observance frequently ignored them. As a result, some royal decrees included a detailed description of the severe punishments that would be imposed on negligent and corrupt officials. As we can see, the image of order and hierarchy that emanates from many official texts is contested by *other* official texts, which were also made public and reveal that particular ad hoc measures – rather than sets of general (legal) principles – constituted the very foundations of government. In the end, they point to a rather personalized governmental system in which bureaucracy barely emerges as an autonomous sphere, even less to be guided by normative impersonal principles and sanctioned by laws that aim to define and limit its remit. At best, teachings and other compositions used in the training of scribes tried to instil ethical values into the crown's agents. At a more modest level, things were no different. Many letters exchanged between middle-rank officials and their subordinates contain bitter criticism about laziness, missions accomplished unsatisfactorily or not fulfilled at all, etc. In a society dominated by patronage networks, in which officials were also linked to their superiors through personal bonds of constraint, allegiance and even dependence, loyalties might appear divided in some cases when the interests of the monarchy and those of an official were in conflict (Moreno García 2010b).

The absence of an impersonal referential order, comprised not only of ethical claims but of actual laws and a corpus of regulations, means that the conditions in which the agents of the crown operated left them a great deal of autonomy, which could be open to abuse or, simply, to personal interpretation. Many references, especially in New Kingdom texts, refer to measures taken 'according to law' (Eyre 2013: 55–77). While we cannot be certain whether legal codes ever existed at all, at least until the first millennium BC, justice was in fact dispensed by courts formed by officials on an ad hoc basis, rather than by (professional) judges. These courts would deliberate after hearing petitions from the parties involved and, if needed, after examining documents presented by the parties or preserved in the archives of institutions (as in the case of lawsuits about temple or state land). So 'law' may refer in this context more to a mix of tradition, proper procedure, written or remembered 'precedents', moral behaviour and ethical values, than to actual legal codes. Perhaps 'norms (to be respected)' is a more precise description of the legal system at that time. Inevitably tensions arose between, on the one hand, royal interventions intended to settle a decision 'for ever' through a decree enacted by the king and, on the other hand, exemptions and annulations to the measures taken by other kings. The tensions reveal the extent *and* the limits of enduring royal interventions, the existence of a sort of 'legal vacuum' arising from royal decisions being changed, and their arbitrary (or limited) implementation by the agents of the crown. Under these conditions, royal power appears as a fragile source of authority and legitimation in the long term, buffeted by the changing balance of power between kings and potentates, by factional fighting and conflicts inside the royal family, by revocations of previous royal orders, by favours granted to royal favourites, etc. It will come as no surprise, then, that people sought protection and support for their demands from influential patrons.

These circumstances may also explain the importance of temples. As 'houses of gods', and typically impervious to the ups and downs that affected royal power (dynastic conflict, volatile royal tempers, and even the occasional collapse of the monarchy itself), temples offered long-term institutional security, substantial income as well as the indisputable legitimacy lent by divine support. Temples also helped preserve social position and fortune as their patrimony was – in principle – unaffected by the hazards of buying and selling property, dividing it between family members, and even debt worries that so plagued private fortunes. Temples appear thus as providers of durability and stability in the absence of a normative law, and as a result their role was crucial for the stability and continuity of the monarchy. Let us also not forget their cultural importance as producers and propagators of a common set of values and cultural tools (religion, scribal practices, visual imagery, ideas of social order, etc.). Temples and 'theologies' integrated local cults and royal ideology into an intricate body of myths, composite divinities and religious 'geographies' that provided a kind of cultural homogeneity in an otherwise regionally diverse country. (The royal palace was the other major mainstay of Egyptian culture and values.) Temples were repositories of wealth, legitimacy and cultural values that proved fundamental for the monarchy when it was to be reconstructed and/or unified after episodes of crisis. The long history of many temples consecrated to gods contrasts with the relative volatility of temples dedicated to kings, in particular royal mortuaries. It is hardly surprising, then, that royal annals and literary texts show that the organization of temple life and resources not only regulated access to these institutions but was also a major area of royal intervention. And it is not by chance that many royal decrees and measures sought to provide temples with income, to restore them (if they fell into disrepair, or were destroyed) and to control access to the priesthood. These measures were intended to (re)organize the economic assets and workforce of temples, and would include the occasional exemptions of duties and taxes for the personnel of divine institutions, as well as regulations about royal donations of land to the shrines. Ramesses III, for instance, issued a decree ordering an inventory of Upper Egypt's temples, for them to be purified and their treasuries and granaries inspected. This decree is referred to in inscriptions found at the temples of Tod, Karnak, Elkab, Edfu and Elephantine, which might illustrate the principle of acting 'according to law'. It was also this king who made massive donations of land, people and offerings of all kinds to the temples of Egypt after a period of political turmoil. Divine support in exchange for offerings and the construction of cult buildings formed the very basis of the relation of reciprocity that legitimized kingship, so these measures figure prominently among royal activities and contributed towards the creation of an ideal order of stability, prosperity and social order (Moreno García 2013c and 2013d).

Under these conditions, there was no opposition between 'temples' and 'the state' or between 'priests' and 'agents of the crown'. In fact, many officials also performed priestly functions, and managed to fulfil these duties without clashing with the crown. It might also be the case that the development of temples in some way followed a certain withdrawal of direct interventions on the part of the crown, a sort of decentralization of functions in which temples took on some of the managerial activities hitherto restricted to the crown (for example, the exploitation of temple *and* royal land and of other resources, storage and delivery of goods when needed, remuneration of bureaucrats, etc.), while the king and his council concentrated their efforts on foreign policy and military expansion. This phenomenon, concomitant with the disappearance of the network of royal economic centres scattered all over the country at the very end of the third millennium BC, also helps explain why cities emerged at the very same time as autonomous poles of administrative, economic and social organization. In a way, temples appear to be a complement to the royal administration, as a 'reserve of statehood' less subject to political hazards and via which political power could reorganize itself after periods of monarchical crisis. They also provided the crucial link between local elites and the monarchy. Hence temples and institutions directly controlled by the crown represented the main pillars of the pharaonic monarchy.

Further illustrations of the communication flow between all these spheres of power and the circulation of royal authority can be found in the letters and instructions issued by the king in order to prepare particular arrangements, to organize ordinary activities or even to promote officials (Eyre 2013: 81–53). However, these documents point again to the absence of clear governmental procedures, regulations and protocols characteristic of a bureaucratic-based system of rule within which administrative departments had well-defined competences. It also suggests, once again, that officials enjoyed considerable latitude for discretionary measures, based on their take on specific situations. It was probably in the domain of foreign relations, in which diplomacy was organized according to conventions and cultural codes acceptable for different political entities, at least in the late second millennium BC, that claims to absolute rule became clearly untenable and that the limits of royal power became visible to a wide audience (for instance, soldiers returning home after unsuccessful military campaigns, merchants denied access to a foreign territory, etc.). In such situations, rules that were acceptable to all actors stimulated the consensual emergence of practices that dictated what 'proper' war was, how diplomatic relations should be organized, how gifts might be exchanged between courts, and so on. This was also an environment in which the balance of power between kingdoms limited the claims made by rulers to absolute power so present in texts intended for an internal audience. The best expressions of these practices were treaties, such as that agreed between Ramesses II and the Hittite king, Hattušili III.

The contrast is clear with other contexts, such as the relations between Egypt and Nubia, where such practices were simply absent, treaties and diplomatic contact (if any) not formally expressed in

Figure 6.2 Akhenaten and his wife, Nefertiti, represented in a more affable, even intimate attitude.

monuments, and relations framed within the limits of the alleged superiority of Egypt over 'wretched Kush'.

A final aspect concerns official reaction to misconduct, corruption or incompetence. Many inscriptions describe the severe punishment meted out to negligent and corrupt officials, which usually consisted of corporal punishments, the suppression of privileges and income, assignment to compulsory work – and even death. In theory, officials active in the provinces were subject to some governmental scrutiny, as stated in the inscription of Pepyankh 'the middle' (one of three brothers bearing the same name) from Meir:

> until the end of the time I spent as an official I was occupied with the function of the seal: I never slept with the seal far from my side from the time when I was promoted to be an official. I was never placed under guard, I was never imprisoned. With regard to everything the witnesses said in the presence of the officials, I always came away from the matter with success, the matter having been thrown back on those who spoke (against me), since I had been cleared in the presence of the officials, for they had maliciously spoken against me.
>
> Strudwick 2005: 370

Pepyankh raises two crucial issues: on the one hand, such control could have resulted from intrigues and factional rivalries among the elite; on the other, powerful officials could be reasonably sure that their chances of being exonerated were high. A letter from Elephantine from the late third millennium BC expresses the concern of two local officials about the possibility that another high-ranking local dignitary, Sabni, might have charges of misconduct against him dismissed at the Hall of Horus, the royal council formed by the king and other senior officials (Strudwick 2005: 178–79). In other cases, councils and justice-dispensing courts had little influence given that they were mainly the arena for factional fighting used to discredit rivals, as in the case of the judicial inquiry following the robbery of royal tombs at the end of the second millennium BC. The inquiry shows in detail the bitter rivalry between Paser, the mayor of the Theban East Bank, and Pawero, the mayor of the West Bank, and their respective supporters following an inspection of the tombs in Western Thebes ordered by the vizier and city-governor, Khaemwase. Relatively junior officials, however, were punished severely if found guilty of misconduct, particularly when it concerned theft or the diversion of resources destined for institutions (especially temples, royal funerary endowments, etc). The 'Elephantine scandal', which involved the theft of thousands of sacks of grain from the temple there over several years by an unscrupulous official, also reveals that the robbery was possible only thanks to the complicity of temple personnel.

Counterpower(s)?

Issuing decrees and orders was one aspect of royal power, but actually implementing them was another matter. It might be tempting to consider the pharaohs' great building programmes as the quintessential manifestation of an effective division of tasks, bureaucratic efficiency and managerial skill under the superior control of monarchs and their agents. Nevertheless, things were more complex. The regular involvement of kings in building and decorating temples, at least in the provinces, became significant only from the early second millennium BC onwards, a period during which some provincial nobles were also able to build massive tombs for themselves and to participate in the construction, provision and decoration of local sanctuaries. They were even able to control access to local priesthood, apparently on their own initiative and using mainly their own resources (Bussmann 2015 and 2016). This means that the real story of many monuments was not one of exclusive royal decisions and that, at least in some instances, it conceals interests and goals shared by kings and potentates. It also means that powerful potentates could, in principle, mobilize the symbolic and economic resources necessary to create potential foci of counterpower to royal authority. In the same vein, a recent research trend has suggested that the royal administration had, in fact, barely any impact on the life of rural Egypt, as these areas remained tightly controlled by local chiefs, and any 'central' authority found it almost impossible to penetrate this world effectively.

From this perspective, two main potential foci of alternative authority emerge, one centred around the court and high-ranking officials, and the other on the local nobility. However, as we have seen in previous chapters, both groups shared some characteristics that limited their ability to build up extensive alliances and to challenge the monarchy. The first is that their wealth derived, ultimately, from their service to the state. This means that they could use and manipulate the state to a certain extent, but their own existence as a social privileged group was intrinsically linked to the existence of the state. The second point is that factions seem to have been based on circumstantial alliances between individuals and groups from different backgrounds – the provincial nobility, say, or the army, senior local officials, and so on – rather than on joint interests, so their mobilization apparently never sought to preserve (even expand) collective interests in the long term. In fact, there is no evidence of (for instance) a 'provincial party' that aimed to promote the influence and power of regional officials, organized as a group, against other factions. What the sources reveal, instead, is that the provincial elites' power bases varied widely: in some cases their clout was derived from temples (which provided both wealth and symbolic authority), while others drew their power from trade, service to the state, or even a combination of all of these, but in each case some degree of alliance with the royal family, even at a matrimonial level, would have been important. Furthermore, as we know from the best documented provinces, two or more different powerful families could have co-existed in one place, while specific tasks were entrusted to different branches of the dominant family, thus revealing potential fracture lines that could be exploited by the kings to limit the influence of ambitious local potentates. The sources also point to the existence of particular strategies of power that were limited to a single province, while such strategies were rooted both in a firm local basis and in contacts with the court. Such an inability (or lack of incentive) to co-ordinate strategies between local landlords prevented the transformation of the provincial nobility into an organized group at 'national' scale. In fact, local nobles *were* part of the ruling elite, in that they shared the codes of a common (high) culture and were selectively co-opted to occupy some of the most powerful positions of the state. This may explain why, when the monarchy collapsed, local leaders tried to consolidate their own autonomy in the provinces under their control, but did not seek to acquire power in former centres of royal power, such as Memphis, Itj-tawy or Thebes. The case of some 'great chiefs of a province' in Middle Egypt, in the third and second millennia BC respectively, is a good example; local families (at Akhmim, Bersheh and Beni Hasan) sent some of their members to the Court in the hope of gaining privileged positions close to the king or in the administration, but took care not to neglect their own (home) bases of power. The chiefs from Bersheh and Beni Hasan managed to exert substantial control over foreign contacts and trade in the early second millennium BC, both as autonomous actors – judging by the occasional presence of monuments dedicated to them in the Levant – *and* in the role of high-ranking officials and agents of the king, not as feudal lords (Moreno García 2017). The early centuries of the first millennium BC confirm such configurations of power, with kings progressively reduced to a marginal role, while local potentates claimed to be royalty but showed little interest in expanding their power permanently beyond the limits of their regional kingdoms; hierarchies within their ranks – where they existed at all – were always unstable. We can assume, then, that in some areas (mostly Middle and Lower Egypt), power seems to have been organized as occasional loose confederations of local leaders against external menaces, be they Theban kings or Kushite pharaohs. Little is known about the internal organization of the micro-kingdoms that flourished in periods of political crisis. But the fact that their leaders claimed royal status, that they reproduced royal institutions and practices at a smaller scale (such as educating the sons of their provincial allies at court, as was the case in the Heracleopolitan kingdom), and that they invoked royal values on their own monuments, points to the mimicking of royal structures rather than the formation of a feudal class. These actions may also explain why they were easily integrated into the monarchy once it was reorganized after a period of crisis. At this point, in their role of local leaders, they once again supplied officials to the royal administration and the temples they controlled were decorated by the kings (who used these sanctuaries as vehicles for having their authority recognized and legitimized locally). Their wealth derived once more from royal income and awards in the main, and not (apparently) from substantial private riches amassed during periods of the monarchy's collapse, and preserved thereafter.

Specialized governmental corps almost never became real counter-powers. One might think of military leaders and administrators of justice as potential holders of legitimacy, authority and force on their own account, and people thus capable of wresting these prerogatives from the monarchy. However, they never became autonomous actors. For example, courts were not presided over by 'professional' judges but instead were made up of officials, scribes, priests, high dignitaries and so on, on an ad hoc basis, depending on the importance of specific lawsuits. Furthermore, these formal procedures were not incompatible with the use of 'parallel' channels, such as the mobilization of powerful patrons and influential relations, in order to get satisfaction. This means that there was nothing close to a corps of judges, of specialized jurists or of a corpus of referential legal precepts interpreted by a body of religious or secular authorities, that was able to limit the king's authority. This was particularly evident during the late second and early first millennia BC, a period in which an alternative source of legitimacy emerged, when political (as well as other) matters were submitted to the consideration of divinities that issued a verdict through oracular practices. As regards the use of force, it was only from 1550 onwards that an operational specialized army existed in Egypt (Gnirs 1996). However, some limitations restricted the use of this particular force. First, it was a campaign army, predominantly comprising specialists (foreign mercenaries, charioteers, etc.), partly quartered in fortresses and bases (Eastern Delta, Fayum), partly formed by mobilized peasants and landowners, and deployed in campaigns abroad. Internal security was managed by a type of police force staffed by foreigners (Nubians, people from the Eastern Desert or Medya). The most senior command positions fell to 'generals' who often had other roles, from high priest to vizier. It was only in the second half of the second millennium BC that the army became a significant distinctive branch of the administration and, as such, it was able to provide opportunities for social mobility and the accumulation of riches. As far as we can tell, during the second millennium BC, the army as an institution was not used to support political ambitions in Egypt, other than when a governor of Nubia mobilized an armed force to support his political claims in the Theban area around 1100, only to be defeated.

Obviously, kings were far from being mere spectators of the strategies followed by their subordinates and the nobles. As mediators between factions, their decisions helped to support, block or set one faction against another (Baines & Yoffee 1998). Removing rival dignitaries from key positions was another weapon at their disposal, as were marriage alliances with powerful families. Selecting, promoting and/or honouring particular nobles against the ambitions of their relations, offered kings the opportunity to break the internal solidarity of powerful families. Resorting to foreigners was another tactic. Promoting non-Egyptians to key positions in the kingdom was a strategy that fulfilled two goals: first, it secured the loyalty of these foreign appointees, who had been uprooted from their home territories and kin groups, and who thus owed their position exclusively to the king; it avoided an excessive dependence on powerful Egyptian families eager to increase their wealth and influence. Another tool, and one increasingly important as of the second half of the second millennium BC, was to create an armed force whose elite troops consisted mainly of foreign fighters. According to the papyrus Anastasi I, a division of 5,000 men in Ramesside Egypt included 520 Sherden warriors, at least 1,600 Libyan troops and 880 Nubians, all of whom accounted for just over 60 per cent of its total forces. Later on, contingents of Libyans, Carians, Greeks, etc., were usual in pharaonic armies. As a trained force of specialists who relied on state wages and land allocations for their survival, foreign warriors offered the king the opportunity to avoid local levies raised by provincial leaders, to minimize their military threat and to enjoy an undisputed armed supremacy against any internal rival: employing such a number of foreign troops would have been beyond the means of any Egyptian dignitary or provincial noble. Only in periods of political instability is there evidence of foreign contingents working in the service of provincial nobles.

But what of priests? It was only in the late first millennium BC that they developed a collective sense of their interests vis-à-vis the monarchy. Each temple or, to be more precise, each 'house' of a god (with interests sometimes at quite a remove from the main sanctuary, at least in the case of the more important cults) was an autonomous world in itself, with its own economic assets and personnel, and liable to interventions from kings and magnates, but there was no 'league' of priests, or similar. In fact, 'priests' very often held 'secular' titles and responsibilities, so the very term is rather reductive and misleading, particularly in the case of people of a relatively high social status who typically accumulated many other functions. Even in the case of the more powerful cult institutions, such as the Domain of Amun in the first centuries of the first millennium BC, when it emerged as the dominant political and spiritual power in Upper Egypt, its relation with kings (then residing in Lower Egypt) was ambiguous. Instead of seeing their complex relationship as a kind of rivalry between 'state' and 'temple', it is safer to consider both institutions as representatives of the interests of former elites that had by this time split into two factions thanks to shifting balances of power. Lower Egypt turned to a flourishing Mediterranean world, drawing first of all on existing political structures before later creating its own (including kingship); Upper Egypt, which gradually became rather a marginal area, could only offer to its declining elites the Domain of Amun as an institution powerful enough to protect their interests, wealth and status. Finally, 'citizens' rarely organized themselves collectively into a body supported by institutions (such as urban councils, guilds and so on) or as a league of cities. Just a handful of texts, in particular *The Teaching for (King)*

Merykara, evoke the possibility that urban dwellers might be deceived by demagogues. Otherwise, their political influence seems limited, and it is only at the very end of the third millennium BC that 'citizens' and cities appear as a force to be reckoned with by local rulers. In the end, towns and cities were ruled by powerful families and patrons ('great men') and they were probably prone to the kind of vertical relations, based on hierarchy, patronage and obedience to kings and local nobles, so prevalent in the pharaonic world. The fact that mayors of some cities came from the same dominant local family, and transferred (even sold) their position to other members of their kin, confirms their oligarchical organization.

Inescapable patrons

In the absence of autonomous spheres of political intervention typical of the modern world, spheres based on law, strategic discussions about means *and* goals, civil rights, and substantial collective bodies of political actors, ancient Egyptian society was organized along horizontal and vertical lines. Horizontal structures were formed of family links, relations with peers and membership of a village or an urban neighbourhood; vertical structures were based on hierarchy and patronage. Formal hierarchy is constantly evoked in official texts and scenes: we hear of peasants reporting to scribes, scribes reporting to dignitaries, dignitaries reporting to kings and kings reporting to gods. Texts (*onomastica*) and private monuments describe in detail such a structure, usually framed by the concept of *maat* or preservation of cosmic harmony as a guide for kings and their administration. However, authority could also be exerted via alternative, informal channels. Patronage was perhaps the most important of these. It pervaded both vertical and horizontal relations as it was based on protection and (unequal) reciprocal support. That said, hierarchy was also present where horizontal bounds prevailed. In the case of family relations, it was the kin group that provided support for its members, though the loyalty and respect that needed to be observed (towards elders, male relatives, elder brothers, etc.) restricted the scope for individual agency. Women, for instance (particularly widows: Kóthay 2006), found protection within their kin or in the professional guilds of their husbands, but in many cases it was their male relatives who represented them in private business (such as the acquisition or sale of land). The pursuit of individual strategies that had not been approved by the wider family group was discouraged – if not utterly prohibited, as stated in *The Teaching of Ptahhotep*: 'Do not be greedy towards your kin. The mild man receives more respect than the strong. He who shuns his kin is a miserable man.' The same held true when the impartial behaviour expected of dignitaries in their official capacity clashed with the goals of their family, as outlined in *The Installation of the Vizier*:

> Avoid what was said of the vizier Akhtoy, that he denied his own kin for the sake of others, for fear of being falsely called [partial]. If one of them appealed a judgment, that he had planned to do to him, he persisted in denying him. But that is excess of justice. Do not judge unfairly, God abhors partiality. This is an instruction, plan to act accordingly. Regard one you know like one you don't know, one near you like one far from you. The magistrate who acts like this, he will succeed here in this place.

In terms of the support and protection afforded by superiors, many officials pretended that their careers had advanced by merit alone, and not due to the influence of contacts and powerful patrons. So Hezi (twenty-fourth century BC) claimed that 'His Majesty caused (it) to be done for me because His Majesty knew my name while selecting a scribe because of his hand (= ability), without any backer, (simply because) he remembered the one who had spoken to him wisely', while Simut-Kyky (thirteenth century BC) said that 'I have not made a(ny) protector for myself from (other) men, [I have not attached] myself to (any) from among the notables, not even a son of mine' (Frood 2007: 87). In fact, powerful patrons, well-placed contacts, or membership in influential social networks were informal but nevertheless essential means for furthering one's career or, simply, for securing some protection against potential difficulties, a common practice often concealed by the scribal culture and its insistence on promotion through merit. These practices were also fundamental to ensuring that authority circulated effectively between upper and lower social groups and between the royal palace and the provinces. At the same time, officials boasted constantly that they had behaved appropriately in their role, that they had avoided abuses and that they had protected the poor from the powerful. And abuses *did* exist everywhere, which is why texts used for training scribes stress the appeal of their privileged circumstances when compared to the mistreatment inflicted on peasants and workers: forced requisitions (of food, grain, cattle, etc.), strict grain rations, physical punishment, etc. That such gloomy descriptions were not hyperbolic can be seen in royal decrees and official documents describing these abuses and the punishment doled out to officials. The influence of powerful people, however, not only limited the effectiveness of legal procedures ('do not go to court against your superior when you do not have protection [against] him' (*The Teaching of Ankhsheshonq* 8: 11), but their support was crucial in obtaining justice: 'do not say: "find me a strong superior, for a man in your town has injured me"; do not say: "find me a protector, for one who hates me has injured me"' (*The Teaching of Amenemope* XXII: 1–4). As is evident, then, the webs of informal relations centred on powerful officials and potentates were quite considerable, as can be seen in the names of hundreds of people (servants, relatives, subordinates, clients) carved in the tombs of the highest elite. Their extended households allowed them to be a significant influence in the local sphere as nodes of power, influence and protection. This model was reproduced, at a lesser scale, by middle-rank dignitaries. Yet in both cases, marriages, funerary ceremonies, banquets and the exchange of gifts reinforced horizontal links of social relations and ensured that their protagonists were recognized officially as people of status by their peers. Other practices sought the same goal, such as when the wealthy landowner Heqanakhte leased land to and from other affluent tenants in his neighbourhood. His aim was probably not just economic but also social, to be accepted as a peer by people of similar status (Allen 2002).

Contrary to the practices common among the elite, many Egyptians were forced instead to depend on powerful or influential fellow citizens and to join the patronage networks they headed, to the point of being considered part of their households. Such networks provided a kind of 'vertical integration' in addition to the horizontal path constituted by family and neighbours, which is how senior officials could be linked to minor ones, local potentates to courtiers, officials to ordinary workers and citizens, and so on. A Late Bronze Age ostracon, for instance, reports that fugitive oarsmen were found in the company (under the protection?) of prominent officials at various locations in the Delta. Other sources refer to tenants acting as agents for scribes or dignitaries, like 'the house(hold) of the cultivator Paysen attached to the scribe Aanery'. As recompense for their services, the superior would take care of his subjects (for example, if they fell ill or were caught up in lawsuit). Such bonds were explicitly marked by the use of kinship terms: compulsory workers were described as the 'sons' of prominent citizens ('N, he is called the son of Senbebu, a priest of Thinis') or when officials were labelled 'friends' or '(pseudo-)children' of their superior (in horizontal relations between peers, 'brother' was the term used). Sometimes, the patron/client relationship was formalized by means of legal contracts, even by fictitious adoptions which masked what was actually the voluntary servitude of the person referred to as a 'son'. Finally, people in trouble sold themselves or handed over all their possessions to a patron in exchange for protection.

Local authorities

Any consideration of the organization of power and the exercise of authority in ancient Egypt would be incomplete without considering local potentates, 'mayors' and 'chiefs', all of whom constituted a body of formal and informal authority in the territories they controlled. Many texts refer to 'great men' and 'great ones' as prominent members of their communities, in contrast with 'modest/humble ones', while literary texts from the first millennium BC evoke the notables of the villages as the main local authority, as if the localities were entirely in their hands – no royal authority is even mentioned: 'the notables of a town are its walls', 'the lord of a town is its potentate.' In a world of secluded rural communities, where internal solidarity in time of strife was expected, and foreigners routinely distrusted ('do not stay in a town in which you have no one; if you stay in a town in which you have no one, your character is your (only) family'; 'do not let your son marry a woman from another town, lest he be taken from you'), the role of such potentates at the core of local life meant that their support and protection was essential, especially as their ties with the temple(s) linked to their village or town strengthened their authority even further (Agut-Labordère 2011).

It is likely that town mayors and village chiefs came from the social milieu of rural potentates and wealthy peasants, and their status of genuine local power-brokers in troubled political times is expressed, for instance, in a papyrus referring to the anarchy that prevailed around 1190 BC: 'the land of Egypt was in the hands of chiefs (literally, 'great ones') and of rulers of towns.' Their social position was further enhanced by their role as mediators between the royal administration and the wider population, particularly with regard to taxation, delivering goods to the king's agents, providing manpower when requested, or cultivating royal and temple land. Nevertheless, and in spite of their local relevance, village chiefs are almost invisible in the archaeological record, and only exceptionally did they have access to the prestigious goods reserved to the elite.

In any case, detecting such elusive sub-elites in the archaeological record – and defining their competences – is relatively difficult, as they very seldom produced documents of their own (Moreno García 2010b). Their support was nevertheless crucial to the enforcement of orders issued by the king and his representatives, despite their stereotypical depiction in art: typically, village chiefs are depicted in the scenes of private tombs in a humiliating pose, dragged before the scribes to whom they should deliver their taxes or justify their accounts by stick-wielding officials. So when the priest Sobekaa boasted about serving noblemen and overseers of Upper Egypt at the end of the third millennium BC, his claim did not sound extraordinary. However, when priests and scribes proudly proclaimed that they worked for simple village governors, 'chiefs' and overseers, they pointed to the real importance of these authorities. The simultaneous existence of several such chiefs in the same province suggests that their authority extended beyond the limits of a single locality and encompassed districts. In fact the 'houses' and 'domains' of prominent men were sometimes considered as equivalent to districts or areas under the authority of a powerful person, and they delivered personnel and offerings to the central administration as any other official would. Finally, the appearance of the title 'member of the council of a district' around 1800 BC, and the definition of its holders as local authorities liable to the vizier in the same vein as mayors and other local officials, casts further light on these elusive sub-elites.

All of the above helps us understand how villages were integrated into the administrative structure of Egypt. Although they might appear at first glance as secluded worlds, controlled by 'great men' and prominent heads of patronage networks, it is also true that local elites provided the indispensable link which connected the rural world to the royal administration and the court (Agut-Labordère 2011). Temples appear as privileged meeting points between these spheres of power, while establishing contact with officials and the court gave the local elites the opportunity to expand their interests and wealth beyond their very local area of influence, a position reinforced when they in turn became scribes, priests, minor officials and informal agents of the crown.

Transfers of sovereignty?

Despite their claims to absolute power, pharaohs' decision-processes were influenced by a range of actors and factors, some formal, some informal. This means that the construction of statehood and kingship was a highly dynamic process subject to considerable changes over three millennia. Although the early monarchy took the form (at least judging from its monumental vestiges) of a highly personalized structure of power, centred on the king, an extremely limited body of (very) high-ranking dignitaries and a network of economic and 'power' centres scattered across the country, such a system proved impractical by about 2500 BC. The enormous pyramids surrounded by the tombs of the elite epitomized the physical and symbolic attachment of a reduced upper class to their master, with the royal cemeteries representing the 'embodiment' of a centralized system of decision-making and of the state itself. This landscape was, of course, an idealized expression of power, one that would be forced to cope, long-term, with a more diversified reality, when other sources of authority (mainly in the provinces) required a more effective integration in the state, both administratively and symbolically. So the move towards a highly centralized concentration of power, workforce and resources (and the idealized landscapes that represented it) was a short-lived experiment (roughly 2613–2532 BC), as was the case under comparable circumstances in Qin China. Running a relatively large state (by the standards of the Early Bronze Age), its people and its resources required a more effective integration of provincial leaders, the creation of unifying cultural values and the promotion of an expanded (and less personalized) bureaucracy, a process that introduced notable changes in the composition of the elites and in decision-making procedures from 2500 BC. Kings could no longer rely on a tiny group of dignitaries, many of them related by blood to the pharaohs; instead they needed to redistribute power, delegate part of their prerogatives to other institutions and promote an increasingly indirect and (at least in some areas) more specialized system of government.

Their first step was to delegate to temples part of the former royal role of mediator between gods and people. Provincial temples, controlled by local nobles, thus gained legitimacy in the eyes of both the king and their fellow citizens as partners in governmental tasks. Temples gradually became more autonomous institutions, especially as kings diverted significant amounts of land (and manpower) to them. As a result, royal funerary temples – as well as sanctuaries closely linked to the monarchy and the capital (at Hieracompolis, Heliopolis, Memphis, etc.) – lost some of their importance, which was now shared with the sanctuaries that flourished in the provinces, that were being richly endowed and whose overseers became closely related to the king, as occurred at Bersheh and Tehna. After the collapse of the monarchy around 2160 BC, the kings who reunified and ruled Egypt around 2040 BC embellished provincial temples, probably as part of a strategy seeking to gain support and loyalty from local leaders. In fact, the power of kings at this time appears to have been somewhat precarious, prone to rebellions, and more ideologically dependent on divine support, as may be inferred from the iconography of temples built during this period. Note that provincial nobles also claimed that they had restored temples. So, the idealized landscapes resulting from this process are marked by a stark reduction in the dimensions (physical and symbolic) of royal tombs as nodes of power whereas temples saw their role as foci of social and cultural identity increased. This process was completed in the first millennium BC, when kings were buried in temples and when decision-making was formally assumed by gods through oracular procedures. In the absence of law(s) as a referential body of norms that delimited the sphere of executive power, such a reduction in the centrality of kings as source of legitimacy had major consequences, particularly when we consider that the lack of distinction between the state and the king gave the latter a marked public character (Arjomand 2005). Indeed the increasing role of temples, cults and elaborate religious beliefs suggests a gradual failure by the crown to cope with the ideal of absolute authority (and to assemble the necessary means of pursuing that) it claimed on royal monuments. Occasional enormous building programmes, a new military ethos or the elaborate court ceremonies so prevalent during the Late Bronze Age hardly obscured the fact that, in the private sphere, officials and common people ended up turning directly to gods for assistance and succour.

The second phase would be to delegate managerial competences and decision-making initiatives to an expanding body of administrators that was increasingly aware of its social status. The formal development of the Chamber of Dignitaries in the very late third millennium BC was the outcome of a process initiated around 2500 BC. This also means that decisions, spheres of influence, division of tasks, etc., became more blurred in order to harmonize not only the activities, but also the ambitions, co-operative and individual interests, and strategies of an expanding body of crown agents. In a society dominated by patronage networks and extended families, this also meant that divided loyalties had the potential to become a challenge for, but also a tool at the service of, kings, especially when rivalries erupted between palace and noble factions. And, as the monarchy and the governmental apparatus collapsed periodically, bureaucrats would have found it difficult to become a durable distinctive sphere of power in themselves. Also note that administrators could always be sourced from within the many branches of the royal family, while the expansion of bureaucracy and governmental departments in periods of 'mature' monarchic rule probably led not to increased efficiency but rather to stifling decision-making procedures. For all these reasons, there are no traces of a *raison d'état* based on a clear separation between state and kingship.

The third approach would be to delegate the use of force to a body of military specialists under the orders of an increasingly threatening international sphere, particularly from 1550 BC. It was at this point that the army became a significant branch of the administration, as well as a source of promotion, wealth and prestige, although it was perhaps more important from a social point of view for commoners than for individuals born into elite families. Generals and senior officers tended to be scions of powerful families, including provincial ones, and they usually accumulated other functions not related to military activities. In some cases, they acceded to the throne, probably less as representatives of 'the army' (as a collective) than as members of the king's inner circle. Yet there is no evidence that the army acted as a political actor of its own volition, with a specific agenda confronting other actors. So, while *coups d'état* are well known, sometimes sought to murder kings (Amenemhat I, Ramesses III) and included military personnel, such conspiracies tended to be promoted nevertheless by courtiers, rather than the army as an institution.

Did delegating power in these ways reduce the authority of kings dramatically? It seems unlikely. Priests never altered the theocratic basis of power from which they ultimately depended and which was based, justified and legitimized by the existence of a semi-divine king, a mediator between gods and humans. When something close to a 'theocratic' political entity emerged in Upper Egypt at the very end of the second millennium BC, it owed more to a redistribution of power in a changing geopolitical environment than to a usurpation of royal prerogatives. That kings chose to establish themselves in Lower Egypt, leaving Upper Egypt in the hands of the Domain of (god) Amun and his High Priest at Thebes (who also frequently held the title of general), is symptomatic of the loss of importance of Upper Egypt for a monarchy ever more oriented towards the Mediterranean and its burgeoning economy. In any case, the High Priests of Amun recognized the authority of the pharaohs and married into the royal family, in what appears to be a renewed division of functions between kings (who retained control over the more dynamic economic and geopolitical region of Egypt) and temples. In fact, Theban High Priests showed no ambition to access power in Lower Egypt, even less to create a kingdom of their own, even when Lower Egypt was at last divided into several relatively small polities. It is also significant that the army played no political role whatsoever when strong rulers were absent, either in Upper or Lower Egypt. It would thus seem that it was political crises within the monarchy – and not the emergence of autonomous power structures – that were the main reasons behind its (repeated) collapses, most likely catalysed by specific events, severe financial challenges, and the subsequent inability of kings to capture wealth (and to redistribute it among the elite), to maintain an equilibrium between the court, the central administration and the provincial nobility, and to mediate effectively between factions and regional interests. In any case, all these factors shared a main characteristic: while fiscal crises reduced the crown's revenue significantly and precipitated its collapse, this process always took the form of a 'soft', rather than traumatic, breakdown.

7

Building Statehood Through Culture

In early Mesopotamia the consolidation of kings as the main authorities in the territories they ruled was a gradual process until they finally bypassed the former primacy of other institutions, such as temples. The trajectory followed by pharaonic Egypt was quite different, though. Here, kings emerged as the dominant authority at the very beginning of Egyptian history, around the middle of the fourth millennium BC, while 'dynastic' temples seem to have played a much more modest role and appear inseparable from (and subordinate to?) the monarchy. Situated far from the main centres of royal power, early provincial temples seem rather modest too, at least judging from the scarce evidence preserved. It was only from the second millennium BC onwards that temples grew in size, economic importance and, especially at the end of that millennium, in political autonomy (Bussmann 2015). The very central position of kings in the national hierarchy, and the autocratic nature of their power as semi-divine beings and mediators between gods and people, contributed to the establishment of a relatively rigid ideology whose most distinctive features were reproduced for many thousands of years, even if the actual nature of royal power changed considerably over time. Two factors contributed to this stability.

First, the monarchy in ancient Egypt had relatively stable and well-defined borders. In ancient Mesopotamia, for instance, territorial control was often sporadic and borders precarious, as states usually encompassed older and well-consolidated social and political entities (city-states, small kingdoms, tribal areas, marsh communities, etc.), scattered over large floodplain and steppe areas where boundaries remained imprecise. This world of strong local traditions, many of which were based on urban societies and their own powerful groups, meant that states were usually precarious and short-lived aggregations of cities and tribal groups tied together under the authority of exceptionally successful leaders (Sargon, Hammurabi, Shamshi-Adad I, etc.). When empires became the predominant political organizations in the first millennium BC, it became even more challenging to integrate very diverse peoples, elites, territories and lifestyles, each with their own distinctive culture. This was not the case in ancient Egypt, however, which was more homogeneous socially and which had a much lower urban population density, at least until the second half of the second millennium BC.

Second, there was an absence, for most of Egyptian history, of potential major counterpowers that could have forced pharaohs to negotiate with them and limited royal authority. Contrary again to ancient Mesopotamia, the number of tribal populations living inside or in close proximity to Egypt was very low, while the political role of cities and urban assemblies (led by their own authorities, such as elders, etc.), trade associations and so on seems negligible. Only provincial nobles had their own political agendas and jostled for power, but this happened only at certain points in Egyptian history and in certain regions, particularly Middle Egypt (Moreno García 2017). Feudalism was never a major challenge for the monarchy. We should also note that dominant cultural mores bore the distinctive mark of the monarchy – sometimes called 'palace culture' or 'high culture' – and included the creation of a unified scribal language or the creation of the artistic codes reproduced so widely (Baines 2013). The success of such cultural values was immense, both in their capacity to integrate and re-interpret (to their profit) alternative values, as well as in their aim to become models that could be emulated and deployed under conditions very different to those that had witnessed their emergence (the periods known as archaism or classicism).

The king

From the earliest times, the king was identified with Horus, the dynastic divinity. As a result, pharaohs were regarded as having a semi-divine nature that placed them in a unique ideological position. Inhabiting this lofty plain inspired an increasingly elaborate body of ritual texts that aimed to define the role of kings as representatives and mediators of gods on earth, and as pivotal elements in crucial functions such as keeping order, harmony and justice (concepts embodied in the term *maat*), protecting Egypt's borders, bringing prosperity to the country and preserving the eternal cycle of legitimate kingship that renewed the alliance between Egyptians and gods (Baines 1995b). When considering the triad of legitimacy, authority and right, as formulated by Saskia Sassen (2008), it appears that kings presented themselves as the key element in maintaining the prevailing social and economic order. This also means that, from an ideological point of view, the delegation of royal authority was inconceivable in a theocratic system that would only allow specialized agents with particular tasks. As sovereignty could simply not be shared, there was little chance that politics would emerge as a truly autonomous sphere of action, or as a deliberative process about long-term *goals* (not about short/middle-term *means*) between actors enjoying executive agency. Hierarchy and subordination were thus essential in an ideal pyramidal order encompassing the entire Egyptian society, in which there was only a place for one actor at the summit (pharaoh) and in which his agents reproduced – on a smaller scale and towards their own subordinates and kin – the same values and duties expected from kings: maintaining prosperity and order.

Given the unique role of kings as mediators between humans and gods, any rearrangement of power would have involved redefining the relationship between kings and gods. If Horus corresponded, originally, to a crude patrimonial concept of the kingdom, whereby pharaohs appeared as heads of an extended (ruling) family that included not only their relatives but also dignitaries considered as their sons/daughters, later on this model revealed itself as inoperative. The increasing complexity of the administration, and the integration of new elite groups beyond the high-ranking families present at court and in key provinces, meant that this ideal of an extended 'royal family' could no longer embrace a large body of officials and low-status dignitaries, never mind the provincial administrators born to provincial families who lived and were buried far from the capital. So as time went by, the main symbol of this ageing ideal, the royal pyramid, lost most of its symbolic importance. Kings had to deal with local potentates and 'new' men who had become dignitaries, and this move was accompanied by the crown's greater involvement in local cults, first by erecting chapels provided with royal statues, then by decorating already existing (modest) provincial temples, and finally by building enormous temples far from the capital. In a sense, and as was the case with administrative tasks, the divine nature of kings became deterritorialized as it had to be present in the provinces, a move that enhanced both the role of local potentates as priests in major cults and the integration of local cults and gods into increasingly complex religious manifestations (myths, pantheons, iconography, ritual compositions, etc.). A further consequence was the need to develop 'national' cults, that would cover all of Egypt, be accessible to everybody and attentive to the feelings, expectations and spiritual needs of ordinary Egyptians, an aspect that royal cults could not fulfil. The rise of the cult of Osiris (linked to Abydos, the ancestral burial place of the monarchy) provided a vital link between this world and the underworld for every Egyptian (Mathieu 2010; Smith 2017), while the attempts to set up major 'national' gods (such as Amun), to be revered everywhere, as well as syncretic cults comprising 'national' and local deities, brought official religion (and its views of the cosmos and order) closer to ordinary Egyptians. Thus domestic cults (and the family values they supported) gradually lost their importance in the construction of personal identities. In return, people addressed their pleas directly to god(s) and communicated directly with them in new forms of personal religion (oracles, personal piety, etc.: Vernus 1993).

The process of creating 'national' cults was very closely linked to political conditions in ancient Egypt (Shafer 1991). The prominence of Amun as a 'national' god would be incomprehensible if we did not consider the rise of potentates (later pharaohs), in the late third and middle second millennia BC, who originated from an area (Thebes) where Amun was worshipped. These events indicate not only political challenges, but also new definitions of kingship. The strange episode of the short-lived monotheist experiment of Akhenaten and the cult of Aton, centred at Tell el-Amarna, in the fifteenth province of Upper Egypt (a traditional power base for influential local families), is probably to be understood (at least partly) as the last stand of some Upper Egyptian nobles eager to retain their influence against the irresistible rise of the (Eastern) Delta as the richest and most powerful region in Egypt. When this shift in the balance of power was finally achieved under the Ramessides (who came from the Delta), their rise was accompanied by that of Seth, a divinity connected to foreigners and trade. In the context of the imperialist expansion and military clashes with other states that characterized the Late Bronze Age (thus revealing the limits of pharaonic authority), kings stressed their role as warriors and expeditionary leaders through the display of highly elaborate artistic evocations of *particular* (not generic) military interventions and extensive descriptions of their military achievements: the expedition to Punt (Hatshepshut), the annals of Thutmose III, the battle of Qadesh and the Egypto-Hittite treaty (Ramesses II), the battles against Libyans and Sea Peoples (Merenptah, Ramesses III), etc. Hundreds of toponyms of 'conquered' foreign lands – or those presented as such – were reproduced on temple walls, alongside representations of foreign tribute. The end of the empire and, with it, of both tributary resources and military glory, undermined some of the most important justifications of the kings' authority. A new era of (imbalanced) relations between kings and gods was about to emerge.

Throughout Egypt's long history, the power of kings was continuously subject to challenges, tensions and disruptions, all of which forced the monarchs to 'reinterpret' the past in order to accommodate such disturbing events within the accepted ideal of order and to secure the legitimacy of their own rule. Divine help was definitely needed, as it procured the ultimate justification for kings' claims to the throne. Yet the mobilization of the past in order to secure the present provided another source of legitimacy, especially when a new line of kings arrived

Figure 7.1 Nefertiti and her husband, Akhenaten, introduced considerable – but ultimately short-lived – religious innovations.

on the throne or when particularly troubled political periods had been definitively left behind. Such legitimization took several forms. One of them consisted in erecting chapels or monuments dedicated to the memory of previous kings, thus positioning one's own reign as the latest in a long chain of supremacy dating back to the very origins of monarchy itself. This practice was replicated by dignitaries on their own tombs and statues, when they represented dozens of their forebears or enumerated long genealogies of holders of specific titles that supported their claims to priesthood, governorship and other functions. Another route was to refer to the immediate past as a time of chaos and turmoil that had been concluded happily when the current king was finally raised to power, restored order at last and resumed the traditional duties of the monarchy, thus ushering in a new period of prosperity. Again, this *topos* was emulated by dignitaries in two ways: either they claimed that neighbouring provinces starved while theirs thrived as a result of their effective administrative skills, or they boasted about having increased the taxes owed to the crown thanks to their zeal, while their predecessors had failed to do so. A third form was the invention of completely new 'traditions', such as claiming royal status for non-royal ancestors who initiated nevertheless a fresh line of pharaohs. This was the case for Mentuhotep I, the alleged (although probably fictional) ancestor of the Theban ruling dynasty during the late third millennium BC; it is also possible that the Heracleopolitan dynasty that ruled in Middle and Lower Egypt at the same time saw its modest history embellished by its later rulers. Another way of achieving a similar goal consisted of denying royal status to rival lines of kings (such as the Hyksos). A fourth form, closely linked to the preceding ones, lay in promoting artistic and visual compositions and monuments directly inspired by a prestigious king or historical period. The prestige thus bestowed on historical personalities in order to present oneself as heir of a noble tradition is also evident in the private sphere, when scribes wrote brief passages from famous literary compositions (usually attributed to long-dead, famous dignitaries) in the tombs of revered officials (Ragazzoli 2016). A fifth form was based on a selected and restricted set of deeds and acts that defined the 'proper' achievement of duties, and thus maintained *maat*. Kings described these in their annals in the form of brief statements that summarized – year by year – the most impressive achievements of their reigns, from building temples to dispatching military expeditions, donating land and offerings to cults, erecting statues, etc. In some cases, such enumerations were reproduced by local authorities, such as the High Priests of Amun at Karnak. In the case of dignitaries and scribes, their inscriptions are rich in colourful details about their promotions, their successful achievement of missions, their managerial skills as well as their moral qualities and irreproachable behaviour, but many other aspects of their lives are barely mentioned. Kings and officials appear thus as particular embodiments of ideal figures (*the* king, *the* official), performing what was expected of them in their respective domains of competence and leaving little space for individuality. When individuality *does* emerge, it also takes a specific form: that of the king or the official who surpasses what his predecessors had accomplished and thus becomes a model for future generations (Assmann 1990).

To conclude, in a theocratic society in which gods were the ultimate source of inspiration and legitimacy, kings enjoyed a position that, ideologically, set them above the rest of society and discouraged any challenge to their decisions. However, kings were not only liable to the gods, but also to people (in the end, good government and divine guidance meant prosperity for everybody), potentates (as local powers or leaders of palatial factions, pharaohs had to cope with their ambitions and gain their support) and priests (even if they acted as representatives of the king, their close contact to divinities gave their actions a particular weight). Egyptian texts and art stress the importance of a hierarchy in which everybody occupied a well-defined position and performed a precise function: 'serfs', artisans, soldiers, priests, scribes, etc. But ultimately the prosperity of the whole social fabric depended on the work of common people who should be allowed to perform their activities undisturbed, under the protection of a paternalist sovereign. Pharaohs thus had to suppress abuse and injustice, eliminate excessive taxes, care for their subjects' needs, promote moral behaviour and ensure their agents ruled justly. Several Egyptian texts insist on this kind of social contract in which people, compared to a flock, are put under the rule of the pharaoh, who was a shepherd for his people: 'fight for people in every way, they are the flock that is good for their lord'. Ultimately, rhetorical statements about the elimination of famine, stamping-out of abuses, and other 'imperfections' show that claims about absolute, unrestricted rule were more an ideal than a reality that, in the end, tested and questioned the actual authority of kings. Yet these same problems forced kings to intervene time and time again in earthly affairs, in what constituted further proof of their irreplaceability. Were such circumstances enough to question the role of kings if they proved unable to fulfil their side of the 'contract', even to spark 'legitimate' uprisings that might lead to their deposition? Not really. While some kings did earn poor reputations as a result of the harsh conditions they imposed on their subjects, or even because of impious deeds, their rule was never challenged. Criticism remained hidden in the private sphere (personal correspondence, caricatures of pharaohs drawn by craftsmen) or emerged only when these kings had died and their successors had condemned their memory in order to legitimize, by contrast, their own deeds.

Religion: A cultural bond for the elite?

Religion represented crucial cultural common ground for the elite, especially in a country with deeply rooted local traditions (Shafer 1991). The concept of 'local' gods was one of them, and a source of both identity and a sense of community. Unlike the sophisticated compositions, rituals and monumental settings that marked the official religion, the beliefs of common people were based mainly on magic, amulets and seeking protection against everyday concerns. The official religion, on the contrary, seems to have been more dynamic over time, able to integrate a diversity of local divinities and myths into a 'national' pantheon and to provide legitimation to the ever-changing authority of kings and officials in Egyptian society.

The decentralization of power as of 2500 BC that was inevitable for practical administrative reasons, meant that royal funerary monuments lost their status as ideological 'assembling points' for the ruling elite, a phenomenon paralleled by a relative loss of the centrality of kings as sole mediators with gods (Moreno García 2010a). With the consolidation of local leaders and local temples, new forms of cultural cohesion were needed, and religion played a fundamental role in that. The rise of the cult of Osiris promoted a new cult geography, centred on pilgrimages to Abydos (not by chance the ancestral burial place of pharaohs) and, with it, a new interest in the underworld. The explosion in the number of funerary compositions (known as 'Coffin Texts') from the very end of the third millennium BC was rooted mainly in provincial reformulations of formerly royal texts ('Pyramid Texts'), and was expressed in a rich diversity of local variants (some of them unique). The diffusion of such texts was concomitant with the new expressions of the self echoed in new designs of private funerary monuments: thus stelae and inscribed coffins introduced themes and concerns common to ordinary Egyptians, from the importance of extended families to the use of contracts or the importance of patronage links. The reunification of the monarchy around 2050 BC brought with it a major challenge, however. The new kings, issued from a modest background – they were a provincial (Theban) family with no links with the old Memphite pharaohs – had barely any credible connection to traditional kingship, even less so after the conquest of the area of Memphis and its rich sacerdotal traditions related to the kings of the past. Significantly, the rival kingdoms of Thebes and Heracleopolis were known as 'The House of Antef' and 'The House of Khety' respectively, from the names of their alleged (provincial) ancestors. So, whereas the pharaohs that ruled again over a reunified Egypt relied mostly on their own provincial god, Amun, who had now been raised to 'national' prominence, they also had to win and incorporate into the ruling elite other provincial families that had their own interests, connections and gods. In a way, the position of the Theban kings appears doubly precarious: not only were they (albeit successful) *parvenus*, but they also had to deal with other regional powers. In this light, the restoration and embellishment by the crown of many provincial sanctuaries, mostly in Upper Egypt, reveals a certain weakness and a feeling of illegitimacy among the new rulers.

Later on, the expulsion of the Hyksos by the descendants of provincial Theban leaders and the reunification of Egypt around 1550 BC would only intensify these trends. The immense importance accorded to Amun, the dynastic god of Thebes, and the impressive wealth his temple there received from pharaohs, could not conceal several major problems. For example, the cult's dominant position was actually rather precarious, as it had to address attempts to develop

Figure 7.2 Pyramid texts from the pyramid of King Pepi I at Saqqara.

'imperial' cults (including solar cults, which culminated with the introduction of the god Aton); in some cases, attempts were even made to transform local cults linked to the fortunes of provincial families into 'national' cults (as the Lower Egyptian Ramessides did for the god Seth). However, although such cults were brought to a wider audience through festivals, processions and lavish ceremonies, access to the temples themselves remained off limits to most Egyptians, so they had to try other ways to establish a more intimate, private relationship between gods and people. Individuals could ask for divine help directly, even for solving a particular issue, with the result that many innovations were made: for example, a shrine of the 'Hearing Ear' was built at Karnak, where common people went to have their prayers heard by the gods, whilst private stelae were built to serve the same purpose for the more affluent. In addition, 'personal piety' became a popular specific composition genre in private inscriptions; statue cults of private individuals could act as intermediaries between the petitioner and

Amun; deified officials, like Imhotep or Amenhotep, son of Hapu, were gradually included into the official pantheon of deities and recognized by the king; and oracles were commonly used by commoners from the eighteenth dynasty onwards in order to solve private concerns. All of these measures show that the role of kings as unique mediators between this world and the divine sphere had gone once and for all, and that official religion had to cope with a population that was not only socially diverse but ever more complex culturally. The sharp distinction drawn between elite and 'popular' religion, including access to temples, meant that beyond the elite (in a broad sense) and the beliefs in life after death, official religion failed to provide a unifying corpus of beliefs that was accessible to everyone (Baines 2000). The cult of Amun (the main divinity) lacked the unifying and hope-filled force that would characterize later religions in other places, which emerged in the 'Axial Age' and diffused through imperial entities, Zoroastrianism in the Achaemenid empire or Buddhism in the Mauryan empire being the best known. Egyptian religion, however, promoted only the 'popular' animal cults while 'high religion' became increasingly conservative, entrenched in traditions and in abstruse theological elaborations, which were often expressed in idiosyncratic and complex hieroglyphics (Borgolte 2015). In other words, there was no single doctrine capable of providing both salvation (in the underworld) and everyday hope and relief to all, as both aspects of spiritual beliefs remained split between Osiris on one side and a myriad divinities on the other side, and were also marked by a bias towards the elite. Preservation of the body (via mummification), access to specialized (and costly) liturgical objects and texts were affordable for just a fraction of Egyptian society. In this way, Egyptian religion failed to provide a sense of (religious) community for every citizen, irrespective of his/her social, cultural and geographical background.

In this sense, one aspect still to be explored is the absence of significant ritual plazas in Egyptian cities (at least, judging from the very limited archaeological evidence). For example, in Chuera, an ancient Mesopotamian city, the public plaza was the focal point that unified the households of the residents, the palace and the temple. Yet, a few hundred years after its construction, the central plaza began to fill with refuse from adjacent residential areas, revealing that its original purpose and meaning changed significantly as the city evolved. The remarkable shift from open to closed space indicates that the use and meaning of this square were changing, perhaps due to significant transformations in the social organization of urban life. In other cities, though, temples and palaces did remain the focal point. Plazas facilitated regular face-to-face interactions between urban dwellers and concentrated flows of people, information and goods into a public area. In this role, they were used for a variety of purposes, from religious observance to trading. As foci of community life and the symbolic embodiment of community cohesion, plazas were essential to community integration. That they had such an important role might point to the relative autonomy of urban actors and corporate groups, and to the fact that either they shared power with rulers, or that those rulers needed them – if only as spectators – to legitimize their own authority. In turn, the absence of plazas suggests a more hierarchical and oligarchical society, where 'citizens' were politically irrelevant. That Egyptian temples very rarely fulfilled a similar role, given that access to them was so restricted, provides another clue about the inability of the country's religion to integrate people (Baines 2006). The importance of beliefs in the afterlife (a leitmotif of ancient Egyptian civilization) was probably intended to fill this crucial gap.

Imperial conquest provided pharaohs with additional means to assert their importance in the religious and cult sphere, but they paid a price: such a policy led, inevitably, to the exhibition of the their own fragile position. Conquests funded the building and endowments of temples on an unprecedented scale, but they also revealed that kings, their palaces and their initiatives would all come to an end, while temples remained standing. The funerary temples erected by specific kings were often subject to decay and appropriation of their economic assets by subsequent sovereigns. One way to compensate such fragility was to propagate an exaggerated image of kings as warriors and the 'military wing' of the divine, as well as providers of tribute and offerings. Temple walls were thus inscribed and decorated with meticulous narratives and depictions of military campaigns in addition to extensive lists of offerings and festivals in honour of gods. Kings also used temples to provide social identities to members of the elite (in a broad sense): placing one's statue(s) in a temple, becoming the priest responsible for a king's statue erected in a temple or simply being appointed as priest because of one's position as noble or military man, expressed such status. However, with the loss of the empire at the very end of the second millennium BC, the political and ideological basis of power of kings was reduced considerably.

One final aspect to mention is that regionalism always remained a powerful force in ancient Egypt, and this too was partly expressed through local gods and beliefs. Its importance in cults (and the original syncretism, even 'religious geographies', it produced) contributed to a failure to create enduring 'national' cults outside the funerary sphere. It also prevented the emergence of a 'national' priesthood in the same way as there was a 'national' elite formed of senior dignitaries and courtiers whose interests and social networks extended everywhere. Priesthood, on the contrary, remained mostly local, entrenched in provincial temples and cults, and its members guarded their privileges jealously. Access to priesthood was severely restricted, as was access to their religious compositions (drawn up in increasingly complex writing systems that proved incomprehensible even to learned scribes, except for a very small number of specialists). In the end, localism, coupled with the failure to create a unified 'popular' belief system, precipitated the extinction of Egyptian religon.

All the king's men: Values and training of scribes

The failure of religion to produce a common set of spiritual beliefs and hopes that were accessible to and shared by all, stands in sharp contrast with the success of the Egyptian monarchy in creating solid cultural values and traditions that would be transmitted through millennia. Writing systems, representational codes, literary compositions and ethical values (based on *maat*) prove the endurance of pharaonic culture. However, these were reserved for a tiny cohort of specialists (mainly administrators and courtiers) who were more comfortable when claiming cultural links with their historical peers than with their (mostly illiterate) fellow citizens. Many literary compositions emphasize the privileged existence of scribes in comparison to the hardships and abuses endured by many other professions, from peasants to merchants and craftsmen. Other texts, usually known as 'teachings' and attributed to famous dignitaries of the past (*The Teaching of Ptahotep, The Teaching of Kagemni*), even to kings (*The Teaching for (King) Merykara, The Teaching of Amenemhat*), set the accepted standards for appropriate behaviour, morality and efficiency expected from any servant of the king and gave pharaohs useful advice on good government (including how to cope with potentially unworthy nobles). Other compositions evoked in vivid terms the calamitous consequences that followed the collapse of the monarchy, when social order was ineluctably turned upside down in the absence of royal guidance. These texts, usually referred to as 'pessimistic' literature, in some cases take the form of prophecies that foresee the end of disorder and the reintroduction of justice once kingship is restored (Parkinson 1997).

These compositions were copied and recopied as part of the training of young scribes (Vernus 2016). Not only did the students learn how to write and become acquainted with venerated texts, but they were also introduced to the moral and behavioural codes that would guide their relations towards superiors and subordinates, and also acquired the rhetorical skills they would need to express their opinions cogently in the presence of their colleagues and superiors alike. Written in a highly formalized and unified official language, these texts also furnished the cultural tools indicative of the superiority of scribes, or at least that of those with higher levels of competence. In fact, there is also evidence that the writing and reading ability of many scribes was less than satisfactory, limited to keeping basic accounts and little else. At a slightly higher level, other texts (such as the *Book of Kemit*) recorded sets of polite formulae that could be used to address a superior or to begin and conclude a letter, among other formalities (although superiors typically addressed their assistants by letter in rather peremptory terms). Finally, model letters showing how to write reports about any topic imaginable (from lists of cities and goods to requests and petitions) introduced young scribes to geographical and practical knowledge that would prove useful for their future activities. All these texts were written in hieratic, the writing system normally used in everyday activities; hieroglyphs, by contrast, were reserved for a rather select minority of scholars – its informative and ornamental function was well suited to religious and monument-related texts.

Belles lettres were thus essential to the training of middle- and high-ranking officials. Despite the fact that texts and illustrations present officials as instrumental agents of the royal will, there are many references to councils and boards of dignitaries that advised kings and took an active part in decision-making processes alongside their sovereigns. On such occasions, eloquence and a skilful presentation of facts and personal points of view gave officials the chance to win the king's favour and to enhance their careers – or at least gain the attention of powerful patrons. These competences were crucial in a highly competitive environment such as the royal court, where the top echelons of both administration and courtiers comprised only several dozens of people. Intrigues, conspiracies and slander were current currency there and opened many opportunities for promotion and reward, but also for disgrace and dismissal. A strict etiquette, reinforced by a complex set of honorific titles, indicated how officials fit into a broader hierarchy of peers and superiors. Other ceremonies, such as the giving of gifts and awards by the king to a particular official, in the presence of the court, would enhance that person's position further.

Nevertheless it would be too simplistic to regard kings as the *sole* source of honours and promotion. Many officials also kept their own networks of relations and contacts, cemented by intermarriage, as well as their own bases of power. In some cases, they held their position because their families had occupied key roles for generations; in others, provincial officials born into families with strong local roots benefited from both a privileged starting point from which to promote their careers at the court and a comfortable place to withdraw to, should things go awry. Kings had to work with these families as they were essential to the stability of the throne (Moreno García 2013a; Raedler 2004 and 2006). This means that in periods of monarchical crisis, some provinces excelled as repositories of traditional culture and cradles of innovation, and would later be incorporated into the mainstream of a renewed 'high' culture centred once more around the king.

The combined weight of provincial forces, of a highly personalized and oligarchical organization of power and of a strong sense of royal continuity might explain a peculiarity of Egyptian culture, in that there is nothing along the lines of 'Pharaonic Confucianism', despite the rich corpus of texts providing moral and strategic advice to officials. The central point is probably the absence of a true sense of history. In fact, history (chronicles, memoirs, histories of particular reigns, periods or institutions, etc.) would have introduced a dangerous and all too human perspective for a monarchy whose ultimate source of legitimacy was descent from gods themselves and the continuous re-enactment of kingship by individual pharaohs. Unlike the Chinese empire, which was born in the late first millennium BC after long and painful struggles between kingdoms with their own traditions and legitimacies, expressed through a rich historical legacy, the early consolidation of Egypt as a unique monarchy was quite different. Emerging in a period (the late fourth millennium BC) in which the use of writing was very restricted and continuous texts were simply absent, the monarchy had no competitors offering alternative justifications of power and interpretations of the past. Given the exceptional longevity of the first Egyptian monarchy, an uninterrupted succession of monarchs from 3100 to 2150 BC, pharaohs produced, imposed and consolidated a unique (high) culture as well as traditions of power that were subsequently adapted, reinterpreted and developed by their successors, but never seriously challenged, even by local powers aspiring to kingship. Pharaohs epitomized social order, political stability and the cyclical repetition of acts that maintained cosmic order within an undisturbed sequence of time. As a result, there were few opportunities for the emergence of an autonomous idea of the state embodied by its civil servants, framed by laws (both moral and juridical) and able to operate in the absence of kings, even less to limit the authority of the sovereign. In theory, the king was identified with the state (the term *per-aa*, 'great house', which designated the palace originally, became synonymous with 'pharaoh', and even with the state) and the continuity of kingship through an uninterrupted line of sovereigns constituted the very backbone of the state. Perhaps the most 'Confucian moment' of Egyptian history (in the sense of Pines 2015b) occurred in the late third millennium BC, when the monarchy was rebuilt and the country reunified after a period of political division and conflict between two kingdoms, Heracleopolis and Thebes. Heracleopolis apparently preserved more effectively the old traditions of the monarchy and its scribal institutions, as young provincial nobles still frequented the royal palace to be educated with princes (Lichtheim 1988: 29). However, the victorious Theban kings who finally reunified Egypt incorporated into their administration many scribes and managers from the north, at least judging from their name, 'Khety', typical of the Heracleopolitan kings. It was also at the very beginning of the second millennium BC that literary texts appeared for the first time, intended to train scribes and to instil fresh values to a new class of civil servants. The fact that some of these texts were attributed to a scribe also named Khety (*The Teaching of Khety, The Teaching of (King) Amenemhat I*), celebrated as a great scholar many centuries later, and that a treaty on the art of government had an Heracleopolitan king as its main protagonist (*The Teaching for (King) Merykara*), may point to a corps of dignitaries that circulated between courts and whose cultural competences and values served their new masters at Thebes. However, their own experience of government, statehood and kingship, as well as of the limits and vulnerability of these institutions, vanished rapidly behind a new palace-based culture and a restored monarchy that aspired, once more, to an eternal cycle (of legitimate kings succeeding one another on the throne of a unified Egypt), which left no (official) place for doubts and questions about its capacities and authority.

Monumentality, ornamentalism and ceremonialism: Landscapes of power

Monumentality – that is, the commissioning and construction of monuments – is a distinctive trait of ancient Egypt. By using stone to build well-constructed monuments and to create perdurable symbolic landscapes, the Egyptian state expressed its wish to transmit an ideal of order, hierarchy and territoriality that was further supported by a rich iconography which included hieroglyphs themselves. Tombs and temples were the pivotal elements of such landscapes, accompanied by impressive inscriptions and scenes carved in liminal areas intended to delimit the borders of the kingdom and to glorify the active intervention of kings as peace-keepers, and to prevent intrusions (identified with disorder and chaos). Perhaps the most unusual aspect of such monumentality in its earlier stages, especially when compared with Mesopotamia, is the *weight* of funerary monuments compared with 'civil' architecture (such as royal palaces) and even temples (although monumental reed architecture might also have been quite significant; Bussmann 2015). Being the most conspicuous landmark, the tomb of the ruler, surrounded by the burials of his/her officials, epitomized the strength of personal bonds and personal power in an otherwise poorly urbanized society. It also expressed the monarch's capacity to rally the elite of the kingdom around him. In Mesopotamia, by contrast, temples as well as monumental structures (perhaps used to host urban councils formed by prominent people) were the most important constructions, while royal tombs lacked the significance they enjoyed in Egypt. Monumentality expressed thus two very different configurations of power in these two different areas. Not by chance, Mesopotamia was an urbanized region in which kingship took a long time to consolidate itself compared with more impersonal but divinely rooted authorities.

Early Egypt, on the other hand, was organized as a network of royal centres and personal bonds centred around kings and spread over a relatively large area (from Elephantine to the Mediterranean). It was only from around 2500 BC that a more complex system of power, based on an increasing bureaucracy and an inevitable decentralization in a country with strong regional traditions, led to the gradual reduction of the symbolic monumental centrality of kings. The outcome was the increasing visibility of temples and decorated tombs in the provinces; note that senior dignitaries based at Memphis did not necessarily build their tombs around the pyramid of the reigning king.

This trend continued during the early second millennium BC, when powerful provincial families built their tombs on an impressive, almost royal scale, and when provincial temples were built and decorated with high-quality materials. Royal pyramids failed to produce durable symbolic landscapes comparable to those of the third millennium. It would be too simplistic to establish a direct link between the dimensions and setting of royal funerary monuments and the actual extent of the authority of kings, although both phenomena probably point to a monarchy whose power base had weakened. Temples – and in particular those dedicated to Amun at Thebes (cradle of the new royal dynasty) and Osiris at Abydos (ancestral burial place of kings) – emerged as focal points of a new symbolic landscape aiming to create a sort of 'national' religion, supported by pilgrimages and an innovative funerary culture (Nyord 2018). In a way, this meant that kingship was no longer the primary source of legitimation and authority. Later on, from around 1500 BC, this trend deepened despite an ostensibly more favourable context for kings. For the first time, Egypt created an empire that encompassed Nubia, Egypt and the Southern Levant and which monitored crucial trade routes between inner Africa, the Red Sea, the Eastern Mediterranean and the Near East. The arrival of foreign tribute was but one manifestation of this change, others being a new militarist ethos in which kings celebrated their victories at the head of their troops, and the development of diplomacy and imperial expansion, which put Egypt in contact with foreign powers.

However, the central position of kings in the hierarchy under these new conditions was not followed by an increased *symbolic* centrality of kings in their relations with gods and temples. Royal tombs were now isolated and hidden in a remote desert area near Thebes, while royal palaces retained their residential and ceremonial role, and provided the setting for military parades, the reception of tribute from colourful foreign delegations, the public delivery of awards to dignitaries, etc. Not by chance, this was the time when the palace (the Great House) became synonymous with the king and the state (in the vein of the Sublime Porte in the Ottoman Empire). But palaces remained short-lived structures, built with perishable materials (bricks) at a time when temples became truly massive, at a scale never seen before, and when their managerial and economic activities transformed them into the most important economic institutions in the country. So when kings decided to immortalize their deeds, they chose to do so precisely – on the walls of temples. The ideal landscapes thus built in the second half of the second millennium BC suggest two major weaknesses in an otherwise apparently 'powerful' monarchy. Given their own modest origins in provincial Thebes, kings needed the support of powerful families from Elkab, Edfu and other localities between 1650 and 1400 BC, as well as the legitimacy provided by the gods, to consolidate and expand their authority. Later on, when a new provincial family was raised to the throne (the Ramessides, from the Eastern Delta), they also promoted massive temple-construction programmes and the appropriation of other kings' monuments in order to legitimate their power. In the mid-second millennium BC, though, the ruling kings were in the precarious position of having *no* apparent links with previous monarchs. So the importance bestowed on Amun and on military success might hide, paradoxically, the lack of a solid basis for kingship; here, rulers tried to make themselves 'useful' by stressing their role as protectors of the gods and as military leaders. The emphasis put in recruiting nobles and soldiers as priests in the temples founded by pharaohs everywhere may point to their need to gain support from traditional and new elites. It is also noteworthy that temples became the main foci of organization in conquered Nubia and they also helped reinforce the links between the local elite and the king, as donation stelae show. When the empire collapsed, the monarchy and its resources also weakened, while temples survived and remained as nodes of wealth and institutional stability. The stability of the country might go on without kings, but it would surely falter without temples and the elites that controlled them.

Temples also became increasingly important in the construction of social identities (Bussmann 2015). Oracles, processions, pilgrimages, 'visits' by gods from one sanctuary to another, the transport of ceremonial boats, etc., were special occasions that served to display the pageantry surrounding the most important divinities. As of the end of the third millennium BC, temples became key builders of social identities (from 'city-gods' and local sanctuaries to experiments in creating 'national' cults), while the priesthood remained an indispensable source of income and prestige for local elites. And when the monarchy weakened in the late second millennium BC, this tendency was most visible in the less economically dynamic areas (such as southern-most Egypt), situated far from the burgeoning Mediterranean coast. Contrary with the conditions prevailing in the Middle and Late Bronze Age, when foreign monarchs became pharaohs in the first millennium BC, such as the Persian and Greek kings, they were much less dependent on the support of temples to assert their authority in Egypt, probably due to the tools at their disposal (such as military force and increased fiscal resources). This change raises many questions about the real basis of power of Bronze Age pharaohs and their dependence on temples and their symbolic paraphernalia. Ultimately, the construction of temples might point less to the strength of kings than to their need to assert symbolically their presence in areas with strong local interests and power groups. The link between the small step pyramids built around 2600 BC and the provincial temples embellished or restored by Mentuhotep II, Ramesses II and Ramesses III, may thus provide a crucial connection between royal power, local autonomy and the construction of ideal landscapes.

State values and lower society

Many official inscriptions express the concern of superiors about the well-being of their subordinates, from the prevention of abuses and injustice to debt cancellation and protection. In an elaborate tale such as *The Eloquent Peasant*, the main character, a man living in a remote area, delineates with vibrant oratory what subordinates expected from superiors and agents of the king in order to preserve social harmony. Of course, this text was a creation of the scribal class, not a real account of the opinions, concerns and expectations of common people, but it is crucial to understanding how Egyptians understood social order and prosperity within a firm but paternalistic hierarchy in which everybody found his/her place.

To begin with, social hierarchy and restricted social networks were the very things that prevented the emergence of something close to modern concepts of individuality, freedom of choice or 'public opinion', all of which are fundamental to the emergence of a body of *citizens* capable of influencing the political agenda through their claims, opinions and actions. In fact, extended families, patronage networks, communal reciprocity and village solidarity under the control of local potentates and, finally, state paternalism (at best) hampered the emergence of an autonomous political sphere or just simply individualism. This was a relatively 'small' world in which individual action was framed by a dense network of social obligations and constraints. Direct contact with the state was unilateral, not reciprocal, and took the form either of interventions by royal agents whose orders and arbitrary measures were not up for discussion, or religious activities centred around temples under the control of local authorities. Under these circumstances, the penetration of state values among common people (in the form of propaganda, etc.) was hardly a political priority for the authorities. What is known as 'sapiential' literature, which was intended to train scribes, describes in vivid terms what could be expected in periods of turmoil and subversion of legitimate order: chaos. It was never considered that the restoration of order would be based on dialogue and political deliberation between rulers and subjects; rather it hinged on a new and legitimate sovereign gaining access to the throne and being able to reconstruct the apparatus of government. Divine support would then again bring prosperity and proper rule.

Material culture provides some clues about the degree of penetration of official culture among common people. Their religious values (the most accessible for us) seem quite different to the complex system of beliefs reproduced in papyri, temples and scenes in tombs. They were much more practical and aimed at solving everyday concerns, while the occasional use of coffins, statues, etc., reveals at least a desire to imitate the cultural standards and prestige of the elite. Furthermore, such imitation was limited to people of a relatively lofty status who could afford good-quality objects and who wanted to reproduce – if only at a modest level – the practices of the elite, including the occasional building of mastabas intended for collective, not individual, burials. However, evidence also reveals that people reproduced cultural values that differed dramatically from those proclaimed by the elite and were still able, on occasion, to penetrate into high culture: economic autonomy meant that ostensibly 'humble' people could nonetheless support themselves; seals were used in private, domestic and other economic spheres not necessarily controlled by the state; houses built originally by the state could be modified to meet the needs of extended families; amulets and crude figurines of the gods were manufactured and bought; ancestor cults became the foci of group identities, etc. Ideals such as hierarchy and subordination to officials were somewhat challenged by private monuments that stress seemingly opposing concepts such as family links and other forms of solidarity that were certainly not devoid of tensions, but capable in the end of providing protection and comfort to people. The penetration of such practices (particularly the use of seals and contracts, importance of family and patronage networks) in the sphere of religious compositions (such as the Coffin Texts) prove the vitality of some values independent of, but ultimately not incompatible with, those promoted by the state. Culinary and clothing practices (the consumption of 'impure' pork and fish versus elite beef; use of wool and cloaks versus elite linen, etc.) also express further differences that are represented rarely (if at all) in the picturesque scenes of 'everyday life' painted onto tomb walls.

The contradictions embodied by these different sets of values became more evident when they came into close proximity. One example concerns the use of silver and the increasing importance of commerce in Egyptian society during the early first millennium BC. Literary compositions from this period warned people against greediness and an excessive love for wealth. However, there is also evidence that traders formally accepted these dominant cultural values, to the point that they and their activities are practically invisible in the monumental record. This cannot be explained by an assumption that traders could not afford quality monuments for themselves (stelae, statues, coffins, decorated tombs), but probably that they preferred to present themselves as holders of other, more respectable, positions within their communities (priests, administrators, etc.). Written evidence reveals nevertheless that they built their tombs and houses close to those of other members of the elite (priests, officials, etc.). Another example concerns the importance of village life and village identity, also evoked in literary texts of the first millennium BC that explicitly warned people against the inhabitants of neighbouring villages. Finally, oracles like those preserved from the small community of artists at Deir el-Medina reveal a world in which petitions addressed to the gods aimed at settling commonplace disputes that, apparently, the community could not address or was not interested in sufficiently to solve through other means. The pharaoh's justice was probably too expensive (in terms of the costs associated with ad hoc courts formed by dignitaries, not professional judges) and reserved for conflicts between people of a certain status, while internal mechanisms to enact authority did not always prove efficient in this particular area. Finally, mentions of people who escaped their obligations towards the state, or who returned to nomadic lifestyles when royal authority collapsed, point to a kind of 'silent resistance' that stands in sharp contrast to the supposed benevolence of kings towards their subjects.

8

Sociopolitical Change and the State

In his memoirs, published posthumously in 1867, the Italian politician Massimo d'Azeglio made his famous statement that 'we have made Italy. Now we must make Italians'. In my opinion, this sentence could be easily paraphrased to define the early Egyptian monarchy: kings from Abydos were successful enough to create (around 3100 BC) the earliest and most stable *territorial* state of the ancient Near East, claiming exclusive control over the area stretching from Elephantine to the Mediterranean along 1,000 kilometres. They also succeeded in laying the foundations of a sophisticated culture that would thrive in this area, the most conspicuous elements of which (writing, visual codes) were to last for millennia. However, royal control was far from homogeneous over such territory, and the backbone of the early state consisted of little more that a network of crown-controlled centres scattered across the country. The support and the collaboration of the local potentates was thus crucial, while local populations in the north seem to have enjoyed a good deal of autonomy. In other words, the early state bore (in a way) the taint of a peculiar original sin: a very early territorial unity, loosely controlled via a network of hubs and in search of stable institutions that would help support an otherwise highly personalized exercise of power. This process was the exact opposite of that operational in early Mesopotamia, where supra-regional powers (the Akkadian empire) appeared relatively late and had to cope with a myriad city-states, each with established traditions and identities, well-rooted administrative and economic institutions as well as an impressive degree of economic integration with the immediate territory under the control of each city-state. In Egypt, though, pharaohs created a state *first*, then struggled to assert and effectively expand their authority in a barely urbanized provincial world.

Regionalism always remained a powerful force hidden behind the apparent monolithic authority of kings. However, this was only part of the story. Due to Egypt's strategic geographical position, the influence from the trade and economic networks crossing the Nile Valley was another force that could have altered the balance of power between regions, between the capital and the provinces, and between local nodes of wealth-accumulation. This influence left a strong mark in some periods of Egyptian history, and helped orientate the state and its interests toward one area or another (the Mediterranean, the Levant, Nubia). The impact of these forces on Egyptian society was considerable and may explain long-term dynamics that are much more important than those derived from brief political struggles between court factions and the succession of monarchs and 'dynasties'. But the very nature of pharaonic ideology, with its emphasis on durability, stability and (royal) order, often succeeded in obscuring the influence derived from these forces. Their influence, nevertheless, was unavoidable, especially in the organization of kingship and high culture, both of which had to adapt in response, as can be seen in the composition of literary texts, in attempts to restore traditions, in the integration of local nobles into the core of the state decision-making ruling elite, etc. From this perspective, the conspicuous near-absence of traders, cities, urban dwellers and so on in artistic representations, despite their increasing importance over the centuries, stands in strong contrast with the overwhelming presence of an idealized rural world dominated by large noble households, agricultural activities and a traditional hierarchy. Far from this idealized world, however, the significance of trade, urban expansion and geopolitics shaped the state and underpinned the rise of Thebes around 2000 BC, the shift of political and economic power from Upper Egypt to the Delta around 1300 BC and a definitive integration into the Mediterranean sphere from 1000 BC onwards. Finally, it was in periods of political crisis when cultural innovation flourished and that more realistic assessments of social organization and values (trade and merchants, economic profitability, personal initiative) left their trace in literary compositions.

So, far from being a monolithic structure ruled by an absolute sovereign, the pharaonic state was a dynamic structure within which the monarchy flexed and adapted itself in search of stability and for the best conditions to guarantee the reproduction of the ruling elite. Social and economic forces shaped the state and justified the many forms it took throughout three millennia.

Regional powers and new social dynamics: The second half of the third millennium BC

The early organization of the state seems based on a loose network of crown centers dispersed across the country and on the alliance and collaboration of the local elites (Moreno García 2013b). The most conspicuous of these centers were the *ḥwt*, a kind of tower that acted as the centre of an agricultural and productive unit which included fields, workers and cattle, and which also played the role of storage facilities and even defensive structures. From the analysis of the geographical distribution of the dignitaries in charge, it appears that the *ḥwt* network covered virtually all of Upper and Lower Egypt around 2300 and 2200 BC and that they replaced older centres constructed in the first centuries of the third millennium BC (the 'great-*ḥwt*' was the most prominent of them). As they concentrated agricultural wealth and their administrators were sourced from the local nobility, they probably helped concentrate people at specific points along the Nile. Temples constituted another pole of social and economic power that complemented the role played by these crown centres and which, quite possibly, provided the royal administration with the legitimacy it needed to penetrate into and influence the local sphere. Finally, a tax-system based on the control of workforces and mobile wealth (gold, cattle) completed this administrative structure. Note that when the *ḥwt* network disappeared at around 2000 BC, never to be restored, towns and cities became conspicuous landmarks and fiscal units. Tell el-Daba, in the eastern Delta, a trading centre and locality that developed originally from a ḥwt, is a good example of the way in which these centres concentrated population and wealth in strategic areas.

The implementation of these networks of authority would have been impossible without the support of the local elites. As temples benefited from royal donations of land, temples and ḥwt helped rally provincial leaders to the monarchy, and the expansion of both institutions in the regions was concomitant with major changes in the composition of the elites of the kingdom about 2500/2450 BC. These changes were twofold. First, kings began delegating authority to dignitaries from outside the 'royal family' (in a broad sense). Their number increased, as did their visibility in the monumental record at the same time that kings married and incorporated women from this social background into the ruling elite (Bárta & Dulíková 2015). Second, this shift also reached the provinces, as local nobles were co-opted into the highest elite and allowed to build decorated tombs in their homelands.

Figure 8.1 Lists of titles of rank and function expressed the social position of officials and their place in the hierarchical structure of the kingdom.

These transformations paved the way for two major developments. First was the expansion of the *ḥwt* in the provinces, and the creation of new administrative departments and functions supporting the administration of Upper Egypt. The fact that local nobles boasted about their ability to increase the resources and fiscal revenue of the territories under their care suggests that kings were seeking to expand the crown's income. Second, this goal seems related to the creation of the logistics needed to supply expeditions along the Nile and beyond, to Nubia, the Western Desert and the Levant. There is evidence that trade activities were becoming increasingly important in Egypt from around 2500 BC, so adequate logistic support for merchants, royal agents and armies sent abroad was a major concern for the monarchy. Trade, the expansion of income and provincial prosperity went hand in hand, but an expanding provincial bureaucracy focused squarely on assimilating the codes of 'high' culture (decorated tombs, costly funerary equipment, lavish lifestyles, substantial retinues, etc.), also led to the growth of wealth spent and invested in the provinces.

Finally, the (presumably) new lineage of pharaohs (about 2345 BC) who arrived on the throne engendered some opposition from some sectors of the court (several senior officials were deposed and a queen put on trial) in what can be perceived as a weak basis for royal power. Moreover, the rapid succession of many dignitaries (some of them quite young) at the head of the main offices of state points to some instability, an impression confirmed by the traces of intentional destruction of the depictions installed by some officials in their own tombs, as a sort of punishment. In this tumultuous context, kings chose to reinforce their links with the provincial nobility: they married provincial women (whose families were raised to a prominent position in the kingdom), they promoted provincial officials to the highest offices in the land and many Upper Egyptian leaders were granted the title of 'great chief of the province'. These developments only continued and deepened tendencies that had emerged well before. The outcome was the gradual weakening of the monarchy while some provincial leaders reinforced their own power, particularly those residing at strategic crossroads – such as

Coptos, Thebes and Elephantine – at a time when trade with foreign territories flourished. In the end, these regional rulers succeeded in controlling foreign trade and tribute and followed their own politics irrespective of any royal initiative, as kings proved unable to curb their increasing autonomy. The fall of the monarchy and the political fragmentation of the country would come as no surprise at around 2160 BC.

Two lessons may be inferred from this process. The first, common to other societies and periods of the ancient Near East, is that changes in the sphere of trade had the potential to destabilize political structures and to inspire new, adaptive political responses to the challenges they posed. The second is that the very survival of the monarchy depended on its capacity to maintain a delicate equilibrium between different forces (regional powers, the court, local nodes of accumulation of wealth), as well as to control the circulation of wealth in the country and avoid the emergence of substantial alternative poles of wealth-accumulation. When the monarchy failed in both roles, it collapsed and new institutional arrangements were necessary to restore kingship and territorial unity. Behind the ideological façade of a monolithic power and a rigidly centralized economy, the reality was much more dynamic.

Coping with new social forces: The failure of the monarchy (2050–1750 BC)

The end of the monarchy, and the emergence of several regional powers, did not halt trade and Egypt's integration in the sphere of international exchanges. This means that Egyptian commercial activities with foreign territories were not based uniquely on the initiatives promoted by the state but that such activities continued, even thrived, in the absence of any central authority, a process that only deepened socio-political and economic trends that had surfaced long before. Four (perhaps five) major nodes of political power are now discernable between 2160 and 2050 BC. Elephantine, in the south, kept its traditional role as gateway to Nubia, and its elites developed their own forms of legitimation (principally a cult that venerated an ancestor, Heqaib, a caravan leader) while, on the political front, they traded with Heracleopolis while being loosely integrated into the Theban kingdom. Thebes consolidated itself as the major political centre in southern Egypt, its fortune in all probability linked to its geographical position at the crossroads of desert routes leading into the Western Desert as well as to the Red Sea and the port of Mersa/Wadi Gawasis. Further north, the area between Asyut and Bersheh/Beni Hasan became a major focus of political power, and its leaders provided crucial support to the Heracleopolitan rulers. It seems that the fortunes of this locale were closely related to its contacts with the Levant and to the control of fluvial trade. The fourth node was Heracleopolis itself, and its prosperity and political importance seem linked to the development of a new trade axis between the Western Delta, the Fayum, Middle Egypt and, quite probably, Nubia. Finally, the area of Tell el-Daba, in the Eastern Delta, also grew as a major trade hub, apparently under Heracleopolitan political influence.

It was also in this period (2150–2050 BC) that Asian peoples settled in Egypt – in some cases serving in the Heracleopolitan armies – while Levantine 'warrior tombs' appear at Kom el-Hisn, in the Western Delta. It is possible that the sudden importance of Asian populations and the trade axis through the Western Delta may correspond to the increase of Egyptian contact with the Aegean at a time when Cyprus became one of the main providers of copper in the Near East. The previously influential network of *ḥwt* centres declined and finally disappeared, but harbours (*dmj*) and the settlements that surrounded them flourished, to the point that the very word *dmj* became synonymous with 'city, town'. It could well be that both phenomena are connected as archaeology reveals that some cities expanded (Edfu), others witnessed the creation of new areas inhabited by a 'middle class' (Dendera, Elephantine, Abu Ghalib, etc.) and others flourished, judging from the construction, for the first time, of richly decorated tombs and from modest burials containing small objects created from precious metals (Barnugi, Kom el-Hisn, Middle Egypt, etc.). The increasing use of seals and of mentions of sealed documents in private transactions suggest the expansion of private transactions, a fact concomitant with the popularity of the feminine title 'lady of the house', borne by women who managed their own financial affairs. Archaeological forays have also revealed the expansion of patronage networks centred on powerful local potentates, as well as the emergence of an affluent 'middle class', particularly at sites such as Abydos. Not by chance, a new ideological motif was introduced in private inscriptions, celebrating people who had accumulated wealth from their own efforts, rather than due to help or favour from the monarchy, and who could provide for themselves, for their families and for their households. Also for the first time, people boasted in their inscriptions about the personal accumulation of wealth, mainly the acquisition of land, serfs, cattle and ships. Far from being a period of shortage and social unrest, it seems that private wealth expanded in a context of expanding trade networks and of a weakened state-run taxation system.

When Thebes finally prevailed, Egypt was reunified and the monarchy restored (c. 2050 BC), the new pharaohs had to cope with a social and political environment very different to that faced by their predecessors in the late third millennium BC. To begin with, the reunification of the country seems based more on negotiation and mutual agreements than on total military conquest. The provincial potentates of Middle Egypt switched sides, retained their privileged position (they were practically the only holders of the old title of 'great chief' of a province) and seem to have inherited the control over trade networks formerly in the hands of Heracleopolis. Thus, the chiefs of Bersheh boasted about their control of and links with myrrh, but their colleagues from Beni Hasan, Meir and Asyut were also involved in international trade, foreign relations and control over 'gateways' to external territories (Moreno García 2017). As for the potentates' monumental (almost royal) tombs, they displayed their wealth, power and autonomy. Elephantine's rulers enjoyed a similarly privileged position, to the point that one of them, Sarenput I, celebrated in his inscriptions that pharaohs now ruled for his own benefit! Not by chance, the inscriptions of King Mentuhotep II, who reunified Egypt, as well as those of his main dignitaries, reveal a real concern about foreign commerce, the supply of precious goods and the opening-up of trade routes. Pharaohs also depended on the good will of provincial potentates to assert their authority, even to face down 'usurpers' and consolidate their position on the throne. Even the burgeoning 'middle class' of this period constructed costly monuments and its values penetrated into high culture, in particular those of the importance of extended families, patronage networks and private patrimonies at the disposal of affluent household heads.

The very existence of such a 'middle class' and of autonomous provincial potentates, all of whom were able to acquire and control substantial riches for themselves, points to a major problem – the monarch's apparent inability to implement an efficient tax system. This was an issue not only because the old network of *ḥwt* centres was never restored, but also because royal monuments (pyramids, temples) appear somewhat modest in size and kings were eager to embellish and make donations to provincial sanctuaries, dominated by local elites. It is perhaps significant that one of the most important displays of architectural monumentality was the network of fortresses/trading centres built in Nubia near to the Nile's second cataract. These impressive buildings aimed to concentrate, regulate and tax trade with Nubia, as Tell el-Daba did with regard to the Levant. Trade had become a major concern for the crown and for provincial potentates alike, a circumstance that raises many questions about the very nature of power in Egypt in the early second millennium BC. Were kings mere instruments in the hands of provincial potentates, implementing the policies these leaders pursued? Were the very continuity and autonomy of these potentates proof of the commonality of interests between them and the monarchy, or just an expression of royal powerlessness? The fact that kings introduced co-regencies in order to ensure an orderly transmission of power from the reigning ruler to his intended successor and that, when this system expired, kingship took the form of an oligarchical system before its final gentle collapse (kings came from a restricted number of noble families), point to a monarchy that encountered many difficulties in consolidating itself and in monitoring the flows of wealth across Egypt. When the monarchy collapsed, the fortresses/emporia in Nubia continued to be used, trade continued to flourish between Upper Egypt and the now-independent Eastern Delta, the trade routes that linked Nubia to the Mediterranean remained open and rich tombs in the Fayum region, with costly foreign goods, reveal that wealth was still held in private hands. Thus the monarchy appears to be somewhat secondary in terms of traders' interests. Ultimately, it seems as though the monarchy of the early second millennium BC failed to cope with the challenges of the late third millennium BC, when it proved unable to control effectively the consequences of expanding trade, of the growth of the logistics and bureaucracy necessary to support it (in which local potentates were indispensable) and of the flows of wealth derived from it.

Temples and empire: A definitive solution (1550–1070 BC)?

When the monarchy was reunified again, around 1550 BC, its foundations were very different from those of previous periods. Military expansion abroad was a feature that marked the second half of the second millennium BC (Gnirs 1996). It led to the creation of an empire that encompassed Nubia and most of the Levant and that, for the first time, put Egypt in direct contact with the main powers of the Near East (Liverani 2001; O'Connor & Cline 1998; Cline & O'Connor 2006; Cline & O'Connor 2012). Temples also emerged as massive economic structures, judging not only from their impressive architecture but also from the abundant epigraphic and papyrological information they produced. As pivotal elements in the organization of the territory and of the economy, it is significant that temples gained in prominence not only in Egypt but also in Nubia. A further element is that a major shift in the regional balance of power resulted in the consolidation of Lower

Egypt as the most dynamic economic area in Egypt, given that it was open to the Mediterranean and thus to international trade, particularly from the Ramesside era onwards. Another consequence was that traditional foci of political influence, such as the area between Asyut and Bersheh/Beni Hasan, in Middle Egypt, seem to have lost most of their former importance. Finally, cities began to become prominent in the documentary record. What do these phenomena reveal about the social, economic and political forces that shaped Egypt for five centuries?

Coming after a period of political division, the reunification of Egypt was once again steered by Thebes, but it took a very different path from that followed at the end of the third millennium BC. Several inscriptions found in the core area of the Theban kingdom prior to the reunification (Elkab, Coptos, Medamud, Ermant, Thebes itself) reveal that the reorganization and endowment of the temples in this area, including regulations about access to their goods, were a major concern for the monarchy and its provincial allies. Temples played a crucial role in integrating elites and territories into the nascent kingdom, and this policy was continued and expanded in the next centuries. In fact, many inscriptions mention that kings founded temples, provided them with income and appointed nobles and military personnel as priests. Administrative papyri, such as the Wilbour Papyrus, list thousands of modest temple land tenures granted to priests, soldiers but also to prominent members of the provincial society, such as moderately wealthy peasants, 'ladies', etc. It is clear that kings used temples as tools via which to rally the local elites to their support, and to control and administer the resources of the kingdom. Finally, statues dedicated to kings, placed in temples and endowed with fields and offerings, were granted to distinguished officials who performed cults in exchange for revenue. Even the cultivation of temple land was assured in part by wealthy peasants able to deliver thousands of sacks of grain to the sanctuaries, in all probability in return for a share of the harvest.

Why temples? A close insight into the circumstances that led Theban kings to power gives some clues (Shafer 1997). Unlike the reunification process that occurred half a millennium before, and which was presumably based on negotiation and the integration of local elites into a nascent unified administration, Theban kings now derived their power solely from war. Apparently, this was not the time to find common ground, but rather to ruthlessly eliminate any potential rivals. War was launched against the northern kingdom ruled by the Hyksos until it was destroyed and their monarchs forced to exile themselves in the southern Levant. Internal opposition was also suppressed through repressive measures, as revealed by the cases of Teti, son of Minhotep (at Coptos), Teti, son of Pepi (defeated at Nefrusi, close to Beni Hasan), and Teti-an (defeated and killed in Nubia). These examples show that, other than a possible family link (although names formed with the element 'Teti' were common at this time), these rebels operated at the very ends of the route that connected Middle Egypt (Beni Hasan) and Nubia through the oases and that some of them expected a degree of support from Nubia. And it was precisely along that route that the Theban king Kamose intercepted a message sent by the Hyksos king to the Nubian ruler of Kush asking for his help against the menacing power of a rising Thebes. However, contrary to what had happened five centuries before, Theban kings avoided the mistake made by their predecessors, who were recognized as sovereigns of a unified Egypt but at the price of preserving the power and interests of the elites rooted in Middle Egypt. The intransigence now shown by the rulers of Thebes was based on the use of warfare on a scale previously unknown, leading campaigns deep into Nubia and the Levant and transforming the army into an essential institution under their control. Finally, if an apparent division of areas of influence between Egypt and Nubia had justified the construction of a network of fortresses/emporia in previous centuries, now Nubia was simply conquered and the kingdom of Kush suppressed. Negotiation and co-existence with potential rivals were no longer tolerated on the Nile.

However, building this kind of power required new tools. One of them was military, while the other one was more integrative, a sort of carrot-and-stick policy. An expansionist policy opened new paths for wealth, position and integration into a burgeoning state and its bureaucratic apparatus, the ideal conditions in which to shape a new elite who owed everything to the king and whose influence and expectations could now expand well beyond their original limited local background. The destruction of the existing powers of Middle and Lower Egypt during the wars of reunification (the Hyksos and their allies) also made it possible for the new rulers to confiscate land, to settle soldiers and administrators and to found temples in the newly acquired territories. Small 'islands' of loyal officers and soldiers thus dotted the countryside, as the Wilbour Papyrus or the inscription of Mose reveal (Eyre 2013: 155–232).

In this context, the expansion of temples, richly endowed by the crown, prevented one of the major risks that pharaohs faced in the early second millennium BC, that of a monarchy confronted by an independent 'middle class' and by powerful local lords. Temples helped to build loyalties and integrate wealthy local elites and sub-elites. Under divine protection and disposing (theoretically) of inalienable resources, temples guaranteed income and institutional stability for the new elite, free from the hazards of partition and inheritance that weakened private patrimonies. Their beneficiaries were also able to follow individual strategies and to escape from any potential interference from their kin, on the principles of reciprocity and solidarity. Finally, as new temples were built, richly endowed and put under the protection of kings, they also promoted the emergence of a class of 'rentiers' whose prosperity was closely linked to royal support. As relatively stable institutions, temples were able to harmonize individualist strategies with state interests and to reorganize the elites of the kingdom and their very bases of power and wealth, which were now closely attached to the monarchy (Moreno García 2013c).

The success of this system becomes apparent when considering the fate of provincial potentates. The inscription of Sataimau of Edfu (around 1550 BC) provides an excellent example of the patronage provided by the king to provincial temples as well as of the rewards bestowed on local potentates, especially in a period of war, reunification and reorganization for Egypt, when their collaboration and support were crucial. Appointed as priest of a statue of the king in the temple of Horus at Edfu, he received substantial income both in offerings and land (at least 10 ha). His case is similar to that of his contemporary Iuf, also from Edfu, and confirms that temples provided substantial income, prestige and rank to local elites. In the long term, these elites became closely linked to temples and kings, in some cases through endowed royal statue-cults (Wenennefer of Abydos, a contemporary of Ramesses II, is an excellent example), but their political power in the affairs of the kingdom seems rather limited and had, apparently, little to do with the prominent position attained by provincial 'great chiefs' and nobles in the late third and early second millennium BC. Only in particular periods of political turmoil did they reappear – briefly. This certainly was the case in Elkab. The nobles of this locality supported the Theban kings in their wars of reunification and their inscriptions provide vivid and detailed narratives about these events. However, these texts (like those of Ahmose, son of Ebana, and of Ahmose Pennekhbet) were inscribed decades after their death, around the reign of Thutmose III (1479–1425 BC). Curiously, it was also under this king that the title of 'great chief' of a province reappeared briefly at Qaw, Bersheh and Beni Hasan, in Middle Egypt, that the title of 'great chief of Upper Egypt' was adopted by dignitaries from Qaw and Thinis, and that some provincial leaders – such as Satepihu and Min of Thinis, Iamnefer of Nefrusi and Montuherkhepeshef of Qaw – were active members of the royal households of Hatshepsut and Thutmose III. Bearing in mind that this king's accession to the throne was marked by unusual circumstances (his father's queen, Hatshepsut, proclaimed herself pharaoh), and that it was he who launched a continuous and unprecedented series of military campaigns against the Levant, it is possible that the eminent role of provincial rulers corresponded to a very specific political situation. So, in order to consolidate his own authority, Thutmose III could well have found support among provincial leaders while continuous warfare procured him the tribute, wealth and paths for promotion that helped inspire loyalty towards him. Temples were again richly endowed with tribute and captives and profitable priesthood positions were granted to local elites and military personnel. Shortly afterwards, nobles from Akhmim were raised to a prominent position thanks to their family connections with Pharaoh Amenhotep III. These events were concomitant with the development of new forms of ideological integration (sun cults, epitomized by Aton), by the construction of a new but ephemeral capital at Tell el-Amarna (close to Bersheh), and by the efforts of Hatshepsut and Thutmose III to connect their reigns with prestigious periods of the past, such as the reigns of Senusret I (1956–1911 BC) and Sahure (2487–2475 BC). In all, it is tempting to see in these events the first traces of a reorganization of power in Egypt, marked shortly after by the definitive shift of the political and economic core of the kingdom from Upper Egypt to the Delta, catalysed by the rise to power of senior military figures (Horemheb, Ramesses I) and by the definitive loss of power among Middle Egypt's elites. In these circumstances, temples guaranteed stability, as would be the case some time later, when a brief period of political crisis brought to the throne a new line of pharaohs (Setnakht and Ramesses III) and when Ramesses III implemented measures to endow temples with land, workers and offerings on a massive scale.

The Delta's replacement of Upper Egypt as the most dynamic region in Egypt probably reinforced the role of temples in the former as the principal remaining poles of wealth and prestige for local magnates (Moreno García 2016b). As of the late second millennium BC, the Eastern Delta became the monarchy's primary site, and the region experienced steady growth in population and in urban life. Upper Egypt and – most notably – Thebes felt the resulting blow on two different fronts. Not only was it a long way away from the Mediterranean and its burgeoning trading activities, but it also lost its traditional role of gateway for the goods arriving by sea from the southern Red Sea. In fact, the introduction of camels and the development of the land way in Western Arabia known as the 'Incense Route', were heavy blows for Thebes and probably explains the ruralization of its elites during the first centuries of the first millennium BC. The complete collapse of gold extraction in Nubia around the very end of the second millennium BC could only exacerbate Upper Egypt's decline. Under these conditions, exports of grain might have provided an alternative venue to obtain wealth. Unfortunately, Egyptian sources barely mention what Egypt sold in exchange for its imports. However, literary texts boast (for the first time) about cities' agricultural wealth, and even mention affluent people who sent ships loaded with agricultural produce to the Levant. The huge amounts of silver paid as taxes to the temples by the cultivators of their land meant that substantial amounts of temple products were being commercialized. The Harris I Papyrus (dating from 1150 BC) evaluates the annual contribution in silver of cultivators and other temple personnel as 18,254 *deben* of silver (1661 kg). If all of this silver came exclusively from the sale of grain (which is pure conjecture), it would amount to 1,095,240 *deben* of copper (at a rate of 1:60, typical of the Ramesside period) or 547,620 sacks of grain, that is to say, slightly over 42 million litres of grain (compare to the Egyptian *annona* during the fourth century AD, evaluated as 20 million *modii* or 174.6 million litres). Egyptian texts mention exports of grain to the Hittite empire and it is very possible that this trade did compensate for the loss of pharaonic control over the traffic of Nubian and South Arabian goods at the end of the second millennium BC. As most of the cultivable land of Egypt was located in the Delta and Middle Egypt, the Delta – together with the Fayum – became an increasingly strategic source of income for the monarchy and an area of increasing agricultural expansion and urbanization. Judging from architectural remains and from documents recording donations of land to temples in the early first millennium BC, Lower Egypt was the region that benefited by far the most from the building of new temples and from the expansion of agriculture.

Temples also played an important role as providers of revenue and subsistence for the army. The holders of about one-third of the plots of land recorded in the Wilbour Papyrus were military personnel, including foreign soldiers, and their landholdings were often quite substantial. The creation of a sizeable army for the first time, from 1550

BC onwards, raised a significant problem, namely how to remunerate thousands of soldiers. In other Near Eastern societies, ancient and pre-modern, it was usual to grant land to officials and soldiers as 'payment' for their military services (Mesopotamian *ilku*, early Islamic *iqta'*, Ottoman *tımar*, etc.). In the case of Egypt, the state introduced a system of standardized landholdings based on plots of five arouras (about 1.37 ha) and on multiples of this amount. In some cases such tenures seem to be independent of temples, as when Ahmose, son of Ebana, received extensive estates, including one comprising sixty arouras in the locality of Hadja, and another of five arouras in his hometown of Elkab. Mose traced the history of a land grant awarded by the king four centuries before to his ancestor, the ship-master Neshi, veteran of the wars against the Hyksos and contemporary of Ahmose, son of Ebana. The land was located just south of the Fayum, at Wehit-Neshi ('the village of Neshi') and was kept intact within his family for centuries. However, the Wilbour Papyrus and many other Ramesside administrative documents reveal that temples granted land tenures to both soldiers and officials, thereby assuming functions that, in other cultures, depended on the state. This practice promoted a particular culture in which a modest elite formed of military personnel, low-ranking priests, 'ladies', wealthy peasants, etc., reinforced their status, which was regularly expressed by the erection of votive stelae that proclaimed their links with the king and with gods. This social sector constituted a solid and broad social basis for pharaohs, as their members were present in key areas within Egypt and enabled the penetration of royal values and authority in areas usually dominated by local traditional authorities (village chiefs, etc.). It is not by chance that the Wilbour Papyrus reveals a concentration of land attached to royal statue-cults close to Sharope (Middle Egypt), where many military personnel resided. These estates represented only 1.6 per cent of the total recorded in this document, but they were linked with the funerary cults of Ramesses III and Ramesses V and with royal institutions (Moreno García 2016b). Modest but not unsubstantial (around 5.5 ha on average, but sometimes as large as 27.5 ha), they enhanced their owners' social prestige.

However, votive stelae and other monuments betray a certain failure by the crown to provide protection and help, as they reveal the emergence of new and more direct forms of personal relationships with the gods, as well as more individualist feelings ('personal piety'). Their owners cited illness and personal distress in their inscriptions and requested help directly from gods (Vernus 1993). Such individualism probably underpins the popularity of other cultural manifestations: scribes who left their names in the tombs of prestigious scholars of the past, the popularity of love songs that expressed intimate feelings, perhaps a wider use of letters, etc. It is also apparent in the contrast between these stelae and the 'typical' stelae of the early second millennium BC, which were dominated by representations of extended families and kin groups. Furthermore, royal tombs, now hidden in a remote desert valley, definitively lost their role as visible symbolic referents of kings' authority. Even the funerary temples of kings and their goods suffered from looting that exposed their fragility. Finally, unusual political episodes (such as the rise to power of Hatshepsut, the Amarna episode during Akhenaten's reign, an Egyptian queen's petition for a foreign husband, the troubled reign of Queen Twosret and the execution of her allies – Chancellor Bay and an Asian rebel called Irsu – not to mention the murder of Ramesses III, the rise to power of generals not linked to the royal family, and so on) reveal a certain weakness in the crown that could only enhance the role of temples as providers of institutional stability.

A final word concerns cities and their social life, one of the greatest unknowns in Egyptian history. Only in two cases (Tell el-Amarna and Pi-Ramesses) is it possible to discern in detail the urban layout of an Egyptian capital city, though it is quite probable that ceremonial architecture was somewhat overrepresented there in comparison with other conurbations. In any case, this was a period in which frequent mentions of merchants and their activities, massive building projects, workshops operating on a large scale in order to supply armies, the development of an intensive peri-urban horticulture, references to wealthy peasants and ladies, the very circulation of precious metals and scattered references to markets and trade all point to a burgeoning urban life about which we know very little. A scene in the tomb of vizier Rekhmire describes about eighty cities and towns as being tax payers, while the Harris I Papyrus mentions 160 'cities of Egypt' that were transferred to the gods. It is also around this time that inscriptions drew a clear distinction between different types of settlement, mostly *dmj* ('harbour/city'), *wḥyt* '((clan) village)' and the most generic *nwt* ('settlement'). Occasional discoveries of small hoards of precious metals, official letters and archives concerning the looting of temples and royal tombs at the end of the second millennium BC (and how the thieves laundered their booty) show that gold and silver circulated and were used in private economic transactions.

Given the scarcity of sources relating to private finances, it is difficult to analyse the impact of private economic activities and urban life on Egypt's internal life. Certainly the Delta became the most dynamic economic centre while the area around Thebes was gradually reduced to a sort of conservative, increasingly ruralized and ceremonial backwater. Kings chose to reside in the Delta and trade continued to thrive there even after the empire collapsed. Hence, the king of Byblos stated in the *Story of Wenamun* that trade between Egypt and the cities of Lebanon, controlled both by pharaohs (such as Smendes) and private traders (such as Werekter), was in excellent health, to the point that 'twenty ships here in my harbour do business with Smendes. As for Sidon, that other (place) you passed, are there not another fifty ships there that do business with Werekter and haul to his house?' That a son of Ramesses II married the daughter of a Syrian ship-owner (as noted in an earlier chapter) is further testimony of the wealth and status accumulated by rich merchants about whom we know virtually nothing. This shift to the north also explains subsequent events, such as a wider use of silver and the involvement of pharaohs in Levantine affairs (Sheshonq's campaign into Canaan, and the astonishing amounts of precious metals he sent back to Egypt subsequently, are just one example). Shortly afterwards, sapiential texts reveal a change of mentality, whereby wealth-seeking and cupidity were regarded as reprehensible, but increasingly popular, values. The settlement of foreign traders in Delta (Naucratis is perhaps the most famous case in point) further increased the integration of the Delta in the international trade sphere and its participation in the politics of the Eastern Mediterranean and the Near East.

The loss of the empire: Weakness exposed?

The loss of empire around 1080 BC and the attendant drop in revenue (taxes, tribute, direct access to coveted goods, remunerated administrative positions), as well as the dislocation of foreign trade networks, inaugurated a period of political division and of rearrangements in the distribution of power in Egypt. These aspects were inextricably linked and raise crucial questions about the failure of the Egyptian monarchy to reproduce itself in the last years of the Late Bronze Age, a characteristic shared with other Near Eastern political entities: in an allegedly overwhelmingly agrarian society, why did the loss of empire and the decrease in international trade *between royal powers* have such devastating political consequences across the Near East? What can the structure of crown institutions reveal about the organization of political power in Egypt, when the unified monarchy (1550–1069 BC) was a kind of stop-gap between two long periods of political division? Why did autonomous political powers in the Delta turn repeatedly to foreign values (Hyksos, Libyans) in order to build and to assert their identities instead of adapting 'classical' monarchical values? In short, why were political unity and imperialism so inextricably linked in the Late Bronze Age?

The loss of Nubia (and its gold reserves) and the shift of the traffic of myrrh and incense from a maritime (Red Sea) to a land (Western Arabia) route diminished Egypt's traditional role as a vital commercial mediator between inner Africa and the Mediterranean. The immediate consequence was the decline of the Theban crossroads, while the balance of power between the area around Thebes and the Delta shifted definitively to the advantage of the latter. The interruption of the flows of foreign workers employed in the cultivation of institutional land may have provoked a manpower shortage and the abandonment of land that had hitherto been farmed successfully. Furthermore, the opportunities offered by imperial bureaucracy and the army in terms of promotion and income vanished, depriving kings of powerful tools that helped them co-opt, integrate and guarantee the social reproduction of the elites of the country. The structure of the state suffered as a result, and moved towards a more flexible and pragmatic organization of power that accepted political division and the co-existence (not always peaceful) of several foci of authority. Although 'empire' had meant expansion by means of capturing territories and trade routes that could be integrated into a single polity, its goals and tools (army, bureaucracy, co-option of foreign elites, etc.) probably became too expensive and proved ineffective in the new scenario created when foreign rivals collapsed and new, lucrative trade routes shifted away from the areas traditionally controlled by Egypt. In this revised setting, kings had apparently no objection to focusing their attention on the Delta (the most dynamic region), to sharing their power with military leaders based at Thebes, and who enjoyed considerable autonomy (they were also High Priests of Amun), and to delegating supreme political authority to Amun by the use of oracular procedures, when the god decided between different options submitted to him. Later, pharaohs virtually disappeared in the north, replaced by a multitude of petty kings who claimed Libyan ancestry. In terms of the exercise of power, bureaucratic proceedings declined, while personal relations became central. That is why dense networks of marriage alliances between the royal family and prominent potentates helped shore up kings' (precarious) power bases and, later, those of pretenders to royal status. These circumstances could only reinforce the role of temples as sources of institutional stability, status, legitimacy and wealth, especially in the north.

What emerges from this picture is that, despite a powerful cultural *koiné* common to all Egypt, the political structures of Late Bronze Age

Egypt did not result in the emergence of a 'national state' in the aftermath of empire. On the contrary, decentralization prevailed, to the point that statehood in northern Egypt took the form of confederations of regional powers under the occasional supremacy of a *primus inter pares* (Heracleopolis, Hermopolis, etc.). The abundant diffusion of Egyptian and Egyptianized objects in the Mediterranean and the Levant reveals that exports helped keep Egypt well integrated in Iron-Age international trade. And, judging from the *Story of Wenamun*, it is possible that other, 'invisible', exports (grain, textiles, fish, papyri, linen, etc.) constituted, in fact, the bulk of Egyptian exports and promoted some kind of economic specialization that consolidated Lower Egypt as the country's most dynamic region (the Delta and the Fayum comprised almost 60 per cent of all potential cultivable land of Egypt).

It is significant that when Egypt was reunified again (about 655 BC), the initiative came from Sais, a city in the Delta, and not from Thebes. This offered the new pharaohs several advantages: their military power was based on the use of foreign mercenaries (mostly Greek); excellent relations with some Greek cities that not only acted as allies, but also helped create a powerful fleet; the establishment of trade centres frequented by foreign merchants (for example, Naucratis); and a renewed geopolitical view that sought to take control of international trade routes and crossroads. Among these were the desert route that linked the Nile Valley to the oasis of Siwa and Cyrenaica; the area of the southern tip of Levant (point of arrival of the Incense Route); and a renewed interest in the Red Sea trade that might explain the legends of a maritime expedition sent by Pharaoh Necho II to circumvent Africa, the Achaemenid (re?-)construction of a canal between the Nile Valley and the Gulf of Suez; or the Egyptian expeditions launched against Nubia. Obviously, building up an army, a fleet, a new administration and an ambitious foreign policy demanded considerable resources that could not help but reinforce Egypt's integration in Iron Age trade networks. Private documents from the Theban area suggest that, in an impoverished Upper Egypt, far from the more dynamic areas of Egypt (the Delta), local elites turned to land holdings as their main source of income, pricipally as holders of temple property in the absence of any other substantial source of income.

Ultimately, military expansion, territorial conquest, and opportunities to increase revenue were crucial to keeping Egypt unified. When this was no longer possible, Egypt regularly divided into a multitude of regions, each of which followed its own interests. In other words, regions and temples appear as true long-term resilient nodes of authority and identity, while the unified state appears, as of the end of the second millennium BC, as a fragile political construct that survived as long as it was able to harmonize the ambitions of the pharaohs and those of the local elites through imperial conquest. As Anievas and Nişancıoğlu have argued (Anievas & Nişancıoğlu 2015: 101–04), imperial expansion became a necessity if tributary states were to obtain the taxes, tribute and the resources needed to reproduce themselves and to harmonize the interests of the ruling elite. In the case of Egypt this meant, from 650 BC onwards, pursuing a policy of imperial expansion (Cyrenaica, Cyprus, southern Levant) that opened up the kingdom to foreign powers competing for similar goals but capable, for the first time, of seriously menacing the country's integrity, as the Assyrians, Neo-Babylonians and Achaemenids did. Far from being an exception, Egypt was simply one among other tributary states and its 'natural' condition was in no way that of political unity. In fact it was only religious beliefs, temples and 'religious geographies' that connected regions and localities through myths and gods, that then helped to preserve a certain cultural identity and to legitimize in some way the authority of kings in a fragmented country subject, moreover, to periodical foreign domination. However, the religious sphere failed too to produce a 'national' religion or a 'national' sense of community, as the belief system it promoted was based on local cults and sanctuaries deeply rooted in provincial identities. This characteristic did not go among foreign rulers, who suppressed private donations to temples in order to break the fundamental link between temples and local elites that enabled the autonomous social reproduction of the latter (Agut-Labordère & Gorre 2014).

9

The Pharaonic State(s) in Comparative Perspective

What is an ancient state?

Was ancient Egypt a state? In the preceding chapters I have focused my analysis on specific features usually ascribed to statehood, from territorial control to the implementation of a tax system or the creation of particular cultural values. Now I would like to conclude my study by addressing a crucial issue: are these characteristics enough to characterize pharaonic Egypt as a state? The question is far from being purely rhetorical. Western political science and political philosophy have traditionally considered that the modern state which emerged in Europe around 1648 is the model and measure of 'true' statehood (in terms of sovereignty, frontiers, rule of law, etc.), and that the political formations that do not fit this model or share its main features should not be considered as states. The problem becomes even more acute in the case of ancient 'oriental' political formations. There, the patrimonialization of power by a tiny ruling class close to kings, the absence of organized, political 'citizen' bodies, of a normative corpus of laws intended to regulate social relations, of autonomous bureaucratic spheres and the need to constantly face the threats posed by factions of the nobility, meant in the end that such 'states' were somewhat primitive. While arbitrary power dominated the top echelons of the state, there was limited scope for action locally and never enough resources to consistently manage the territory that, theoretically, they controlled. This view is quite problematic for two reasons. First, it is eurocentric and ignores other alternative systems of power and sovereignty, not to mention other operative relationships between law, political power and economic activities, that integrated territories and populations so successfully for centuries and which provided a stable basis of power for its rulers. It would be unjust, if not utterly misleading, to dismiss these simply because they do not conform to what a state should 'look like' *according to Western values* and historical evolution. Second, it introduces a difficult notion of 'efficiency' as being synonymous with 'modernity' and with the development of the instruments of power that, in a Weberian perspective, define states. However, such tools (law, specialized bureaucracy, increasing division of powers, formal recognition of counterpowers, etc.) correspond to the very particular circumstances in which European states consolidated themselves once the legitimacy derived from religion and dynastic principles vanished, when capitalist economies and the new social relations they promoted (including individualism) expanded and traditional customs and social bonds collapsed. Inevitably, law and regulations replaced the security and stability formerly guaranteed by traditional social hierarchies and informal networks of obligation and reciprocity. As we can see, the lineages of state are diverse, and cannot be reduced to one single model or path.

So what is a state, then? Endless discussions have tried to whittle down a definition of the state and define its principal characteristics. The definition proposed by Jessop (Jessop 2016 and 2018) is perhaps the most operative one, and is valid not only for modern but also for ancient states. He identifies three basic features in any state: first, a clearly demarcated core territory under the more or less uncontested and continuous control of the state apparatus; second, a politically organized coercive, administrative and symbolic apparatus endowed with both general and specific powers; third, a permanent or stable population that is subject to the state's political authority, and which is regarded, at least by that apparatus, if not its subjects, as binding. The state is then a variable ensemble of technologies and practices that produce, naturalize and manage territorial space as a bounded container within which political power is exercised with a view to achieving various, more or less well integrated, and shifting policy objectives, which may include maintaining, transforming or overthrowing the state itself. In his view the state is *not just* an institutional ensemble, the repository of specific political capacities and resources, a real subject, a passive instrument nor a neutral actor *but also* a social relation. This means that the power of the state is an institutionally mediated reflection and refraction of the changing balance of forces that seek to advance their respective interests in, through and in opposition to the state. So a state is never neutral because it is marked by biases that make state institutions, capacities and resources more accessible to some political forces, some identities, some interests, some strategies, some spatio-temporal horizons and some actions than others. Hence the powers of the state are activated by changing sets of politicians and state officials located in specific parts of the state system. The *structural selectivity* of the state and its powers are thus always conditional or relational. Their realization depends on the complex web of structural interdependencies and strategic networks linking the state and political system to its broader environment, the strategic links among state managers and other political forces, and the action, reaction and interaction of specific social forces located within and beyond this ensemble (Jessop 2016 and 2018). The state's structural powers and capacities, its structural and strategic biases, and their realization do not depend solely on the nature of the state as a juridico-political apparatus, but also on the diverse capacities, liabilities and forces that lie beyond it. In fact, the state is shot through with contradictions and class struggles, and its political agents must always take account of (potential) mobilization by a wide range of forces beyond the state that may include, for example, ethnicity, religion, regional location, etc. Consequently, the historical and formal constitution of a state is related to its dominant principles of social organization (religion, military security, economy, law, etc.). In the end, all forms of the state tend to fail due to the paradox that the state is just one part of a complex social order with limited capacities to intervene in other parts of the whole and is, at the same time, held responsible for the whole and expected to intervene in the last instance to maintain social cohesion and institutional integration. Finally, as a strategic social relation, the state is strategically selective, the site where strategies are elaborated and codified. In this view, the state can be analysed as a strategic terrain with structural, discursive and strategic biases with asymmetrical effects on the capacities of different social forces to pursue their interests over specific spatio-temporal horizons – capacities that depend in turn on their ability to read conjunctures and develop appropriate strategies (the art of the possible).

When contrasted with the Egyptian state, the parameters provided by Jessop not only prove extremely useful but also help us understand the different configurations of power that characterized a succession of diverse monarchical systems over three millennia, under the appearance of a single state. Jessop's theory stresses the importance of the development of specific sets of institutions and their continuity over time but, at the same time, points out that states cannot be reduced to formal sets of institutions and configurations of power (monarchy, oligarchy, etc.). Ancient states relied on a complex set of interactions between formal and non-formal actors, differentiated strategies and configurations of power in which kings and courts were far from being the only repositories of political agency. The strategic and dynamic perspective gleaned from this helps us avoid the usual approaches to ancient Egypt that rely mainly on the ruling elite's assertions and justifications, which (not surprisingly) tended to highlight their centrality while concealing the role played by many other actors. The equilibrium between elite factions, between regions, between the centre and the provinces, between the most prominent elite and an elusive world of local powers and authorities with which kings and potentates had to cope if their authority was to be recognized and their decisions implemented, was fragile and changed over time (Moreno García 2010b and 2013a). It can be safely concluded that Egypt was a state indeed and that this political formation took many forms and covered a diverse array of political configurations over three millennia, even if formal art and official culture stressed continuity and tradition more as a desideratum than a reality. In this vein, Jessop's characterization of the state goes a step further than that provided by Mann and his sources of social power (economic, political, ideological and military), whose changing articulation over time tends to an increasing progress of infrastructural power, that is to say, the capacity of these sources of power to penetrate into and shape society (Mann 1986). His perspective suffers from a somewhat evolutionist bias in which human action and social transformation are moved by a pursuit of increasing rationality (in a Western sense) that shares many common aspects with the ideals proclaimed by New Institutionalism. By contrast, Jessop insists that the social dynamics which crystallized in particular forms of the state were the expression of shifting balances of power between different actors and institutions, and that such balances were deprived of any innate 'superior' human tendency towards greater rationality; instead they depended on their interests, strategies, capacities for forging alliances and their ability to profit from the 'windows of opportunity' opened to them. The history of ancient Egypt thus represents an excellent example of the forces driving the different monarchies established in the Nile valley, and explains not only how the monarchies stayed so stable for so long, but also their periodical crises.

Was Egypt a tributary state?

The concept of a 'tributary state' is a recurrent one in the study of pre-modern and modern political formations, particularly those in the East. In recent years, this has been a subject of interest once more for historians and has inspired fresh analysis that has helped categorize societies that shared some common characteristics. Banaji, for instance, emphasizes the peculiar absence, in tributary states, of a ruling class that emerges *organically* from the depths of society and achieves sufficient stature to control and dominate the state. So, the best way to analyse tributary states is through the diverse configurations of the ruling class that the sovereign had to contend with and the historically distinct ways in which the relationship between ruler and ruling class was configured. It was the unusual dominance of the state that set these regimes apart from those in Western Europe, as the state controlled *both the means of production and the ruling class*, and had unlimited disposal over the population's total surplus labour. In other words, tributary states were characterized both by the control of peasant-labour by the state (the state-apparatus being the chief instrument of exploitation) and by the drive to forge a unified imperial service based on the subordination of a disciplined ruling class to the will of the ruler. The bond between the ruler and the *ruling elite* within the wider circles of the ruling class was the basis on which new states were constructed and the state itself bureaucratized to create an efficient tool of administration. The autocratic centralism of the tributary state and its backbone in the recruitment of a pliant nobility were essential moments of the structuring and organization of the economy. Moreover, tributary economies had considerable vitality, with prosperous powerful states with a vast financial capacity, so that the entire government apparatus was built, and constantly rebuilt, in the interests of the treasury. The conflict between ruler and individual factions of the nobility was typical of tributary regimes and was a struggle not primarily for control of the peasantry but for power, waged not by a monolithic and unified class of aristocrats on one side and absolutism on the other, but by factions or alliances among magnate families who were themselves divided, and where individual rulers could always count on the support of leading nobles. The general form of exploitation was simply one that subjected the peasantry to taxation by the state. The preponderance of tax as a mechanism for surplus appropriation was distinct from the European lord–peasant rent nexus of exploitation because taxation was regulated by regional and central agents of the state. This general form of domination of the peasantry could take a variety of forms because of the way tributary modes were configured in class terms (Banaji 2010: 1–44).

To this basic model Anievas and Nişancıoğlu have contributed some observations based on the Ottoman and Mughal empires. According to them, although the state established control over provincial notables and land, central authority was relatively dispersed. The Ottoman state was able to regulate both production and exploitation by devolving power to its agents in the rural provinces through the *timar* system. A *timar* was the predominant form of land division, an allocation of land from which the holder could extract revenue and that provided the basic income for officials in return for their performing state services. Some larger *timars* were assigned to the highest elite and to those close to the house of the Sultan and, in these cases, the holding was often passed on to the *timar*-holder's son, establishing a degree of hereditary ownership in some sections of the ruling class. Nonetheless, *timar*-holders were fundamentally dependent on and constrained by the Ottoman central state functions for their social reproduction, as *timar* holdings were assigned by the Sultan and tax registers kept a strict record of the size of *timars*, their contents and the level of taxes that could be levied by the *timar*-holder from the peasantry. Moreover, the rotation of *timar* allocations helped to remove potentially discontented holders from their local environment. These mechanisms enabled the Ottomans to institutionalize the social reproduction of *timar*-holders into a relationship of dependence to the Sultan. Consequently, the *timar* embodied the crucial distinction in tributary ruling-class relations between the patrimonial authority of the king and his household, and the local nobility, in which the former controlled the latter. The primary contradiction of the tributary state therefore lay in the structure of the ruling class itself, which could potentially come into conflict over the distribution of surplus between its central and provincial sections. Preventing this conflict, and hence ensuring the continued reproduction of the tributary mode, was achievable only through a policy of military and economic expansion that guaranteed the ruling elite expanded access to more land, taxes, tribute and population. The social reproduction of the tributary state thus took place not only through 'internal' relations of surplus appropriation, but also through geopolitical accumulation. Conquest facilitated the renewal of the ruling class by co-opting subservient elites who were offered access to more land and to contacts with the centre of power, while discontented members of the ruling elite could be expropriated, replaced or relocated away from the imperial centre. In short, becoming part of the ruling class guaranteed privilege, security and social reproduction. Furthermore, such incorporation could foster competition between different sections of the ruling class with differential relations of dependence on – and autonomy from – the imperial system. Imperial geopolitical accumulation was therefore crucial to maintaining state power over sections of the ruling class. This made tributary societies particularly sensitive to external conditions – either through conquest, assimilation, diplomacy, secession or conflict – as a fundamental component of their social reproduction. The centralized nature of the tributary state, along with its ability to effectively monopolize the means of violence, made for a cohesive and unified ruling class. Nonetheless, the potential for conflict remained, particularly between local state officials, private landowners and the centralized state. Local agents might have developed into feudal-like lords with their own landed estates (and armed contingents), and wealthy landowners may have become significant independent economic and political powers. Both tendencies could be countered by divorcing state officials from any permanent rights to the land through constant transfers to different territorial assignments after short periods of time (Anievas and Nişancıoğlu 2015).

Some of these characteristics can be found easily in ancient Egypt, most particularly the considerable effort made by kings to integrate a provincial nobility that, in some areas and periods (Middle Egypt around 2000–1800 BC), exhibited a considerable degree of autonomy and influence in key areas of the state. Despite this, the Egyptian nobility seems to have depended on the state for its social reproduction and it never led, in periods of crisis, to the emergence of a feudal class issued organically from society and capable of dominating the state and capturing its revenue (or substantial shares thereof). Quite the contrary: what emerged was a multiplicity of powers, each one trying to preserve and replicate the features of the monarchy, from fiscality to a court system, in an effort to co-opt local nobles and to monitor resources. This model has been found in other parts of world, such as when the

Umayyad Caliphate of Córdoba (medieval Spain) collapsed in 1031 AD and was replaced by about thirty-three small kingdoms rather than a feudal system similar to that operative in the Christian kingdoms of northern Spain during the same period (Guichard & Soravia 2007: 79–105). Officials' remuneration consisted basically of allotments of land and, occasionally, entire villages, scattered across the country. Similar to the *tımar* (Ottoman), *iqta'*, *jāgīr* (Mughal) holdings prevalent in the Islamic world, the 'domains' thus granted to dignitaries, courtiers and administrators remained under state ownership and were carefully distinguished from their holders' private patrimony. Furthermore, the assets of these domains remained at the crown's disposal and could revert if required, particularly the mobilization of their population in order to complete state-sanctioned work, as the Gebelein Papyri (around 2500 BC) and other sources reveal.

However, one aspect took on an increasing importance in ancient Egypt, when temples became crucial providers of income for the elite and for the kings' officials, but also morphed into managing agencies not just for their own assets but also for those of the crown (such as the *khato*-fields). This move was particularly evident in the second half of the second millennium BC, and concomitant with the reduction – even the disappearance – of the agricultural centres and domains of the crown, and it raises many questions about the 'Egyptian way' of remunerating officials and organizing institutional agriculture when compared with holdings like *tımar*, *iqta'*, *jāgīr* or Mesopotamian *ilku*-allotments of land. The preference in Egypt for a more temple-based, decentralized managerial system may point to a structural weakness of the state, as state land and royal rewards that took the form of land had to be 'anchored' to temples. As is thus evident, temples were an essential link between a monarchy trying to assert its authority and a country with huge regional differences, and in which local nobles enjoyed great power, particularly at Edfu, Elkab, Abydos and across Middle Egypt. The unification of Egypt in around 1550 BC and its subsequent expansion into Nubia and the Levant was achieved in a very short period of time from a modest base in Thebes. Under these conditions, temples became indispensable poles of authority that helped connect the nascent monarchy to the regional nobility and to an expanding bureaucracy. Temples also provided institutional stability for the assets of the ruling class, a significant issue in a monarchy that expanded extremely quickly, that showed signs of instability as it faced periodic episodes of political turmoil (as during the Amarna era), that needed land to remunerate an army that grew considerably in size during the Late Bronze Age and that, in the end, needed to find a formula to acquire and manage land in the provinces without hurting the interests of the local nobility. Another key aspect is that the importance of temples may also correspond to the (apparent) reduced size of *organic* cities, especially when compared with those in the ancient Near East (Moeller 2016). This may explain why, with the exception of capital cities, temples were the main 'theatres of power' because of the absence of high-quality monumental buildings (palaces, plazas, ceremonial avenues, etc.) that displayed the power and pageantry of the state. Temples appear to be nodes of authority essential for the reproduction of the ruling class and of the state itself, rather than independent institutions whose interests collided with those of the monarchy. Being part of a specialized branch of the state, in which 'religion' procured the institutional and legitimate stability that law provided in other societies, temples represented a type of long-term social and economic stability for the ruling class, being repositories of wealth, legitimacy and income in hard times (such as when the monarchy collapsed) and the basis from which royal authority could reconstruct its power over its territory. As their landed assets depended, at least partially, on royal donations, kings thus had at their disposal an ideal tool with which to modulate the growth of institutions controlled, in the provinces, by local nobles. It was in the interest of these nobles to be on good terms with the monarchs if their wealth was to increase.

Two final points are that in ancient Egypt tax (and not rent) was also the main mechanism for surplus appropriation, and that taxation was regulated by the agents of the state (for the implications of this distinction, see Wickham 1984 and 1985). Taxes made it possible to distribute income, to control and to shape a subordinate and disciplined ruling class whose interests thus coincided with those of the king. An indirect clue about the importance of royal taxation is that private contributions played only a very minor role in financing and organizing the major enterprises managed by the crown, such as the construction of (even local) temples, the organization of expeditions (military or other), guaranteeing operational supplies (to harbours such as Ayn Sukhna, the Egyptian fortresses in Nubia, etc.), and so on. Private citizens tended to display their wealth only in private funerary and domestic equipment, while their initiatives (such as leading local contingents of workers or soldiers) were subordinated to royal enterprises. When mayors, cities and towns, chiefs of villages, etc., paid taxes, they delivered them to the crown and its officials, not to an intermediate class of feudal landlords.

Pharaonic Egypt: An ancient state in a comparative perspective

Recent discussions about the infrastuctural power of ancient states, about alternative forms of political organization and on the role played by urban economies and institutions, private business, trade networks, economic integration and informal authorities, among others, help us understand how ancient states were organized and point to the limits of previous interpretations that emphasized centralism, sedentary life, royal agency and law. These discussions also expose the limits of Neo-Institutionalism in its aim to analyse world history within the framework of Western modern patterns of the organization of power and the role played by law, contracts, Western concepts of rationality and efficiency and individualism. That is why ancient Egypt may provide fertile ground for comparative research about how particular configurations of power finally crystallized in states and how these changing configurations produced diverse forms of the state (Baines & Yoffee 1998; Richards & Van Buren 2000; Moreno García 2010c and 2014b).

'Territorial' states?

Ancient Egypt differs from the type of Near East state that prevailed for most of the Bronze Age. In Mesopotamia, Syria, the Levant and Anatolia, states were usually organized around great cities that formed the core of a more or less extensive (but usually discontinuous) territory. When several of them became integrated into a bigger state or 'empire', these political entities remained fragile and short-lived. Only in the Late Bronze Age did some of them consolidate themselves into states that lasted for centuries, rather than just a few generations, Kassite Babylonia and – at a more modest level – Assyria being the best examples. Egypt, by contrast, appeared from even very early history as a unified and long-lived state, stretching for nearly a thousand kilometres. While cities were surprisingly modest in size until the Late Bronze Age, regions emerge nevertheless as powerful nodes of identity and authority, and with their own political and economic goals. This opens a fascinating arena for comparative research about the political role played by regions and cities in the ancient Near East, why regions were, perhaps, a more favourable environment than cities for the preservation of noble lines (ancient Elam and Persia are another case in point), how states coped both with cities and (poorly urbanized) regions in order to build their power, and to what extent the construction of political power in Egypt was different from other regions with strong regional idiosyncrasies.

'Oriental' cities?

There is another (related) question, with regard to the relationship between 'organic cities' and urban settlements founded as administrative and ceremonial royal centres. Egyptian cities acted as administrative centres of districts, as well as taxation units. However, the modest dimensions of many cities (judging from the extant evidence), coupled with their homogeneous distribution along the Nile, suggest that many of them emerged 'organically' as hubs of their districts, as markets, harbours and tax-collecting centres (the word 'town', *dmj*, originally meant 'harbour, harbour area of a settlement'). The Great Dedicatory inscription of Ramesses II makes an interesting point when it distinguishes the territorial organization of 'the foreign lands of Retenu (= Levant)', comprising 'villages (*wḥyt*) and strongholds (*nakhtw*)' from the 'towns (*dmj*) supplied with people' founded by the king. So, *dmj*-towns constituted what a 'proper' Egyptian landscape should be, especially after the decline of the royal *ḥwt* centres around 2000 BC, and when pharaohs settled foreign peoples (for instance, Libyans) in Egypt, they did so in towns (*dmj*). In sharp contrast, ceremonial cities (including the Nubian temple-towns founded in the Late Bronze Age) were rare, restricted mostly to the capital cities of the kingdom (Memphis, Thebes, Pi-Ramesses), so provincial temples assumed most of the role being the local 'stages' for royal power. That said, royal foundations were rather fragile, subject to political ups and downs, the short-lived existence of Tell el-Amarna being a good example, as is the speedy abandonment of royal palaces such as Deir el-Ballas (deserted during the middle sixteenth century BC), Malqata (1390–1352 BC), the Ramesseum (built by Ramesses II, partially demolished by Ramesses III), etc. Temples seem thus to compensate, in a way, for the modest urban network of Bronze Age Egypt and point to an original way of organizing the landscape and creating social identities in contrast with the more urbanized environment of other regions of the Near East.

Bureaucracy and *raison d'état*

The development of the first writing systems in Mesopotamia and Egypt was concomitant with the emergence of a class of scribes alongside administrative procedures and intellectual tools that enabled them to interpret and fix particular forms of exercising power. Lists of kings, annals, 'literary' works, formulations of divine pantheons, myths, etc., shaped and transmitted official social memories and selected the more convenient types of information that helped building those official social memories in order to support the accepted 'normal' order of the world. However, the rich body of written material derived both from Mesopotamia and Egypt is surprisingly light in political thought. In contrast, unstable political conditions, and the multiplication of political entities prior to the emergence of the first emperor, led in China, for instance, to a thorough reflection on what power was and how it should be exercised (Pines 2015a and 2015b). Ancient India has also provided a wealth of treatises on statecraft and government (the *Arthashastra* being the most prominent; Arjomand 2001). Under such diverse conditions, Egyptian compositions such as *The Teaching for (King) Merykara* (Parkinson 1997: 212–34) offer fertile ground for comparative research about how power was conceived in ancient Egypt. In this light, the organization of pharaonic bureaucracy, its values and its structural role within the state may also help explain why an Egyptian *raison d'état* never emerged (apparently) from this cadre of civil servants or why bureaucracy never became an autonomous sphere of action, capable of challenging the social and political influence of other actors, such as the local nobility.

Trade and power

Trade networks helped integrate Eurasia into a dense web of economic interaction that left its imprint on the organization of power. Political entities grew out of local leaders' ambition to capture flows of wealth and trade routes, empires being the ultimate and largest expressions of such attempts to control an increasing number of strategic areas. However, other actors also intervened in these activities, from pastoral populations to itinerant merchants and craftsmen, from fishermen to peoples in control of challenging but strategic areas (oases, deltaic environments, mountain passes, etc.). It was they who, in many cases, opened new routes and facilitated the circulation of goods and ideas independent of any state initiative, thereby nourishing local leaders' appetite for territorial conquest and for putting under their control these new sources of riches. The reaction of non-institutional actors usually consisted of bypassing the authority of states by using new, alternative routes, by smuggling goods, or even by promoting the diffusion of cheaper but mass-produced imitations of valuable and fashionable items that helped expand demand and trade. The internal consequences for states were obvious as they provoked shifts in the balance of power between regions, between regional nobles and their kings, and between new and old poles of wealth accumulation, not to mention the crystallization of new political entities in areas that produced highly prized goods or that became unavoidable crossroads, or the specialized lifestyles promoted by increasing demand and trade. Phenomena such as piracy, sometimes associated with the movement of peoples and trade expansion (for example, the Sea Peoples, Vikings, pre-modern South Asian pirates, etc.) have inspired the term 'maritime mode of production' (Ling, Earle & Kristiansen 2018). One final aspect is that some periods witnessed an increase in private trade and business, partly based on the production of commodities such as textiles. Can such operations be categorized as commercial capitalism? It this was the case, why did they not initiate a process of sustained 'primitive accumulation' that might have resulted in the expansion of private enterprise, credit and capitalist relations (Banaji 2018; Tedesco 2018)?

Misleading cartographies and the complexity of ancient sovereignty

Modern cartography inevitably transposes contemporary notions of state control, borders and sovereignty to ancient societies (Smith 2005). In doing so, they blur the actual extent and nature of political power. What about territories controlled by pastoral peoples whose allegiance to their (nominal) rulers was superficial at best? What about discontinuous areas of state control, intersected by zones in which kings had little or no authority (independent villages, marsh areas, steppes inhabited by nomadic populations, etc.)? Ancient states (and Egypt was no exception), particularly those of the Bronze Age, included many areas that made real control by a political centre difficult because of their low population density (such as the Western Delta), their lifestyles (Bedouins, fiercely independent mountain people) or their lack of taxable resources. As for the real extent of royal rule, its 'density' varied and might consist in a mix of 'islands of authority' with a strong presence of royal institutions and royal intervention, of areas effectively controlled by the state and, finally, of areas that formally recognized the authority of kings but which enjoyed, in practical terms, considerable autonomy. Direct exploitation, tax and tribute may symbolize these three forms of political subjection. Finally, founding temples, cities and palaces helped to create poles of royal presence (at least symbolically) and to restrict local autonomy, especially in areas dominated by powerful nobles.

Towards a theory of temples?

Temples figure as major institutions across the ancient Near East (Kaniut 2013). However, the analysis of their structural role as stabilizers of power for the states of this area has been barely attempted. Their (theoretically) inviolable and indivisible economic assets protected their economic basis from the uncertainties of heritage division and individualist strategies. As providers of income and recipients of royal donations, they helped rally local support for the monarchy. In the absence of a normative corpus of laws, universally accepted and imposed by specialized bodies of judges, religion helped in providing an alternative legitimacy of power, based on divine support and intervention, not laws. At the same time, temples served the interests and strategies of the social sectors that controlled them: urban notables, local potentates, etc. Even their durability (in contrast with the much more 'mobile' and short-lived palaces) points in some way to a certain precariousness of royal power, as if temples were partial repositories of wealth, legitimacy and power that were actually more stable than kings and dynasties, subject to the hazards of politics, factional fights, usurpation and periodic collapse. Seen in this light, temples hold a political valency not always easily compatible with other sources of social power, such as law and organized citizen bodies.

Bibliography

Agut-Labordère, D. (2011), 'Les "petites citadelles": La sociabilité du *tmy* "ville", "village" à travers les sagesses démotiques', in G. Gorre and P. Kosmann (eds), *Espaces et territoires de l'Égypte gréco-romaine*, 107–22, Paris: Librairie Droz.

Agut-Labordère, D. and G. Gorre (2014), 'De l'autonomie à l'intégration. Les temples égyptiens face à la couronne des Saïtes aux Ptolémées', *Topoi. Orient-Occident*, 19: 17–55.

Agut-Labordère, D. and J. C. Moreno García (2016), *Pharaon. Histoire politique des monarchies pharaoniques (3150 av.–340 ap. J.-C.)*, Paris: Éditions Belin.

Allen, J. (2002), *The Heqanakht Papyri*, New York: Metropolitan Museum of Art.

Ando, C. and S. Richardson, eds (2017), *Ancient States and Infrastructural Power: Europe, Asia, and America*, Philadelphia: University of Pennsylvania Press.

Anievas, A. and K. Nişancıoğlu (2015), *How the West Came to Rule: The Geopolitical Origins of Capitalism*, London: Pluto Press.

Antoine, J.-C. (2015), 'Landholding and Agriculture in Late Ramesside Theban Documents', *Zeitschrift für ägyptische Sprache und Altertumskunde*, 142: 104–19.

Arjomand, S. A. (2001), 'Perso-Indian Statecraft, Greek Political Science and the Muslim Idea of Government', *International Sociology*, 16 (2001): 455–73.

Arjomand, S. A. (2005), 'Coffeehouses, Guilds and Oriental Despotism: Government and Civil Society in Late 17th to Early 18th Century Istanbul and Isfahan, and as seen from Paris and London', in H. Bruhns and D. Gosewinkel (eds), *Europe and the Other: Non-European Concepts of Civil Society*, 12–28, Berlin: Wissenschaftszentrum Berlin für Sozialforschung.

Assmann, J. (1990), *Ma'at: Gerechtigkeit und Unstserblichkeit im Alten Ägypten*, Munich: C. H. Beck.

Baines, J. (1995a), 'Kingship, Definition of Culture, and Legitimation', in D. O'Connor and D. P. Silverman (eds), *Ancient Egyptian Kingship*, 3–47, Leiden: Brill.

Baines, J. (1995b), 'Origins of Egyptian Kingship', in D. O'Connor and D. P. Silverman (eds), *Ancient Egyptian Kingship*, 95–156, Leiden: Brill.

Baines, J. (2000), 'Egyptian Deities in Context: Multiplicity, Unity, and the Problem of Change', in Barbara Nevling Porter (ed.), *One God or Many? Concepts of Divinity in the Ancient World*, 9–78, Chebeague, ME: Casco Bay Assyriological Institute.

Baines, J. (2006), 'Public Ceremonial Performance in Ancient Egypt: Exclusion and Integration', in T. Inomata and L. S. Coben (eds), *Archaeology of Performance: Theaters of Power, Community, and Politics*, 261–302, Lanham, MD: Altamira Press.

Baines, J. (2011), 'Egyptology and the Social Sciences: Thirty Years on', in A. Verbovsek, B. Backes and C. Jones (eds), *Methodik und Didaktik in der Ägyptologie. Herausforderungen eines Kulturwissenschaftlichen Paradigmenwechsels in den Altertumwissenschaften*, 573–97, Munich: Wilhelm Fink.

Baines, J. (2013), *High Culture and Experience in Ancient Egypt*, Sheffield: Equinox.

Baines, J. (2014), 'Civilizations and Empires: A Perspective on Erligang from Early Egypt', in K. Steinke and D. C. Y. Ching (eds), *Art and Archaeology of the Erligang Civilization*, 99–119, Princeton, NJ: Princeton University Press.

Baines, J. and N. Yoffee (1998), 'Order, Legitimacy, and Wealth in Ancient Egypt and Mesopotamia', in G. Feinman and J. Marcus (eds), *Archaic States*, 199–260, Sante Fe, NM: School of American Research Press.

Banaji, J. (2010), *Theory as History: Essays on Modes of Production and Exploitation*, Leiden/Boston: Brill.

Banaji, J. (2018), 'Globalising the History of Capital: Ways Forward', *Historical Materialism*, 26: 143–66.

Bang, P. F. and C. A. Bayly, eds (2011), *Tributary Empires in Global History*, New York: Palgrave Macmillan.

Bárta, M. and V. Dulíková (2015), 'Divine and Terrestrial: The Rhetoric of Power in Ancient Egypt (The Case of Nyuserra)', in F. Coppens, J. Janák and H. Vymazalová (eds), *Royal versus Divine Authority: Acquisition, Legitimization and Renewal of Power*, 31–47, Wiesbaden: Harrassowitz Verlag.

Borgolte, M. (2015), 'Foundations "for the Salvation of the Soul": An Exception in World History?', *Medieval Worlds*, 1: 86–105.

Bryant, J. M. (2006), 'The West and the Rest Revisited: Debating Capitalist Origins, European Colonialism, and the Advent of Modernity', *Canadian Journal of Sociology*, 31: 403–44.

Bussmann, R. (2015), 'Egyptian Archaeology and Social Anthropology', in *Oxford Handbooks Online* [DOI: 10.1093/oxfordhb/9780199935413.013.24].

Bussmann, R. (2016), 'Great and Little Traditions in Egyptology', in *10. Ägyptologische Tempeltagung: Ägyptische Tempel zwischen Normierung und Individualität*, 37–48, Wiesbaden: Harrassowitz Verlag.

Chabal, P., G. M. Feinman and P. Skalník (2017), 'Beyond States and Empires: Chiefdoms and Informal Politics Fifteen Years Later', in R. L. Carneiro, L. E. Grinin and A. V. Korotayev (eds), *Chiefdoms Yesterday and Today*, 309–24, Clinton Corners, NY: Eliot Werner Publications.

Cline, E. and D. O'Connor, eds (2006), *Thutmose III: A New Biography*, Ann Arbor, MI: The University of Michigan Press.

Cline, E. and D. O'Connor, eds (2012), *Ramesses III: The Life and Times of Egypt's Last Hero*, Ann Arbor, MI: The University of Michigan Press.

Coulon, L. (1999), 'La rhétorique et ses fictions: Pouvoirs et duplicité du discours à travers la littérature égyptienne du Moyen et du Nouvel Empire', *Bulletin de l'Institut Français d'Archéologie Orientale*, 99: 103–32.

Coulon, L. (2010), 'Célébrer l'élite, louer Pharaon: Éloquence et cérémoniel de cour au Nouvel Empire', in J. C. Moreno García (ed.), *Élites et pouvoir en Égypte ancienne*, 211–38, Villeneuve d'Ascq: Université Lille 3.

Da Graca, L. and A. Zingarelli, eds (2015), *Studies on Pre-Capitalist Modes of Production*, Chicago: Haymarket Books.

Dodson, A. (2012), *Afterglow of Empire: Egypt from the Fall of the New Kingdom to the Saite Renaissance*, Cairo: The American University in Cairo Press.

Düring, B. S. and T. D. Stek, eds (2018), *The Archaeology of Imperial Landscapes. A Comparative Study of Empires in the Ancient Near East and Mediterranean World*, Cambridge: Cambridge University Press.

Eidem, J. (2014), 'The Kingdom of Šamšī-Adad and Its Legacies', in E. Cancik-Kirschbaum, N. Brisch and J. Eidem (eds), *Constituent, Confederate, and Conquered Space: The Emergence of the Mittani State*, 137–46, Berlin/Boston: De Gruyter.

Eyre, C. J. (1999), 'The village economy in Pharaonic Egypt', in A. Bowman and E. Rogan (eds), *Agriculture in Egypt: From Pharaonic to Modern Times*, 33–60, Oxford: Oxford University Press.

Eyre, C. J. (2004), 'How Relevant Was Personal Status to the Functioning of the Rural Economy in Pharaonic Egypt?', in B. Menu (ed.), *La dépendance rurale dans l'Antiquité égyptienne et proche-orientale*, 157–86, Cairo: Institut Français d'Archéologie Orientale.

Eyre, C. J. (2013), *The Use of Documents in Pharaonic Egypt*, Oxford: Oxford University Press.

Ezzamel, M. (2012), *Accounting and Order*, New York: Routledge.

Feinman, G. M. and L. M. Nicholas (2016), 'Framing the Rise and Variability of Past Complex Societies', in L. F. Farghe and V. V. Heredia Espinoza (eds.), *Alternative Pathways to Complexity: A Collection of Essays on Architecture, Economics, Power, and Cross-Cultural Analysis*, 271–89, Boulder: University Press of Colorado.

Frood, E. (2007), *Biographical Texts from Ramessid Egypt*, Atlanta: Society of Biblical Literature.

Gnirs, A. M. (1996), *Militär und Gesellschaft. Ein Beitrag zur Sozialgeschichte des Neuen Reiches*, Heidelberg: Heidelberger Orientverlag.

Goelet, O. (2015), 'Problems of Authority, Compulsion, and Compensation in Ancient Egyptian Labor Practices', in P. Steinkeller and M. Hudson (eds), *Labor in the Ancient World*, 523–82, Dresden: ISLET Verlag.

Guichard, P. and B. Soravia (2007), *Les royaumes de Taifas. Apogée culturel et déclin politique des émirats andalous du XIe siècle*, Paris: Librairie orientaliste Paul Geuthner.

Gundlach, R. and J. H. Taylor, eds (2009), *4th Symposium on Egyptian Royal Ideology. Egyptian Royal Residences*, Wiesbaden: Harrassowitz Verlag.

Gundlach, R. and A. Klug, eds (2006), *Der ägyptische Hof des Neuen Reiches: Seine Gesellschaft und Kultur im Spannungsfeld zwischen Innen- und Außenpolitik*, Wiesbaden: Harrassowitz Verlag.

Haldon, J. (1993), *The State and the Tributary Mode of Production*, London/ New York: Verso.

Inomata, T. (2016), 'Theories of Power and Legitimacy in Archaeological Contexts: The Emergent Regime of Power at the Formative Maya Community of Ceibal, Guatemala', in S. Kurnick and J. Baron (eds), *Political Strategies in Pre-Columbian Mesoamerica*, 37–60, Boulder: University Press of Colorado.

Islamoğlu, H. and P. C. Perdue, eds (2009), *Shared Histories of Modernity: China, India and the Ottoman Empire*, New Delhi: Routledge.

Jessop, B. (2016), *The State: Past, Present, Future*, Cambridge: Polity Press.

Jessop, B. (2018), 'The State as a Social Relation', in J. L. Brooke, J. C. Strauss and G. Anderson (eds), *State Formations: Global Histories and Cultures of Statehood*, 45–57, Cambridge: Cambridge University Press.

Jursa, M. and J. C. Moreno García, (2015), 'The Ancient Near East and Egypt', in A. Monson and W. Scheidel (eds), *Fiscal Regimes and the Political*

Economy of Premodern States, 115–65, Cambridge: Cambridge University Press.

Kanawati, N. (2003), Conspiracies in the Egyptian Palace: Unis to Pepy I, London: Routledge.

Kaniut, K. et al., eds, (2013), Tempel im Alten Orient. 7, Internationales Colloquium der Deutschen Orient-Gesellschaft, Wiesbaden: Harrasowitz Verlag.

Katary, S. L. D. (2011), 'Taxation (until the end of the Third Intermediate Period)', in J. C. Moreno García and W. Wendrich (eds), Los Angeles: UCLA Encyclopedia of Egyptology.

Katary, S. L. D. (2012), 'Land Tenure (to the End of the Ptolemaic Period)', in J. C. Moreno García and W. Wendrich (eds), Los Angeles: UCLA Encyclopedia of Egyptology.

Kóthay, K. A. (2006), 'The Widow and Orphan in Egypt Before the New Kingdom', Acta Antiqua Academiae Sciantiarum Hungaricae, 46: 151–64.

Kron, G. (forthcoming), 'Growth and Decline. Forms of Growth. Estimating Growth in the Greek World', in E. Lo Cascio, A. Bresson and F. Velde (eds), The Oxford Handbook of Economies in the Classical World, Oxford/New York: Oxford University Press.

Lavan, M., R. E. Payne and J. Weisweiler, eds (2016), Cosmopolitanism and Empire: Universal Rulers, Local Elites, and Cultural Integration in the Ancient Near East and Mediterranean, Oxford: Oxford University Press.

Lehner, M. (2000), 'Fractal House of Pharaoh', in T. A. Kohler and G. J. Humerman (eds), Dynamics in Human and Primate Societies. Agent-based Modeling of Social and Spatial Processes, 275–353, New York: Oxford University Press.

Lichtheim, M. (1998), Ancient Egyptian Autobiographies, Chiefly of the Middle Kingdom: A Study and an Anthology, Freiburg-Göttingen: Academic Press and Vandenhoeck and Ruprecht.

Ling, J., T. Earle and K. Kristiansen (2018), 'Maritime Mode of Production: Raiding and Trading in Seafaring Chiefdoms', Current Anthropology, 59: 488–524.

Liverani, M. (2001), International Relations in the Ancient Near East, 1600–1100 BC, Basingstoke/New York: Palgrave.

Liverani, M. (2013), Immaginare Babele. Due secoli di studi sulla città orientale antica, Rome: Laterza.

Mann, M. (1986), The Sources of Social Power. Vol. I: A History of Power from the Beginning to A.D. 1760, Cambridge: Cambridge University Press.

Manzano, E. (2015), 'Why Did Islamic Medieval Institutions *Become* So Different from Western Medieval Institutions?', *Medieval Worlds*, 1: 118–37.

Mathieu, B. (2010), 'Mais qui est donc Osiris? Ou la politique sous le linceul de la religion', *Égypte Nilotique et Méditerranéenne*, 3: 77–107.

Mazé, C. (2017), 'À la recherche des "classes moyennes". Les espaces de la différentiation sociale dans l'Égypte du IIIe millénaire av. J.-C.', *Bulletin de l'Institut Français d'Archéologie Orientale*, 116: 123–76.

Miniaci, G., J. C. Moreno García, S. Quirke and A. Stauder, eds (2018), *The Arts of Making in Ancient Egypt: Voices, Images, and Objects of Material Producers 2000–1500 BC*, Leiden: Sidestone Press.

Moeller, N. (2016), *The Archaeology of Urbanism in Ancient Egypt: From the Predynastic Period to the End of the Middle Kingdom*, Cambridge: Cambridge University Press.

Monson, A. and W. Scheidel, eds (2015), *Fiscal Regimes and the Political Economy of Premodern States*, Cambridge: Cambridge University Press.

Moreno García, J. C. (2010a), 'Oracles, Ancestor Cults and Letters to the Dead: The Involvement of the Dead in the Public and Private Family Affairs in Pharaonic Egypt', in A. Storch (ed.), *Perception of the Invisible: Religion, Historical Semantics and the Role of Perceptive Verbs*, 133–53, Cologne: Rüdiger Köppe Verlag.

Moreno García, J. C., ed. (2010b), *Élites et pouvoir dans l'Égypte ancienne*, Villeneuve d'Ascq: Université Lille 3.

Moreno García, J. C. (2010c), 'Introduction: Les élites, le pouvoir et l'État dans les sociétés antiques. Le cas de l'Égypte pharaonique', in J.C. Moreno García (ed.), *Élites et pouvoir en Égypte ancienne*, 11–50, Villeneuve d'Ascq: Université Lille.

Moreno García, J. C., ed. (2013a), *Ancient Egyptian Administration*, Leiden/Boston: Brill.

Moreno García, J. C. (2013b), 'Building the Pharaonic State: Territory, Elite, and Power in Ancient Egypt During the 3rd Millennium BCE', in J. A. Hill, P. H. Jones and A. J. Morales (eds), *Experiencing Power, Generating Authority: Cosmos, Politics, and the Ideology of Kingship in Ancient Egypt and Mesopotamia*, 185–217, Philadelphia: University of Pennsylvania Museum of Archaeology and Anthropology.

Moreno García, J. C. (2013c), 'Land Donations', in E. Frood and W. Wendrich (eds), Los Angeles: *UCLA Encyclopedia of Egyptology*.

Moreno García, J. C. (2013d), 'Conflicting Interests Over the Possession and Transfer of Institutional Land: Individual *versus* Family Strategies', in

E. Frood and A. McDonald (eds), *Decorum and Experience: Essays in Ancient Culture for John Baines*, 258–63, Oxford: Griffith Institute.

Moreno García, J. C. (2014a), 'The Cursed Discipline? The Peculiarities of Egyptology at the Turn of the 21st Century', in W. Carruthers (ed.), *Histories of Egyptology: Interdisciplinary Measures*, 50–63, London: Routledge.

Moreno García, J. C. (2014b), 'Ancient Empires and Pharaonic Egypt: An Agenda for Future Research', *Journal of Egyptian History* 7: 203–40.

Moreno García, J. C. (2016a), 'Economies in Transition: Trade, "Money", Labour and Nomads at the Turn of the 1st Millennium BC', in J. C. Moreno García (ed.), *Dynamics of Production in the Ancient Near East, 1300–500 BC*, 1–39, Oxford: Oxbow Books.

Moreno García, J. C. (2016b), 'Temples and Agricultural Labour in Egypt, From the Late New Kingdom to the Saite Period', in J. C. Moreno García (ed.), *Dynamics of Production in the Ancient Near East, 1300–500 BC*, 223–56, Oxford: Oxbow Books.

Moreno García, J. C. (2017), 'Trade and Power in Ancient Egypt: Middle Egypt at the Turn of the 3rd Millennium BC", *Journal of Archaeological Research*, 25 (2): 87–132.

Moreno García, J. C. (forthcoming), 'Marketplaces, Customs and Hubs of Trade in Bronze Age Egypt', in L. Rahmstorf (ed.), *Weights and Market-Places: The Phenomenology of Places of Exchange within a Diachronic and Multi-cultural Perspective*.

Narotzky, S. and E. Manzano (2014), 'The Ḥisba, the Muḥtasib and the Struggle Over Political Power and a Moral Economy: An Enquiry into Institutions', in J. Hudson and A. Rodríguez (eds), *Diverging Paths? The Shapes of Power and Institutions in Medieval Christendom and Islam*, 30–54, Leiden/Boston: Brill.

North, D. C., J. J. Wallis and B. R. Weingast (2009), *Violence and Social Orders: A Conceptual Framework for Interpreting Recorded Human History*, New York: Cambridge University Press.

Nyord, R. (2018), 'Taking Ancient Egyptian Mortuary Religion Seriously: Why Would We, and How Could We?', *Journal of Ancient Egyptian Interconnections*, 17: 73–87.

O'Connor, D. and E. Cline (1998), *Amenhotep III: Perspectives on His Reign*, Ann Arbor, MI: The University of Michigan Press.

Otto, A. (2012), 'Archaeological Evidence for Collective Governance Along the Upper Syrian Euphrates During the Late and Middle Bronze Age', in

G. Wilhelm (ed.), *Organization, Representation, and Symbols of Power in the Ancient Near East*, 87–99, Winona Lake: Eisenbrauns.

Parkinson, R. B. (1997), *The Tale of Sinuhe and Other Ancient Egyptian Poems, 1940–1640 BC*, Oxford: Clarendon Press.

Pines, Y. (2015a), 'Zhou History and Historiography: Introducing the Bamboo Manuscript Xinian', *T'oung Pao*, 100 (2014): 287–324.

Pines, Y. (2015b), 'Introduction: Ideology and Power in Early China', in Y. Pines, P. R. Goldin and M. Kern (eds), *Ideology of Power and Power of Ideology in Early China*, 1–28, Leiden/Boston: Brill.

Quirke, S. (1991), 'Royal Power in the 13th Dynasty', in S. Quirke (ed.), *Middle Kingdom Studies*, 123–139, New Malden, Survey: SIA Publishing.

Raedler C. (2004), 'Die Wesire Ramses' II. – Netzwerke der Macht', in R. Gundlach and A. Klug (eds), *Das ägyptische Königtum im Spannungsfeld zwischen Innen- und Aussenpolitik im 2. Jahrtausend v. Chr.*, 277–316, Wiesbaden: Harrassowitz Verlag.

Raedler C. (2006), 'Zur Struktur der Hofgesellschaft Ramses II', in R. Gundlach and A. Klug (eds), *Der ägyptische Hof des Neuen Reiches: Seine Gesellschaft und Kultur im Spannungsfeld zwischen Innen- und Außenpolitik*, 39–87, Wiesbaden: Harrassowitz Verlag.

Ragazzoli, C. (2016), '"The pen promoted my station": Scholarship and Distinction in New Kingdom Biographies', in K. Ryholt and G. Barjamovic (eds), *Problems of Canonicity and Identity Formation in Ancient Egypt and Mesopotamia*, 153–78, Copenhagen: Museum Tusculanum Press and CNI Publications.

Richards, J. and M. Van Buren, eds (2000), *Order, Legitimacy and Wealth in Ancient States*, Cambridge: Cambridge University Press.

Ristvet, L. (2008), 'Legal and Archaeological Territories of the Second Millennium BC in Northern Mesopotamia', *Antiquity*, 82: 585–99.

Ritner, R. K. (2009), *The Libyan Anarchy. Inscriptions from Egypt's Third Intermediate Period*, Atlanta: Society of Biblical Literature.

Rodríguez López, E. (2018), *La política contra el estado. Sobre la política de parte*, Madrid: Traficantes de Sueños.

Routledge, B. (2014), *Archaeology and State Theory: Subjects and Objects of Power*, London/New York: Bloomsbury.

Sánchez León, P. and J. Izquierdo Martín (2002), 'L'autismo della microeconomia. Per un'interpretazione non utilitarista della storia agraria', *Meridiana*, 45: 179–97.

Sassen, S. (2008), *Territory, Authority, Rights from Medieval to Global Assemblages*, Princeton, NJ/Oxford: Princeton University Press.

Scheidel, W., ed. (2015), *State Power in Ancient China and Rome*, Oxford: Oxford University Press.
Scheidel, W. (2017), *The Great Leveler. Violence and the History of Inequality from the Stone Age to the Twenty-First Century*, Princeton, NJ: Princeton University Press.
Scott, J. C. (2009), *The Art of Not Being Governed: An Anarchist History of Upland Southeast Asia*, New Haven, CT: Yale University Press.
Shafer, B. E., ed. (1991), *Religion in Ancient Egypt: Gods, Myths, and Personal Practice*, London: Routledge.
Shafer, B. E., ed. (1997), *Temples in Ancient Egypt*, London/New York: I. B. Tauris.
Shirley, J. J. (2010), 'Viceroys, Viziers and the Amun Precinct: The Power of Heredity and Strategic Marriage in the Early 18th Dynasty', *Journal of Egyptian History*, 3: 73–113.
Smith, M. L. (2005), 'Networks, Territories, and the Cartography of Ancient States', *Annals of the Association of American Geographers*, 95 (2005): 832–49.
Smith, M. (2017), *Following Osiris: Perspectives on the Osirian Afterlife from Four Millennia*, Oxford: Oxford University Press.
Spalinger, A. (2015), 'Financial Provisions in an Egyptian Court', *Orientalia*, 84: 1–17.
Spence, K. (2007), 'Court and Palace in Ancient Egypt: The Amarna Period and Later Eighteenth Dynasty', in A. J. S. Spawforth (ed.), *The Court and Court Society in Ancient Monarchies*, 267–328, Cambridge: Cambridge University Press.
Stanford, C. (2018), *The New Chimpanzee: A Twenty-First-Century Portrait of Our Closest Kin*, Cambridge, MA: Harvard University Press.
Strudwick, N. (2005), *Texts from the Pyramid Age*, Atlanta: Society of Biblical Literature.
Tedesco, P. (2018), 'Late Antiquity, Early Islam, and the Emergence of a "Precocious Capitalism": A Review Essay', *The Journal of European Economic History*, XLVII, 3: 115–51.
Trigger, B. (2003), *Understanding Early Civilizations: A Comparative Study*, Cambridge: Cambridge University Press.
Van Bavel, B. (2016), *The Invisible Hand? How Market Economies Have Emerged and Declined since AD 500*, Oxford: Oxford University Press.
Vernus, P. (1993), *Affaires et scandales sous les Ramsès. La crise des valeurs dans l'Égypte du Nouvel Empire*, Paris: Éditions Pygmalion/Gérard Watelet.

Vernus, P. (2016), 'L'écrit et la canonicité dans la civilisation pharaonique', in K. Ryholt and G. Barjamovic (eds), *Problems of Canonicity and Identity Formation in Ancient Egypt and Mesopotamia*, 271–347, Copenhagen: Museum Tusculanum Press and CNI Publications.

Warburton, D. (2016), *The Fundamentals of Economics: Lessons from the Bronze Age Near East*, Grand-Saconnex: Recherches et Publications.

Wenke, R. J. (2009), *The Ancient Egyptian State: The Origins of Egyptian Culture (c. 8000–2000 BC)*, Cambridge: Cambridge University Press.

Wickham, C. (1984), 'The Other Transition: From the Ancient World to Feudalism', *Past and Present* 113: 3–36.

Wickham, C. (1985), 'The Uniqueness of the East', *Journal of Peasant Studies*, 12: 166–96.

Yoffee, N. (2005), *Myths of the Archaic State: Evolution of the Earliest Cities, States, and Civilizations*, Cambridge: Cambridge University Press.

Yoffee, N. (ed.) (2015a), *The Cambridge World History. Volume III: Early Cities in Comparative Perspective, 4000 BCE–1200 CE*, Cambridge: Cambridge University Press.

Yoffee, N. (2015b), 'Periphery and Center in Mesopotamia and in Comparative Perspective', 321–348.

Zarakol, A. (2018), 'A Non-eurocentric Approach to Sovereignty', *International Studies Review* 3 (20): 506–09.

Index

Aamu (Asiatic) 103
Aanery 129
Abu Ghalib 24, 49, 169
Abu Ziyar 50
Abusir 75
Abydos 16, 19, 20, 23, 24, 29, 32, 68, 70, 71–72, 74, 81, 112, 140, 145, 156, 163, 170, 176, 195
Achaemenid empire 148, 158, 184, 185
administration 20, 32, 37–39, 109–35
  limits 38, 47–49, 117–18, 120–26, 163–85
  organized in networks 20, 21–23, 29, 39, 41, 45, 67–68, 73, 80, 117, 132, 156, 163, 165–67
  and royal agents 24
Aegean 103, 169
agriculture 20, 28, 39, 44
  and domains 22, 24, 82–83, 178, 184
  and horticulture 27
  and private plantations 27, 49–50, 82–83, 99, 164
  and royal plantations 20, 39, 44, 59, 130, 182, 195
  and temples 33–34, 39–42, 44, 57, 59, 81, 83, 95–98, 99–100, 117, 130, 133, 173, 175, 177–79, 182, 184–85, 195
Ahmose (king) 72
Ahmose Pennekhbet 176
Ahmose son of Ebana 56, 176, 179
Akhenaten 33, 34, 40, 73, 118, 141, 142, 180
Akhmim 58, 70–71, 73, 122, 177
Akkadian empire 163
Alexandria 28, 104
Amarna *see* Tell el-Amarna
Amarna letters 94
Amenemhat (Beni Hasan) *see* Imeny
Amenemhat I 64, 72, 134
Amenemhat II 103
Amenhotep son of Hapu 148
Amenhotep III 55, 70, 177
Amenmose 106
Amenope 96
amulet 145, 160
Amun 33, 46, 83–84, 92–93, 125, 135, 140–41, 143, 146, 148, 156–57, 183
Anatolia 45, 198
ancestors 37, 68, 74–76, 79, 104, 142–43, 145–46, 156, 160, 169
Aniba 72
Anievas, Alexander 185, 192–94
Ankhkhenespepi 70
annona 178
Antef (kings) 146
Antef V 72
Apanage stela 98
Arabia 28, 177–78, 182
aristocracy 8, 62–63, 77, 85
army *see* military
aromatic plants 28, 103, 107
  See also incense; myrrh
Arthashastra 200
artist 48, 58, 89–90, 161
Asia, East 5–6, 8, 201
Asiatics 72, 94, 95, 102–03, 105, 169, 180
Askut 50
Assyria 11, 185, 198
Astarte 94
Asyut 16, 24, 25, 28, 62, 68, 71, 73, 83, 103, 169–70, 173
Aton 141, 147, 177
autonomous populations 11, 30, 105–07, 163, 200
Avaris *see* Tell el-Daba

Axial Age 148
Ayn Sukhna 47, 50, 197

Baal 94
bakery 54
Banaji, Jairus 191–92
Barnugi 24, 169
Bay 64, 105, 113, 180
Bedouins 201
beer 43, 95
Beith Shean 52
Ben-Ia 105
Beni Hasan 47, 68–69, 71, 72, 73, 102–03, 122, 169–70, 173, 174, 176
Berlin Leather Manuscript 111
Bersheh 16, 24, 28, 47, 72, 73, 102–03, 122, 133, 141, 169–70, 173, 176–77
Bilgai 47
biographies (officials) 23, 65, 74–75, 143
borders 8, 11, 93, 101, 104, 137, 139, 155, 187, 201–02
boukoloi 18, 107
bread 43, 54
Buddhism 148
building 48, 58–59, 90–91, 111–12, 120, 133, 143, 180, 197
bureaucracy 2, 32, 38, 48, 50, 60, 66, 76–78, 113–14, 117, 120, 131–35, 156, 167, 172, 183, 187–88, 199–200
bushland 15–16, 18, 30
Byblos 94, 181

camel *see* dromedary
Canaan 181
canals 53, 184
caravans 11, 18, 26, 28, 46, 50, 93, 95, 96, 169
Carchemish (Syria) 106
Carians 124
cattle 16, 18, 19, 22, 23, 30, 41, 43, 44, 52, 53, 54–55, 81–82, 83–84, 90–91, 95, 99, 101–07, 128, 165, 170
cavalry 55
See also chariots
census 19, 39
centralization 1, 2, 12, 32, 57, 77, 131–32
cereals *see* grain
ceremonies 29, 31–36, 64, 88, 133, 147, 152, 157–58
Chamber of Dignitaries *see* council
Chamber of the Documents 38
chariots 52, 55, 99, 123
checkpoint 18, 26–27, 81
and 'gateways' 28, 168, 170, 177
and taxes 45–47, 93
chiefdom 4
chiefs 3, 24, 41, 44, 46, 61, 69, 94, 98, 120–21, 129–31
'children of the *kap*' 66, 105
'children of the king' 53–54, 64, 66, 75, 113, 139
China, ancient 1, 5–6, 12, 55, 75, 132, 153, 200
choachyte (ritualist) 95–96, 99
Chuera (Syria) 148–49
cities 18–19, 20, 21–31, 41, 58–59, 126, 137–38, 163–65, 169, 178, 180–81, 196, 196, 198–99
and administration 23
and city notables 23, 61, 202
and collective bodies of 'citizens' 24, 25, 61, 63, 88–89, 96, 125–26, 138, 149, 159–60, 164, 187, 202
and identities 25, 29, 150
and the monarchy 28–29, 125–26, 137–38, 155
and politics 25, 96, 125–26, 159
and self-government 23, 24, 88–89, 149, 163
and settlement change 30, 41, 164–65, 169, 173, 178
size 24, 196, 198

Index

specialized settlements 29, 48, 58, 91, 198
and taxes 23, 41-43, 45, 55, 81-82, 88, 89, 197
and trade 21-24
city, 'oriental' 7, 88, 198-99
'civil' society 35, 61, 149, 159-60
clientelism 3, 37, 39, 49-50, 74-76, 81, 100, 110-11, 113-14, 123, 126-29, 131, 134, 146, 152, 159-60, 170-71
climatic change 4
Coffin Texts 26, 146, 160
commercial capitalism 6-7, 12, 201
commercialization of production 8, 40, 53, 106, 178
community 29, 32, 145, 148-49, 159, 185
comparison, historical 11-12, 187-202
Confucianism 6, 153-55
conspiracies 33, 64, 74, 119, 152
contract 6, 8, 25, 129, 146, 160, 197
copper 45, 169
ratio copper-silver 45
Coptos 16, 56, 72, 168, 173, 174
co-regencies 33, 66, 171
corruption 3, 37, 47, 59-60, 109-11, 119
council 24, 44, 63, 100-01, 113, 119, 125, 131, 152
Chamber of Dignitaries 65, 111, 134
Great Council 54
court, justice 92, 100, 115, 119, 123, 128
Court, royal 32, 53-54, 61-62, 63-66, 67, 71-72, 74-75, 105, 109, 111, 121-22, 129, 131, 134-35, 139, 150, 152, 154, 167-68, 194
craftsmen 3, 7, 48, 54, 55-56, 58-59, 63, 87-91, 92, 100, 103, 106, 144, 145, 200
and guilds 89-90
and land 91

culture 48, 64, 65, 67, 70, 74-78, 109, 115-16, 122, 128, 132, 137-61, 164, 167, 171, 180, 182, 183-84, 187, 190
customs *see* checkpoint
Cyprus 94, 169, 185
Cyrenaica 104, 184, 185

Dahshur 43, 50, 59, 90
Dakhla (oasis) 101
dams 53
dates 27, 39, 43
deben (unit of measure = 91 gr) 178
debts 85, 97, 159
decentralization 23, 24, 29, 61, 103-04, 117, 132, 140, 145, 156, 184
decree, royal 40, 48, 59-60, 92, 93, 98, 111-15, 116, 120, 128
Deir el-Ballas 199
Deir el-Gebrawy 55, 83, 102, 106
Deir el-Medina 29, 48, 58, 89, 91, 100, 161
Delta, Egypt *see* Lower Egypt
demography 18, 22, 138
Dendera 24, 29, 69, 169
desert routes 16, 17, 52, 57, 104, 169, 177, 182, 184
despotism, oriental 6, 88
and Egypt 16-17, 38, 61-62
dignitaries 23, 32, 41, 60, 63-64, 74-78, 80, 85, 97, 98, 109-11, 113, 123, 126, 128, 132, 139-40, 143, 150, 157, 161, 165, 167, 171
diplomacy 52, 64-65, 72, 96, 106, 117-19, 141, 156, 157, 174, 184-85
district 24, 41, 42, 44, 97, 99, 100, 131, 198
djadjat (council) 24
Djehutihotep (Bersheh) 28
Djekhy 99
Djoser 20, 51, 67

dmj (harbour, city) 22–23, 24, 25, 26, 28, 169, 181, 198–99
dmjw (city people) 25
donkey 18, 52, 91, 99
dromedary 18, 177
Duties of the Vizier 44, 100, 109

Eastern Desert 52, 104, 123–24
economy 34–35, 183–85, 200–01
   economic growth 8, 12, 24
   and Egyptian exports 45, 56, 170, 178, 184
   and 'money' 52, 181
   and personal autonomy 25
   private 45, 49–50, 95–96, 99, 172, 181, 197
   and private transactions 26–27, 49–50, 95–96, 99, 160, 164, 168, 169–70, 181, 201
   and profit 50, 161, 164, 181–82
   and women 25, 27, 49, 52, 81, 91, 95, 97, 98, 102, 179
Edfu 24, 42, 44, 68, 71, 104, 116, 157, 169, 175–76, 195
education 64, 70, 75, 105, 122, 151–52, 154
Egypt, and comparative research 12, 21, 187–202
   as a crossroads 18–19, 45, 103–06, 164, 182
   and geopolitics 13, 163–85
   idealized image of 1–2, 12
   lifestyles 15, 18, 106, 161
   natural environment 15–18, 137, 184
   and political unity 13, 24, 32, 37, 47, 61, 66, 73, 103–04, 117, 122, 124–25, 132–35, 141, 145–46, 153–54, 157–60, 164–85
   and politics 12, 163–85
   regions in 13, 15–18, 23, 34, 163–85, 198
   and social order 1–2, 12, 32, 37, 77, 112, 114, 116, 139–41, 143, 151, 153–55, 159, 164, 199
   in Western imagination 1–3, 38
Egyptology and social sciences 3–4, 12
Eisenstadt, Shmuel 4
Ekallatum 11
Elam 198
Elephantine 16, 17, 20, 23, 24, 26–27, 39, 46, 51–52, 59–60, 75, 91, 93, 95, 97, 116, 119, 120, 156, 163, 168–70
'Elephantine scandal' 59, 120
elites, palatial/central 32–36, 53–54, 61–85, 129, 132–35, 139, 166–85, 190–91
   and collective interests 62, 84, 121–26, 134, 154
   and cultural values 48, 65, 74–78, 109, 143, 150–55, 160, 180
   and factions 35–36, 48, 63–65, 109, 115, 119, 121, 124, 134–35, 144, 152, 164, 187, 190–91
   and political alliances 54, 62, 64, 66, 105, 121–22, 134, 157, 196
   and political autonomy 62, 76–78, 121, 154, 190–91, 200
   and revenue 62, 74, 78–85, 109, 115, 117, 121, 173, 175, 178–79, 183, 195–97
   See also officials
elites, local/provincial 21, 25, 30, 32, 34, 37, 40, 41, 61–85, 96–101, 117, 120–23, 126, 131, 132–35, 139–41, 143, 145–46, 150, 154, 156, 166–85, 194–95, 200
   and armed retinues 25, 125, 197
   and autonomy 63, 71, 87, 102–05, 117, 120–22, 138, 170, 183, 185, 194–95
   and collective interests 63, 76–78, 121–23, 134
   and political alliances 54, 62, 64, 66, 67–71, 121–23, 157–58, 164, 167, 176–77, 190–91, 196
   and trade 28, 46–47, 50, 72–73, 102–05, 122, 168

and wealth 47, 50, 70–71, 77, 78–85, 100, 115, 123, 158, 170–73, 175, 178–79, 183, 184–85, 195
  See also potentates
Elkab 19, 20, 56, 68, 71, 74, 116, 157, 173, 176, 179, 195
Eloquent Peasant, The 59, 110, 159
empire and imperial expansion 33, 59, 61, 105, 117, 138, 141, 147, 149, 156, 172–85, 198, 200–01
enclosure settlement 31
'entrepreneur', rural 34, 41, 97
Ermant 173
etiquette 64, 65, 74, 152
eurocentrism 5, 187–88, 191, 197
expeditions 21, 41, 42, 52, 57–58, 69, 72, 167, 184
exports 45, 56, 170, 178, 184

favourite 64, 115
Fayum 31, 53, 55, 73, 104, 123, 169, 172, 178, 184
feudalism 8, 63, 85, 122–23, 138, 194–95, 197
fields 19, 30, 44, 52, 54, 57, 59–60, 82–84, 95, 97–99, 100, 173, 179, 195
  See also land
fishing and fishermen 30, 40, 45, 52, 91, 101, 106–07, 161, 184, 200
foreigners 31, 46, 55, 64, 88, 92, 94, 101–07, 124–25, 158, 169, 178–79, 182, 184–85
fortress 50, 52, 55, 57, 104, 123, 197
  See also Lower Egypt, Nubia
foundation, private 48
fruits 27, 39

galena 28
garrisons 39, 42, 50, 52, 55
'gateways' (to foreign countries) *see* checkpoint
Gebel el-Asr 51
Gebelein 68, 195

genealogies 68, 74, 81, 142
gezira 15
glass 45
global history 8
goats 28
gold 19, 20, 23, 41, 45, 52, 73, 90, 92, 95, 97, 104, 165, 177–78, 181
  See also metals, precious
gods 7, 29, 34, 81, 95, 125, 126, 133, 137, 138–41, 144, 145–50, 156–58, 161
  city-god 29, 145, 150, 158, 180
government 32, 38, 44, 71, 88–89, 109–35, 144–45, 187–202
grain 39, 43, 45, 48, 49–50, 52–53, 56, 59–60, 97, 128, 178, 184
guilds 63, 88–96, 125, 127
Granary 38, 39, 71
'great chief of a province' 67–69, 70–71, 72, 73, 122, 167, 170, 176
Great Dedicatory Inscription 199
'great' ḥwt 20, 165
Greeks 124, 158, 184
Gurob 39

Haankhef (Edfu) 52
Hadja 56, 179
Hall of Horus 119
  See also council
Hammurabi 2, 138
Hapidjefa (Asyut) 62, 83
harbour 22, 24, 27, 28, 39, 41, 42, 45–46, 50, 52, 57, 93, 103, 181, 197, 198–99
harbour-master 46
Harsaphes 81
Hatnub 25, 42, 103
Hatshepsut 105, 141, 176–77, 180
Hattušili III 118
haty-a (governor) 23, 42, 44, 54, 72, 83, 91–92, 98, 100, 126, 129–31, 142, 197
Hawara 50

Heliopolis 111, 133
hem-nesut (servant of the king) 89
Henqu (Deir el-Gebrawy) 102, 106
Henu (Thebes) 42
Henuttawy 83
Heqaib (Elephantine) 75, 169
Heqanakhte 49–50, 99, 128
Heracleopolis (Magna) 27, 46, 54–55, 72, 73, 81–82, 90, 93, 103, 122, 143, 146, 154, 169–70, 184
Hermopolis 81, 184
heterarchy 11
Hezi 74, 127
hides 45, 73
Hieracompolis 91, 133
hieratic 152
   See also writing
hieroglyph 148, 152, 155
   See also writing
Hittite empire 45, 64–65, 106, 118, 141, 178
ḫnrt (work camp) 41
honey 47
Horemheb 33, 42, 59, 93, 98, 177
Horiherneferher 100
horses 52, 55
horticulture *see* agriculture
Horus 138–39, 176
House of Life 38
House of Weapons 38
house hold 20, 25, 42, 49–50, 58, 68, 83, 90, 99, 128–29, 146, 149, 164, 170–71, 176
   as administrative unit 20, 39, 41, 131
houses 29, 49, 54, 68, 92, 93, 94, 95, 113, 146, 160, 181
   tower-houses 29
ḥwt (royal agricultural centre) 20, 21–24, 26, 29, 41, 51–52, 117, 165–67, 169, 171, 199
   'great' *ḥwt* 20, 165
Hyksos 56, 73, 103–04, 111, 143, 146, 174, 175, 179, 182

Iamnefer (Nefrusy) 176
iawt (penned livestock) 102
Ibi (Deir el-Gebrawy) 55, 83
Ikeni 98
Ikherneferet 112–13
Ilahun 28, 90, 102
ilku 179, 195
Imeny (Beni Hasan) 42, 44, 102
Imhotep 148
incense 28, 73, 182
Incense Route 177, 184
India, ancient 6, 88, 93, 148, 200
Indian Ocean 16, 107
information 37, 77, 109
Installation of the Vizier, The 113, 127
iqta' 179, 195
irrigation 53
   private 27, 178
Irsu 180
Irtenena 105
Irunetjeru 91
Iti-Ibi (Asyut) 23
Itj-tawy 50, 122
Iuf (Edfu) 176
Iuwelot 83
ivory 52, 73, 104

jāgīr 195
Jessop, Bob 9, 188–91
Jezreel Valley 52
justice 32, 77, 109–10, 114–15, 119–20, 123–24, 127–28, 155, 161
   See also court, justice; *maat*

Kamose 72, 104, 111, 174
Kanesh 88, 93
kap (private sector of the palace) 66
Karnak 50, 116, 143, 147
Kassite Babylonia 198
Kemit, Boof of 152
Khaemwase 120
Khafra (*or* Chephren) 31
Kharu (Levant) 94
khato 195

Khayiri 91
khenes (friend) 52
Khety (king) 26, 146, 154
Khnumhotep (vizier) 105
Khnumhotep II (Beni Hasan) 68, 102
Khufu (*or* Cheops) 31, 44
Khuu (Edfu) 68
king 29, 31–36, 135, 137–45, 151,
  155-58
 and authority 33–34, 37, 48,
  61–63, 84, 109–35, 157–58,
  167, 169, 171–72, 179, 183,
  190–91, 196, 201–02
 and councils 54, 63, 65, 100, 111,
  113, 119, 134, 151
 and counterpowers 35, 63, 76–79,
  88, 96, 103, 120–26, 138, 153
 and history 141–43, 145, 146,
  153–54, 157, 177, 182, 199
 and negotiation 33, 37, 61–63,
  109, 138, 144, 168, 170, 174
 and political alliances 54, 62, 64,
  66, 70–71, 121, 153, 157,
  166–67, 173–77, 179, 183,
  185, 201
 and Royal Domain 27, 46
 and royal family 19, 53, 54, 61–62,
  63–66, 69, 74, 105, 115, 124,
  132, 135, 139, 166, 177
 and royal favour 63, 74–75, 84,
  113, 152, 170
 and royal statues 29, 57, 70, 72, 79,
  143, 150, 173, 175–76
 and royal tombs 29, 31–36, 37, 92,
  119–20, 132–35, 140, 145,
  155–58, 180
 See also monarchy
kinship 23, 33, 68–69, 74–75, 79,
  126–27, 129–30, 134, 146,
  152–53, 159–60, 171, 175, 180
 and conflicts 79–80, 84, 124
 and property 56–57, 82–85
Khnum 91
Kom el-Hisn 24, 52, 169
Königsnovelle 65

Kush 119, 122, 174
 See also Nubia

Lahun *see* Ilahun
land 39, 53, 59, 109, 117, 130, 177
 leasing 50, 62, 84, 95–96, 128
 purchase of 26, 52, 62, 82–84,
  96–98, 127, 170
 as remuneration 54–56, 78–85, 91,
  173, 175–76, 178–79, 184–85,
  195
 See also fields
land donation 21, 28, 30, 32, 41, 57,
  70, 79, 85, 116, 143, 158, 166,
  177–78
landscape 15–18, 22, 30
 ceremonial landscapes 31–36,
  66, 131–35, 155–58, 181,
  196, 199
 funerary landscapes 19, 66, 75,
  78–82, 132–35, 140, 145, 156,
  158, 171, 180
Larsa 88
law 5, 6, 7, 48, 77, 88, 114–16, 123,
  126, 133, 154, 187, 196,
  197, 202
lawsuit 24, 56–57, 91, 97, 100–01,
  119–20, 123
Lebanon 94, 102–03, 181
lentils 45
Levant 13, 19, 45, 89, 94, 101, 102,
  105, 122, 156, 167, 169, 171,
  172, 174, 176, 184, 185, 195,
  198, 199
Libya 28, 30
Libyan Desert *see* Western Desert
Libyans 16, 30, 101, 102–04, 106, 124,
  141, 182–83, 199
lifestyles 15, 17, 18, 30, 106, 138, 161,
  167, 201
linen 45, 103, 161, 184
Lisht 50
literature 65, 76, 106, 110, 129–30,
  143, 151–52, 154, 159, 161, 164,
  178, 180, 199

Lower Egypt 13, 15, 20, 30, 69, 165, 175, 178, 181–85
   and fortresses 28, 30, 104, 129
   and mobile populations 18, 106–07, 201
   and political organization 15–16, 34, 103–05, 122, 125, 135, 141, 147, 157, 164, 177
   and trade 24, 26, 28, 34, 52, 103–04, 125, 169–70, 172, 178, 181–82

maat (order, justice) 32, 77, 139, 143, 151
Maatkare 83
Maiherpri 105
Malqata 199
management 20, 37–38, 49, 53, 76, 77, 84–85, 96, 99, 113, 120, 134, 143, 151, 187
   and temples 28, 33–35, 40–41, 57, 80, 97, 117, 132–35, 157, 195, 196
Mann, Michael 4, 190–91
manpower *see* workforce
Mari (Syria) 10, 11
maritime populations 103, 106–07, 201
   'Maritime Mode of Production' 201
markets 22–23, 26–27, 45–46, 53, 93, 98, 106, 170, 181, 198
   See also mryt (quay, market)
marshes 15–16, 18, 30, 137, 201
mastaba 19, 31, 75, 160
Mauryan empire 148
mayors *see haty-a* (governor)
Medamud 84, 173
Medinet Habu 91
Mediterranean 16–17, 19, 24, 26, 28, 50, 56, 73, 93, 104–05, 107, 135, 156, 158, 163–64, 172–73, 177, 182, 184
Medya 27, 124
Megiddo 102

Meir 68, 74, 102–03, 119, 170
Memphis 19, 22, 32, 40, 49, 70, 79, 91, 92, 93, 94, 112, 122, 133, 146, 156, 199
Mendes 81
Menkheperre 84
Mentuhotep (official) 55
Mentuhotep I 143
Mentuhotep II 158, 171
merchants *see* traders
Merenptah 141
Merenre 70
Mersa/Wadi Gawasis 28, 50, 73, 169
Mesopotamia 2, 10, 88, 93, 137–38, 163, 195, 198
messengers 43, 52, 94, 112, 167, 174
metals, precious 23, 28, 45, 53, 59, 92, 103, 169, 180–81
   See also gold; silver
Metjen 82, 97–98
'middle class' 24, 29, 35, 49–50, 169–71, 175
Middle Egypt 13, 15–16, 18, 24, 30, 102–05, 173, 178
   local elites 16, 47, 53, 63, 72, 73, 93, 102, 122, 138, 169–71, 174–76, 178, 179, 195
migration 18, 201
military 33, 34, 40, 42, 52, 54–57, 59, 64, 80, 81–82, 89–92, 97, 103–07, 111, 118, 121, 123–25, 133, 134–35, 141, 143–44, 149, 156–58, 167, 169–70, 172–85, 195–96, 197
Min (Thinis) 176
mines 40, 57, 104, 177–78
mnmnt (itinerant cattle) 30, 102
mobile populations *see* nomads
modernity 1–2, 4–6, 12, 188
modius (unit of volume = 8,73 l) 178
monarchy 24, 87, 109–35, 137–45, 152–54, 160, 163–85, 202
   and accumulation of wealth 47, 50, 163–85

collapse 4, 13, 24, 36, 50, 59, 61, 74, 81, 105, 115, 122, 123, 133–35, 151, 158, 161, 168, 171–72, 181, 183, 196, 202
and political cycles 24, 32, 37, 47, 61, 66, 73, 103–04, 117, 122, 124–25, 132–35, 141, 145–46, 153–54, 157–60, 164–85
and *raison d'état* 76–78, 134, 154, 199–200
money *see* economy; silver
Montuherkhepeshef (Qaw) 176
Mose 56, 91, 100, 175, 179
mryt (quay, market) 26–27, 46, 91, 94
See also markets
Mughal empire 192, 195
Mut 57
myrrh 28, 50, 103, 170, 182
See also aromatic plants

Nakhtefmut 83
nakhtu ('strongholds') 199
Namlot 81
Naqada 19
Naram-Sin 2
natron 45
Naucratis 28, 81, 182, 184
Naunakhte 100
Nauri 42, 59
Nebre (Zawiyet Umm el-Rakham) 30
Nebuchadnezzar 2
Necho II 184
Nedjem 47
nedjes (modest one) 25, 160, 170
Neferabet 57
Neferirkare 40, 69
Nefertiti 118, 142
Nefrusi 72, 174, 176
Nehesi 104
nemeh ('orphan', free tenant) 98
See also peasants, wealthy
Neo-Babylonian, empire 185
neoevolutionism 3–4, 191
Neshi 56, 179
Neshor 81

New Institutionalism 6, 8–9, 191, 197
Nile 15–16
bypassing 17, 104
navigation 17, 43
trade 46, 50, 73, 93, 94, 169
Nişancıoğlu, Kerem 185, 192–94
Nitocris 43, 46
nomads 10, 13, 16, 18, 30, 101–07, 138, 161, 201
and forced settlement 18, 30, 106, 199
nomarch *see* elites, local/provincial
Nubia 13, 16, 50, 51, 52, 57, 69, 72, 73, 89, 91, 95, 101, 104–05, 118, 119, 156, 158, 167, 169, 174, 178, 182, 184, 199
fortresses 28, 29, 51, 55, 171–72, 174, 195, 197
Nubians 16, 72, 104–07, 124
Nubnefer 91
nwt (locality) 22, 24, 25, 26, 28, 30, 181
nwtjw (people from a locality) 25
Nykaure 83

oases 16, 19, 101, 174, 200
officials 32, 38, 41, 61, 91, 100, 101, 106, 109–35, 166, 197
and abuses 59, 85, 109, 110, 112, 114, 119–20, 128, 144
and agricultural domains 42, 96–97, 131
and autonomy 76, 110, 114, 117, 121, 154
and career 74–78, 127, 134, 143, 152–53, 175, 183
and corruption 59–60, 109, 114, 119
and cultural values 65, 74–78, 128, 143–58
deification 68, 75, 148, 169
and ideology 25, 74–78, 109, 143
public and private interests 37, 62–63, 99–100, 105, 110–11, 121, 152–53

and revenue 42, 53–57, 62–63, 74, 78–79, 110, 115, 119, 123, 173, 176, 178–79, 183, 195
trial of 60, 114, 119–20, 167
See also elites, palatial/central; scribes; dignitaries; vizier
oil 46, 93
onomastica 109, 126
Onuris 71
oracles 91, 101, 123, 133, 140, 148, 158, 161, 183
Osiris 32, 68, 71, 79, 112, 140, 145, 148, 156
Osorkon I 83
Osorkon II 66
Ottoman empire 6, 157, 192–93, 195

palace 22, 35, 47, 53–54, 64, 77, 87–88, 109, 116, 134, 149, 154, 155, 157, 196, 199, 202
Pan-Grave 107
papyrus (as commodity) 45, 49, 184
papyrus Anastasi I 124
papyrus Berlin 3047 57
papyrus Berlin 9785 24
papyrus Berlin 10470 24
papyrus Boulaq XI 92
papyrus Boulaq XVIII 54
papyrus British Museum 10335 24, 101
papyrus CGC 58081 92
papyrus Gebelein 195
papyrus Harris I 39, 53, 178, 181
papyrus Rylands IX 59
papyrus St Petersburg 1116A 54, 94
papyrus Turin 1887 91
papyrus Wilbour 53, 57, 81, 96–97, 98, 173, 175, 178, 179
Paser 119–20
pastoralism and pastoral populations 16, 18, 19, 21, 30–31, 41, 51, 101–07, 200–01
pasture land 13, 15, 16, 18, 30, 55, 101–06
Patjauemdiamun 101

patrimony, private 25, 78–85, 95–98, 99, 123, 171–72, 175–76, 178–79, 197
patronage *see* clientelism
Pawero 119–20
Paysen 129
peasants 3, 38, 40, 53, 60, 91, 129, 178
wealthy 45, 49–50, 57, 59, 61, 81, 83–84, 87, 96–101, 123, 126, 128, 130–31, 160, 173, 179, 180
Penniut 57, 72
Pepi I 59, 70, 147
Pepyankh 'the middle' (Meir) 119
per-aa ('great house', pharaoh, state) 154, 157
Per-Ikhekh 26
Persia 8, 148, 198
Peru-Nefer 94
pharaoh *see* king
phyle (priestly service group) 95
Piankhi, Victory Stela of 28
pilgrimages 33, 145, 156, 158
piracy 201
Pi-Ramesses 27, 28, 46, 73, 94, 180, 199
plazas 35, 148–49, 196
politics 7, 9, 25, 61–66, 102–04, 109–35, 139, 159, 182, 187–202
potentates 20, 22, 23, 25, 34, 37, 40, 42, 47, 50, 61–62, 77, 96–102, 105, 109, 115, 120–21, 126–31, 140, 144, 159, 160, 163, 170–71, 175, 202
and collective interests 63
See also chiefs; elites, palatial/central; elites, local/provincial
power 74–79, 96, 100, 109–35, 139, 152–53, 163–85, 187–202
division of powers 4, 77, 117, 120–26, 134–35, 163, 183, 187–88, 190–91
and negotiation 33, 64
and oligarchy 35, 64–66, 113, 153, 170–72

priests 55–56, 59, 64, 71, 74, 79, 81, 82, 87, 89–92, 97–98, 99–100, 116–17, 120, 123, 125–26, 131, 135, 140, 142, 144, 150, 157–58, 161, 173, 179, 183
   associations 89–90, 95–96, 125–26, 135, 150
   High Priest 33, 55, 124, 135, 143, 183
   hiring of 26
prisoners 52, 58–59, 177, 182
progress 5
property (private) 5, 9, 82–85, 89, 171–72, 178
prophecy 151
provinces 12, 21, 32, 34, 38, 67–73, 146, 150, 163–85
   and balance of power 47, 61, 73, 79–80, 102–05, 145, 153, 164–85, 190–91, 195
   and taxes 40, 42, 44
   See also regional powers
provincial lords *see* elites, local/provincial
Psammetichus I 81
Ptah 40
Punt 102, 141
pyramids 19, 31–32, 42, 43, 66, 79, 132, 140, 145, 156, 158, 171
pyramid city 29
Pyramid Texts 26, 146, 147

Qadesh 111, 141
Qar (Edfu) 44
Qareh 104
Qasr el-Sagha 50
Qaw 68, 72, 73, 103, 176
qnbt (council) 23–24, 44, 89, 131
quarries 39, 50, 57

Ramesses I 33, 177
Ramesses II 30, 56, 57, 66, 71, 94, 104, 105, 111, 118, 141, 158, 176, 181, 199

Ramesses III 58, 64, 91, 116, 134, 141, 158, 177, 179, 180, 199
Ramesses IV 58, 179
Ramesses V 179
Ramesses VI 57
Ramesseum 199
rank 54, 60, 62–64, 66, 77, 83, 99, 111–13, 114, 119, 122, 128, 132, 139, 152, 166, 176
rations/wages 49, 50, 51, 52, 53–55, 57–59, 89, 100
rationality 3, 5, 6–7, 41, 49–50, 191, 197
rebellions 66, 72, 109, 133, 134–35, 145, 174, 180
Red Sea 16, 19, 28, 47, 56, 73, 107, 156, 169, 177, 182, 184
redistribution 1, 53, 57
regicide 33, 64, 134, 180
regional powers 23, 24, 63, 73, 102–05, 120, 150, 163–85, 190–91, 198, 201
   See also provinces
Rekhmire 23, 43, 100, 181
religion 7, 34–36, 116, 132–35, 138–41, 145–50, 160–61, 180, 185, 196
   and feasts 33, 35, 150
   and 'national' cults 29, 32–36, 78–82, 116, 140–41, 145–50, 156, 158, 185
requisitions 47, 48, 59, 84, 128
Retenu (Levant) 102, 199
revenue, state 39–60, 135, 158, 167, 182, 184–85
robbery 59–60, 119–20, 181
rock inscriptions 42, 52
Rome, ancient 12, 55, 58
rural society 7, 21–23, 26, 30, 34, 41, 78–79, 81, 96–101, 106, 120–21, 130–31, 164, 175, 177–78, 181
   See also villages

Sabni (Elephantine) 119
Sahure 177

Sais 28, 43, 52, 81, 184
salary *see* rations/wages
Saqqara 51, 147
Sarenput I (Elephantine) 26, 46, 93, 170
Sargon 138
Sataimau (Edfu) 175–76
Satepihu (Thinis) 176
Sayala 91
scribes 34, 54, 65, 75–78, 80, 81, 82, 92, 99, 100, 114, 123, 126, 128–31, 138, 143–44, 150–55, 180, 199
Sea Peoples 141, 201
seals 20, 24, 25, 26, 49, 119, 160, 169–70
sekhetiu ('countrymen') 18, 30, 52, 107
Senbebu 129
Senedjemib (Giza) 75
Sennacherib 2
Senusret I 111, 177
Senusret III 72, 112
Serabit el-Khadim 52
serfs 24, 39, 83, 84, 98, 129, 144, 170
Seshenu 90
Seth 141, 147
Seti I 54, 92
Setnakht 177
sgr (settlement) 31
Shamshi-Adad I 2, 11, 138
Sharope 179
sheep 28, 30, 102
Sherden 124
Sheretnebty 75
Sheshonq 181
ships 27, 39, 44, 52, 56, 59, 84, 93, 94, 104, 170, 178, 181
warships 55, 56, 98, 184
Sidon 94, 181
silphium 104
silver 23, 34, 40, 45, 46, 52, 53, 94, 106, 161, 178, 181
ratio copper-silver 45, 178
See also metals, precious

Simontu 94
Simut-Kyky 74, 127
Sinai 52
Siptah 105, 113
Siwa (oasis) 101, 104, 184
slaves 52, 56, 59, 89, 91, 95, 103, 129
Smendes 181
Smendes II 83
Snofru 21, 31, 90
Sobekaa 130–31
solar cult 34–36, 147
sources, and Egyptian history 2
sovereignty 5, 9, 11, 33, 131–35, 139, 187, 201–02
Spain, medieval Islamic 8, 194–95
states, ancient 3, 4, 187–202
states, modern 4–5, 38, 187–202
statues, royal 29, 55, 57, 70, 72, 79–80, 143, 150, 173, 175–76
Story of Wenamun 45
strike 49
Sublime Porte 157
Suez 184
Syria 22, 94, 181, 198

Taharqa 92–93
Tati 104
taxation 18, 19, 23, 27, 37, 38–53, 59–60, 93, 97, 110, 130–31, 135, 144, 158, 170–72, 178, 181, 182, 185, 187, 194, 196–97, 198, 202
abuses 47, 48, 59, 84, 144, 165, 167
assessment of taxes 47–49, 60, 81–82, 90, 97, 101, 106, 110, 143
efficiency 47–49, 50, 143, 170, 171–72
and state expenditure 50, 53–60
tax exemption 40, 48, 116
Teaching for King Merykara, The 25, 77, 125–26, 151, 154, 200
Teaching of Amenemhat, The 151, 154
Teaching of Amenemope, The 60, 128
Teaching of Ankhsheshonq, The 128
Teaching of Khety, The 154

Index 225

Teaching of Kagemni, The 151
Teaching of Ptahhotep, The 127, 151
Tehna 133
Tell Bazi (Syria) 94
Tell el-Amarna 73, 141, 177, 180,
  196, 199
Tell el-Burak (Lebanon) 102–03
Tell el-Daba 26, 27, 28, 94, 103–05,
  165, 169, 171
Tell Leilan (Syria) 10
temples 21–22, 29, 31–36, 37, 59,
  87–88, 92, 111–12, 115–17,
  125–26, 132–35, 145–50,
  165–66, 171, 195, 199, 202
  accessibility 35, 147–49
  and the crown 32–36, 40, 56–57,
    78–82, 116–17, 120, 125–26,
    132–35, 137, 140–43, 146, 149,
    155–59, 166, 171, 172–82,
    184–85, 195–96, 202
  and economy 29, 34, 39–42, 44, 53,
    54–57, 59, 80, 83–85, 96,
    98–100, 132–35, 172–82,
    185, 202
  and elites 32–36, 56–57, 78–82, 115,
    172–82, 184–85, 195–96, 202
  and foreign deities 94
  and identities 29, 34, 79, 145–50,
    158, 185, 199
  and institutional security 33,
    56–57, 78–82, 85, 115–16, 175,
    177, 180, 183, 196
  and settlement 29, 80
  and taxation 39–41, 45, 48, 59,
    90, 116
  and workforce 39, 40, 53
temple, funerary royal 21, 22, 28, 29,
  31–36, 40, 69–70, 78–82, 116,
  133, 180
temple, Nubian 28, 199
temple, provincial 24, 29, 32, 68–71,
  78–82, 83–85, 120, 123, 130,
  133, 137, 140, 145–46, 150, 158,
  165, 171, 173, 175–76, 183–85,
  195–96, 199

Teti (rebel) 72, 74
Teti (king) 75
Teti-an 72, 174
textiles 22, 26, 27, 39, 43, 49, 51–52,
  53, 59, 102–03, 107, 184, 201
Thebes 16, 28, 33, 42, 43, 46–47, 49,
  72, 73, 94, 103, 119–20, 122,
  124, 135, 140, 143, 146, 154,
  156, 157, 164, 168–69, 173–74,
  176–77, 181–85, 195, 199
Thinis 16, 42, 71, 129, 176
Thutmose (scribe) 99
Thutmose III 105, 141, 176–77
Tili-sarruma 106
tımar 178, 193, 195
timber 52, 55, 56, 92, 94
Tirkak 105
titles 18, 23, 25, 38, 42, 49, 52, 58,
  64, 66–69, 70–71, 73, 79, 93,
  103, 106, 109, 125, 142, 152,
  166, 170
Tiyi 70, 73
Tjeti-Kaihep 70–71, 78
Tod 116
town 22, 85, 100, 106, 126, 130, 165,
  181, 197
trade 24, 26–28, 39, 50–52, 72–73, 88,
  125, 149, 168–85, 200–01
  hubs 50, 52, 102–04, 161, 164,
    167–69, 198
  private 45, 72–73, 102, 169–70,
    178, 181, 201
trade routes 17, 24, 26, 28, 102–04,
  156, 164, 168–85, 200–01
  bypassing of 17–18, 28, 104,
    200–01
traders 3, 17, 21, 28, 40, 46, 61, 87–88,
  91–95, 103–05, 118, 161, 164,
  167, 180–82, 200
  and 'commercial diaspora' 88, 94,
    103, 105
  and cultural values 161, 164,
    181–82
  and guilds 63, 88, 91–95, 96
  and language 94

and 'laundering' of wealth 45, 53, 92, 181
   as mediators for institutions 45
   and taxes 45–46, 93
   and temples 46, 91–93
   and urban neighbourhoods 88, 92, 94
transport 16–17, 27, 39, 53, 57
Treasury 27, 38, 46, 54, 65, 97
tributary states 5, 7, 185, 187–202
tribute 26–27, 52–53, 59, 92, 141, 156, 157, 168, 176–77, 182, 185, 202
Tsenhor (lady) 99
Turin Royal Canon 45–46
Twosret 180

Ugarit 93
Ullaza 94
Uluburun shipwreck 45
Upper Egypt 13, 15–16, 19, 23, 34, 67, 69, 75, 93, 125, 131, 135, 146, 164, 165, 167, 172, 177–78, 184–85
urbanism *see* cities

Valley of the Kings 33, 91, 105
vegetables 27, 39, 43
Vikings 201
Vijayanagara, empire 8
village 22–23, 30, 41, 42, 54, 61, 83, 99, 102, 126, 130, 159, 161, 179, 201
   and taxes 41–44, 57
   and village chiefs 24, **44**, 98, 100–01, 129–31, 179, 197
   See also rural society
vizier 24, 44, 49, 57, 65, 70, 71, 74–75, 89, 91, 100, 105, 109, 112–13, 120, 124, 127, 131, 181

w (district) 23
   See also district
wab (priest) 89

Wadi el-Jarf 28, 44
Wadi Hamammat 42, 54
Wadi Korosko 52
wadis 15–16, 18
wages *see* rations/wages
Wah-Sut 72
waret (trade, guild) 90
wealth 45, 172, 178, 196–97
   accumulation of 47, 50, 61–63, 82–85, 165–70
Weber, Max 4, 6, 88, 188
Wenamun, Story of 94, 181, 184
Weni (Abydos) 40, 47, 74
Wenennefer (Abydos) 68, 71–72, 176
Werekter 94, 181
West in history 6–7, 8–9, 10, 88
Western Desert 16, 18, 19, 101, 104, 167, 169, 174
wḥyt (tribe, village) 23, 26, 30, 102, 181, 199
   Wehit-Neshi 179
wnt (settlement) 31
wine 27, 39, 41, 47, 95
women 25, 51–52, 90, 102, 127, 130
   and economic autonomy 25, 49, 52, 81, 91, 95, 97, 98, 99, 170, 173, 179, 180
wool 102–03, 161
workers and workforce 21, 37, 38–39, 41, 45, 48, 49, 54, 56–59, 83–84, 100, 116, 128–29, 130, 131, 132, 165, 177
workshop 56, 89–90, 96, 180
writing 76, 150, 151–53, 163, 199
wr ('great one', chief) 98

Ya'ammu 104
Yakbim 104

'Zannanza affair' 64, 180
Zawiyet Umm el-Rakham 30, 104
Zoroastrianism 148